SECOND EDITION

# *WILEY* CPA EXAM

# How to Master Simulations

**Includes Free Practice Simulations**

## SECOND EDITION

# WILEY CPA EXAM

# How to Master Simulations

## O. Ray Whittington, CPA, PhD

WILEY

JOHN WILEY & SONS, INC.

# CONTENTS

# CONTENTS

# PREFACE

Passing the CPA exam is within your reach! It just takes focused study and dedication. However, you can improve your chances of success by studying smarter. A critical aspect involves gaining a thorough understanding of the types of problems on the exam, including simulations. Simulations are case studies that are used to assess knowledge and skills by having you address realistic scenarios and tasks. They differ from most types of problems that you are used to answering on your accounting examinations.

Simulations are relatively new to the CPA exam, and nothing worries CPA candidates more than simulations. This book helps to calm those fears. It is a highly focused study aid that features nine practice simulations with a detailed walk-through of how to solve each one and all of the steps required to complete simulations during the exam. More importantly, you are provided with a multi-step approach for performing any simulation. Real-world examples help you perform efficient and effective searches and understand simulation requirements. In addition, the companion CD-ROM contains three additional full simulations that emulate the exam experience. By completing this book you will significantly improve your performance on the CPA exam.

Good luck!

Ray Whittington

# ABOUT THE AUTHOR

**Ray Whittington**, PhD, CPA, CMA, CIA, is the dean of the College of Commerce at DePaul University. Prior to joining the faculty at DePaul, Professor Whittington was the Director of Accountancy at San Diego State University. From 1989 through 1991, he was the Director of Auditing Research for the American Institute of Certified Public Accountants (AICPA), and he previously was on the audit staff of KPMG. He previously served as a member of the Auditing Standards Board of the AICPA and as a member of the Accounting and Review Services Committee and the Board of Regents of the Institute of Internal Auditors. Professor Whittington has published numerous textbooks, articles, monographs, and continuing education courses.

SECOND EDITION

# WILEY CPA EXAM

# How to Master Simulations

# 1 INTRODUCTION

Successful completion of the Uniform CPA Examination is one of the requirements for becoming a Certified Public Accountant (CPA) in one of the 54 jurisdictions in which it is given. Passing the CPA examination can have a significantly positive effect on your career. If you have completed your accounting education, it is imperative that you put forth the effort to complete the exam. Successful completion of the CPA exam is an attainable goal but it takes work. Keep this foremost in your mind as you undertake your study program.

It is important to note that the AICPA expects you to be familiar with the functionality and format of the CPA exam before you report to a testing center to take it. This expectation is set forth in a notice on the AICPA's Web site as shown below.

---

**IMPORTANT NOTICE**

**Candidates are responsible for reviewing the Uniform CPA Examination tutorial and sample tests. Thorough familiarity with the examination's functionality, format, and directions is required before candidates report to test centers. Failure to follow the directions provided in the tutorial and sample tests, including the directions on how to respond, may adversely affect candidate scores.**

---

This book will help you gain the required understanding of the functionality and format of the simulations on the exam. It will also help you to develop an effective approach to completing simulations.

## ADMINISTRATION OF THE CPA EXAM

The four sections of the CPA Examination are delivered in a computer-based format. This provides a significant advantage to you as a candidate. You may take the exam one section at a time. As a result, your studies can be focused on that one section, improving your chances for success. In addition, during eight months of every year, you may take the exam on your schedule, six days a week and in the morning or in the afternoon.

## PURPOSE OF THE CPA EXAM

The CPA exam is designed to test the entry-level knowledge and skills necessary to protect the public interest. The knowledge and skills were identified through Practice Analyses using inputs from practicing CPAs. The skills identified include

- Analysis—the ability to organize, process, and interpret data to develop options for decision making.
- Judgment—the ability to evaluate options for decision-making and provide an appropriate conclusion.
- Communication—the ability to effectively elicit and/or express information through written or oral means.
- Research—the ability to locate and extract relevant information from available resource materials.
- Understanding—the ability to recognize and comprehend the meaning and application of a particular matter.

You should keep these skills foremost in your mind as you prepare and sit for any section of the CPA Exam.

The CPA exam is comprised of four sections: Auditing and Attestation, Financial Accounting and Reporting, Regulation, and Business Environment and Concepts. All four sections contain multiple-choice testlets. The Auditing and Attestation, Financial Accounting and Reporting, and Regulation sections also each include two simulations.

## SCORING THE EXAM

CPA exam scores are reported on a scale from 0 to 99. Except for the Business Environment and Concepts, the total score is a combination of scores from the multiple-choice questions and simulation parts of the exam. The total score for the Business Environment and Concepts section is determined by a candidate's performance on the multiple-choice questions. A total score of 75 is required to pass each section.

Most of the responses on the computer-based CPA examination are objective in nature. Obviously, this includes the responses to the multiple-choice questions. However, it also includes most of the responses to the requirements of simulations. Requirements of simulations include responses involving check boxes, entries into spreadsheets, form completion, graphical responses, drag and drop, transfer to answer, and written communication. All of these responses, with the exception of written communication, are computer graded. Therefore, no consideration is given to any comments or explanations outside of the structured responses. You must provide the correct response and only the correct response.

Graders are used to score the responses involving written communication, (e.g., a written memorandum). Written communication is graded for quality of the writing; not for technical accuracy. However, the communication must be on point to be graded at all. That is, it must be responsive to the requirement. In other words, it must be helpful to the person or persons to whom it is addressed. A second review will be performed for all candidates that earn initial grades that are just below the 75-point cut-off.

On the Auditing and Accounting, Financial Accounting and Reporting, and Regulation sections, the multiple-choice questions account for 70% of the total score. The objective portions of the simulations account for 20% of the total score and the communication parts of the simulations account for 10% of the total score. Therefore, reasonable performance on the simulations is essential to obtaining a passing score on any one of these sections. The historical cumulative pass rates on all parts are of the exam are between 40 and 45%.

### Multiple-Choice Testlets

The multiple-choice questions within each section are organized into three groups, which are referred to as *testlets*. Each multiple-choice testlet is comprised of approximately 30 multiple-choice questions. The multiple-choice testlets vary in overall difficulty. A testlet is labeled either "medium difficult" or "difficult" based on its makeup. A "difficult" testlet has a higher percentage of hard questions than a "medium difficult" testlet. Every candidate's first multiple-choice testlet in each section will be a "medium difficult" testlet. If a candidate scores well on the first testlet, he or she will receive a "difficult" second testlet. Candidates that do not perform well on the first testlet, receive a second "medium difficult" testlet. Because the scoring procedure takes the difficulty of the testlet into account, candidates are scored fairly regardless of the type of testlets they receive.

### Simulations

Simulations are condensed case studies that are designed to test skills and knowledge that cannot effectively be tested with multiple-choice questions. Simulations generally begin with a scenario that provides the basis to perform a number of exercises. The exercises may involve completing spreadsheets or forms, selecting answers to objective questions, researching an issue, or completing a professional communication. While the requirements vary, every simulation will have both a research and a communication requirement. The simulations are the principal ways that practice skills are tested, especially communication and research.

## COMPLETING SIMULATIONS

The simulations are presented in a Windows-based format that navigates similarly to other programs that you have no doubt used. When the simulation is opened, it is presented with a series of tabs across the top. An example of the tabs from a simulation for the Auditing and Attestation section of the exam is illustrated below:

Certain of the tabs are informational in nature.

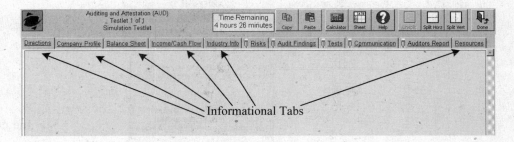

Others, the ones with a pencil logo, contain requirements that must be completed.

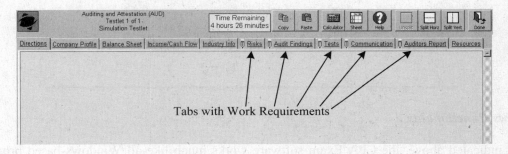

To navigate from tab to tab, you simply use the mouse to click on the desired tab.

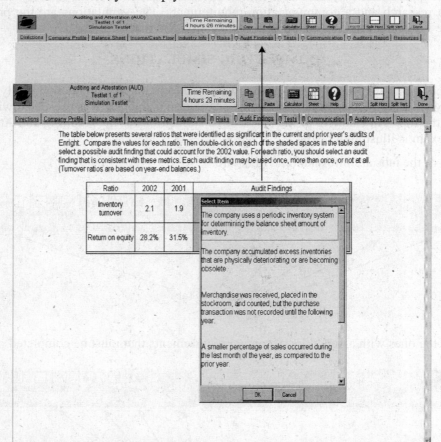

### Windows Functionality

As indicated above, the CPA Exam software works much like all Windows-based programs. Therefore, the more familiar you are with programs such as Microsoft Word and Excel, the easier it will be for you to use the exam software. The following is a summary of some of the functionality important to working simulations. To get more practice, you should review the AICPA tutorials and practice exams (www.cpa-exam.org) and the software included with this text.

The scroll bar allows you to view material in a document that is too large to fit on the screen. On the CPA Exam, the scroll bar will be active whenever all the material in a window will not fit on the screen. To scroll down, you simply click on the down arrow; the up arrow can be clicked on to move up the document.

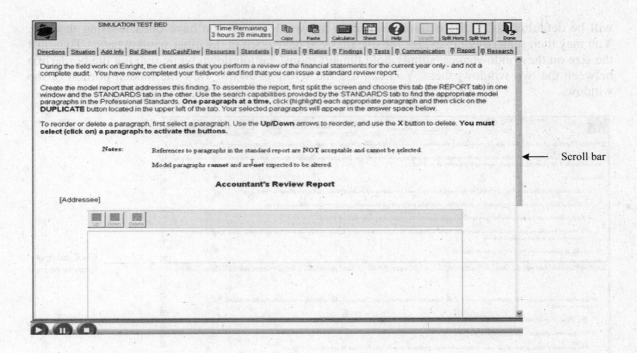

When you have opened a tool or resource (e.g., spreadsheet, depreciation schedule, etc.) over an existing window, you may be able to **resize** the item by holding down the left mouse button while it is positioned on a spreadsheet corner. You can then drag the item to the desired size. You can always **move** the item by holding down the left mouse button on the item's title bar and moving it to the desired location. As with any other Windows-based program, the item may be closed by right clicking on the X in the title bar.

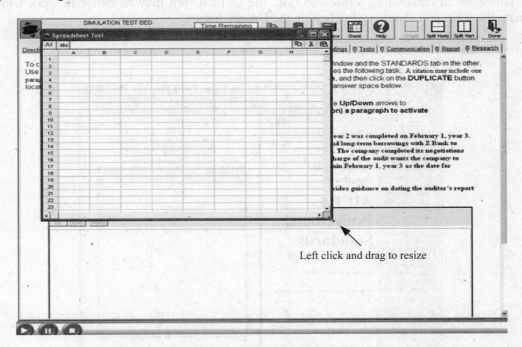

In some cases it will be useful or necessary to view two tabs at one time. **Split screen** functions allow you to split the screen horizontally (Split Horz) or vertically (Split Vert). If you split the screen horizontally, a complete set of new tabs will appear in the new windowpane and you will be defaulted to the **Directions** tab unless the windowpane you have open is using that tab. You may then select any tab except the one that you have open in the other windowpane. To adjust the size on the windowpanes, simply hold the left mouse button down while moving the borderline between the two windowpanes. You can use the scroll arrows to view the hidden portion of the window.

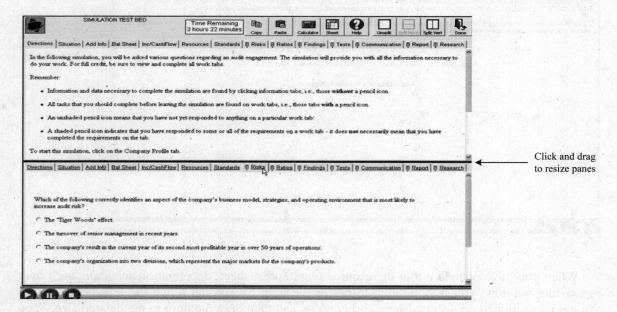

Click and drag to resize panes

You should choose the horizontal or vertical split depending on the task being performed. The horizontal split usually will be more convenient because you can see the entire width of the window. However, in completing a research task, the vertical split may be easier to work with. To eliminate the split, you should right click on the Unsplit button.

Unsplit button

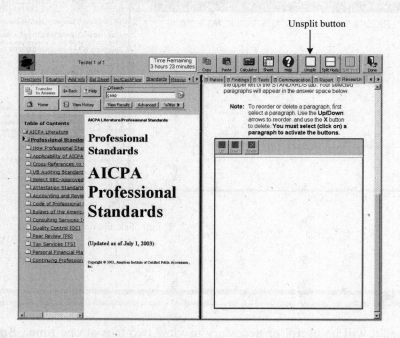

The **copy and paste** buttons work like the same functions in other Windows-based programs. Items or cells that are selected can be copied by right clicking the Copy button, and pasted by right clicking the Paste button after the desired (highlighted) position has been selected. Splitting screens make copying and pasting easy.

Copy  Paste

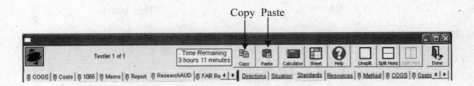

**Tools.** Several tools are available in every simulation, including a scratch spreadsheet and a calculator. The scratch spreadsheet may be called up by left clicking on the Sheet button. The CPA exam spreadsheet functions much like an Excel spreadsheet. Titles, numbers or functions may be put in any blank cell. The size of the cells may be changed by holding the left mouse button down on the cell borderline and dragging it to the desired width or height.

Functions must always begin with an equal sign (=)

| | A | B | C | D | E | F | G |
|---|---|---|---|---|---|---|---|
| 1 | Beginning Inventory | 8000 | | | | | |
| 2 | Purchases 6 months ended 6/30 | 27000 | | | | | |
| 3 | | | | | | | |
| 4 | Total | | | | | | |

Spreadsheet Tool — B4  abc  =SUM(B1:B2)

As with an Excel spreadsheet, you can use a number of **operators** to perform calculations. The Help button may be used to call up the list of operators that can be used as illustrated below.

Help button

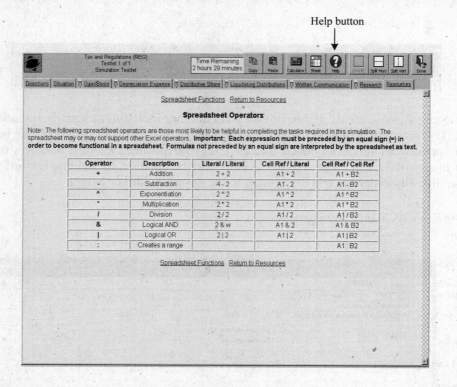

The spreadsheet also can accommodate a number of **functions**. They may also be called up using the Help button at the top of the screen, as illustrated below.

| *Function* | *Description* | *Syntax* | *Example* |
|---|---|---|---|
| PMT | Returns the payment amount given the present value, specified interest rate, and number of terms | PMT (*Amount, Interest, Terms, TermsPerYear*)<br>Where *Amount* = Present value<br>*Interest* = Interest rate expressed as annual percentage<br>*Terms* = Total number of terms<br>*TermsPerYear* = Number of payments per year | PMT (20000, 6, 120, 12) = 222.05 |
| PRODUCT | Multiplies all the arguments and returns the product | PRODUCT (*value1, value2,…*) | PRODUCT (A1: A9)<br>PRODUCT (1, 2, 3, 5) = 30 |
| PV | Returns the present value of an investment based on the interest rate, number and amount of periodic payments, and future value | PV (*Rate, Nper, Pmt, Fv, Type*)<br>Where *Rate* = Interest per period<br>*Nper* = Number of payment periods<br>*Pmt* = Payment made each period<br>*Fv* = (Optional) Future value<br>*Type* = (Optional) 0 if payment at end of period; 1 if payment at beginning of period | PV(0.005, 60, -100, 0, 1) = 5198.42 |
| SUM | Sums cells | SUM (*value1, value2,…*) | SUM (A1: A9)<br>SUM (9, 13, -4) = 18 |

| ADD | Adds two arguments | ADD (*value1, value2*) | ADD (B3, C4) |
|---|---|---|---|
| FV | Returns the future value of an investment based on a present value, periodic payments, and a specified interest rate | FV (*Rate, Nper, Pmt, Pv, Type*)<br>Where *Rate* = interest per period<br>*Nper* = number of payment periods<br>*Pmt* = Payment made each period<br>*Pv* = (Optional) Present value<br>*Type* = (Optional) 0 if payment at end of period; 1 if payment at beginning of period | FV (0.005, 60, -100, 100, 1) = 6877 |
| IF | Returns a value based on a logical value | IF (*value1, value2, value3*)<br>If *value1* is nonzero (True), then *value2* is returned.  IF *value1* is zero (False), then *value3* is returned | IF (1>2, 5, 10) = 10 |
| NPER | Returns the number of periods for an investment based on present value, future value, periodic payments, and specified interest rate | NPER (*Rate, Pmt, Pv, Fv, Type*)<br>Where *Rate* = interest per period<br>*Pmt* = Payment made each period<br>*Pv* = (Optional) Present value<br>*Fv* = (Optional) Future value<br>*Type* = (Optional) 0 if payment at end of period; 1 if payment at beginning of period | NPER (0.005, -790, 90000, 0, 1) = 167.72 |

A **calculator** may be called up by right clicking on the Calculator button.  This calculator works like others that you would be familiar with.  However, at the bottom, the calculator has Copy/Paste function buttons that makes it easy to transfer the calculation to an answer box.

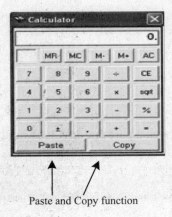

Paste and Copy function

### Simulation Screen Layout

As described above, simulations have multiple parts separated by computer tabs.  Typically they begin with directions and situation tabs and continue with tabs requiring responses and a **Resource** tab.  An example of simulation instructions is shown below.

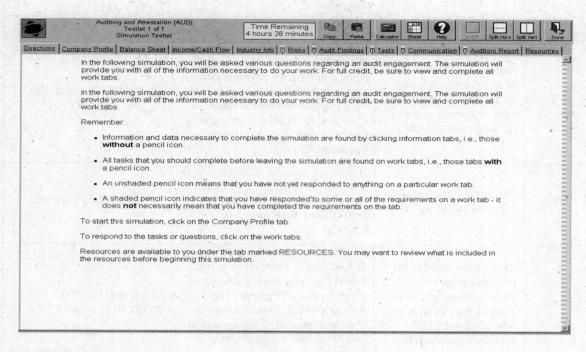

## Types of Responses

The responses required by the tabs of a simulation vary in their nature.  Any of the following types of responses might be required on a simulation's parts:

- Multiple selection
- Drop-down selection
- Numeric and monetary inputs
- Formula answers
- Check box response
- Form completion
- Research results
- Written communication

The following screenshot illustrates a part that involves multiple selections:

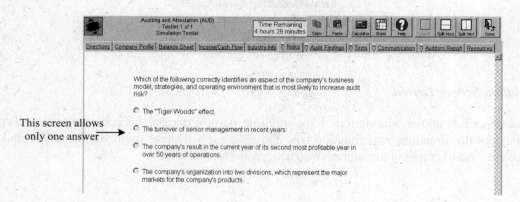

The screenshot below illustrates a tab that requires the candidate to select the response that represents a plausible explanation for the ratio changes using a drop-down menu.

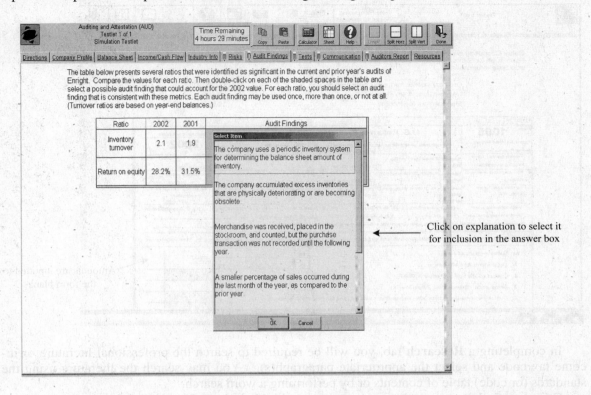

The following screenshot illustrates a part that requires inputting amounts or formulas.  The calculator tool may be used to compute the appropriate input amount.

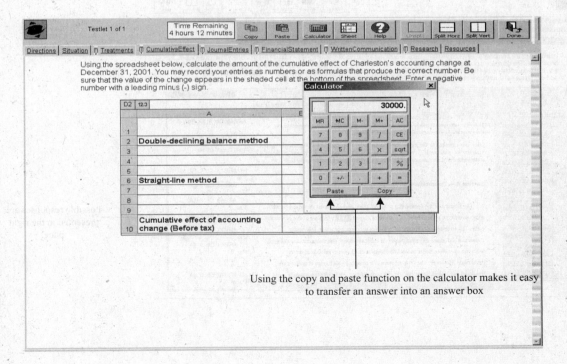

The screenshot below illustrates a part that requires completion of a form.

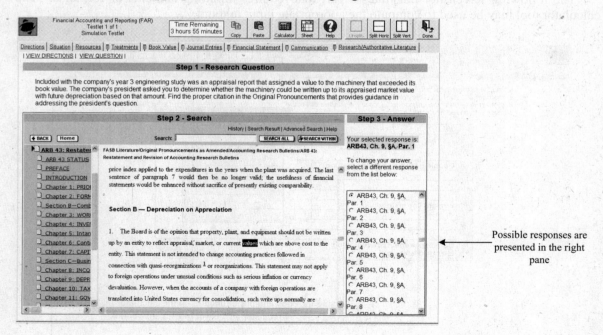

In completing a **Research** tab, you will be required to search the professional literature or income tax code and select the appropriate paragraph(s). You may search the literature using the standards (or code) table of contents or by performing a word search.

Once you find the appropriate section, you can highlight it as shown below.

The **written communications** requirements of simulations will involve some real-world writing assignments that a CPA might have to perform, such as drafting a memorandum to a client explaining a tax or accounting issue, or a memorandum to the working papers addressing an accounting issue. **Remember the communications are not graded for technical accuracy.** However, they must be on point to be graded at all. Therefore, you should not devote a lot of time to considering the technical accuracy of your communication. As long as it is responsive to the requirement it will be graded for writing quality. The screenshot below illustrates a communication requirement for the Financial Accounting and Reporting section of the CPA exam.

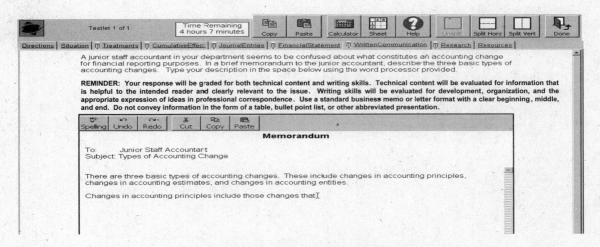

## ORGANIZATION OF THE BOOK

The remainder of the book helps you develop the skills that will make you successful in mastering simulations on the CPA exam. Chapter 2 provides vital strategies for approaching the research requirements of CPA exam simulations. In Chapter 3 you will be provided with a detailed description of how to improve your written communications to maximize your score on those requirements of all sections of the exam. Chapters 4, 5, and 6 provide detailed guidance on how to complete Financial Accounting and Reporting, Regulation, and Auditing and Attestation simulations, respectively.

# **2** RESEARCH REQUIREMENTS OF SIMULATIONS

As discussed in Chapter 1, every simulation will include a research requirement—a tab that will require you to search the professional standards or the tax code and select the appropriate section or sections. The key to performing research requirements effectively is to find the appropriate sections of the literature or the code. In addition to being accurate, you have to be efficient! Time is very limited on all parts of the CPA exam.

The two keys to improving your effectiveness and efficiency in performing a literature search are: (1) become very familiar with the functionality of the AICPA research software, and (2) develop efficient research strategies. This chapter focuses on the functionality of the software and search strategies that will help you with all sections of the examination. Chapters 4, 5, and 6 will apply the skills that you learn here to the simulations in the three sections of the CPA exam.

## FUNCTIONALITY OF THE SEARCH SOFTWARE

The new format of the research requirements is very user friendly. You must merely research the issue, find the appropriate paragraph(s) of the professional standards or code, and select it in the right pane of the search window.

At times you will decide to use a keyword search to find the appropriate literature. When you perform a search you will obtain a list of professional literature that meets the search criteria as illustrated below.

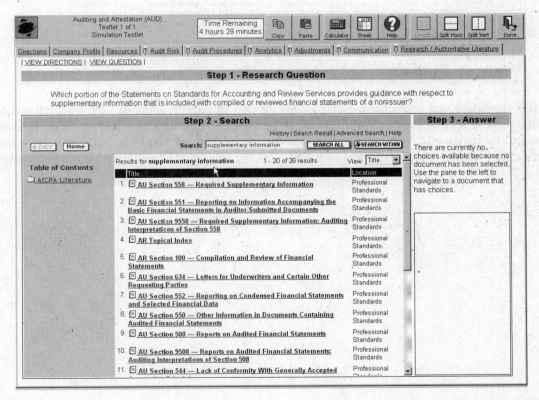

You can then review the titles to identify the standard or section that is most likely to answer the research question. Clicking on the standard or section will allow you to review it. As shown below, the keywords or phrase that you used in your search will be highlighted to help you find the relevant passages. On the top right-hand corner of the **Standards** or **Code** tab, the View is a pull-down menu that allows you to select the detail of your search results. You can just display the title of the document or you can display a short, medium, or long part of the document. More detail may be useful in selecting the relevant document but it takes more time to review.

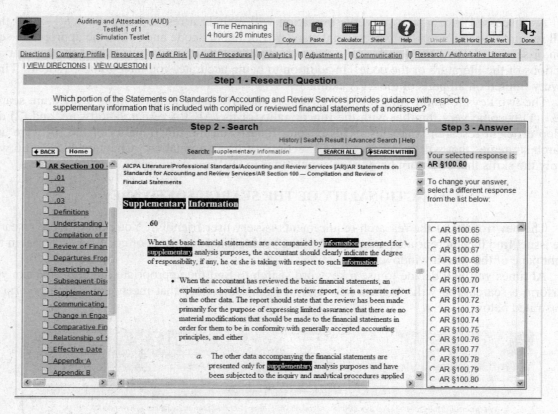

It is important that you review each passage quickly to see if it addresses the research question. If a standard or section is not relevant, you must go back to the titles to select the next standard or section to be reviewed. You can see that if you have not done a good job of developing a search strategy, you could waste a great deal of time reviewing standards or sections that are not relevant.

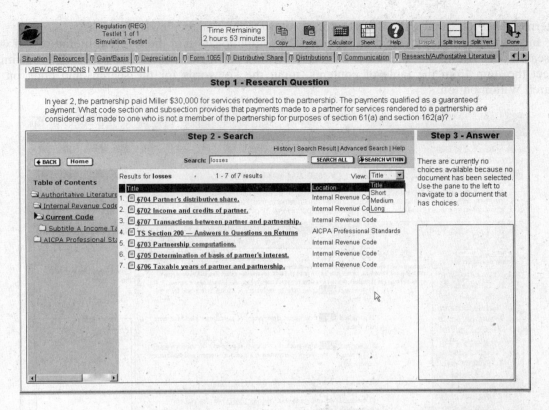

As you are performing your search activities, you will visit various standards and sections. The browser compiles a list of the places that you have visited. In some situations, you may need to revisit one or more of those locations. You can use the View History button to provide a list of the sites that you have visited and click on any of the titles to return to a particular standard or section.

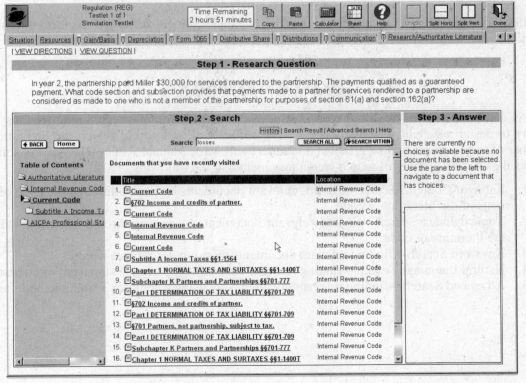

Alternatively, you can use the Back button to return to previously viewed screens.

In some cases you may be able to narrow down the location of the relevant literature and want to search only within that literature. To search within particular standard or code title, you simply select the item from the table of contents, input the keywords for the search, and click on the Search Within button.

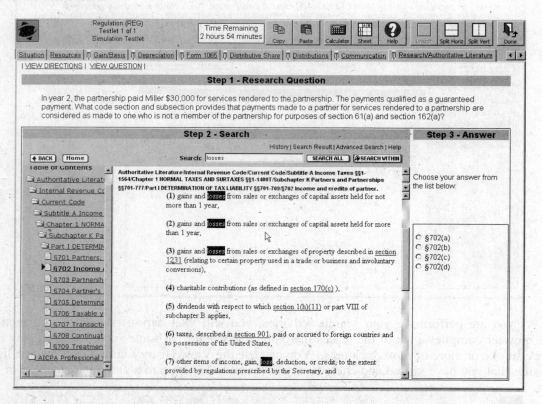

If you find yourself in a situation in which you cannot remember how to perform a particular function, you can always use the Help button to get a description of the major commands.

## SEARCH STRATEGIES

As discussed previously, a key to being successful in performing research requirements is the ability to design efficient search strategies. The software allows you to search the literature in a number of ways. Some will be efficient and others will waste valuable time. The AICPA software allows the use of a number of search techniques including the following:

1. Table of Contents Search—finding relevant documents by paging through the table of contents of the literature or code.
2. Topical Index Search—finding relevant documents by paging through a topical index of the literature or code.
3. Keyword Search—finding relevant documents by using descriptive words.
4. Natural Language Search—finding relevant documents by using a statement or question.
5. Advanced Search—finding relevant documents by using a complex search methodology.

## Table of Contents Search

A table of contents search involves expanding entries in the table of contents of the professional standards or code until you drill down to the relevant document.  To expand the table of contents under a particular table of contents entry, you simply left click on the entry.

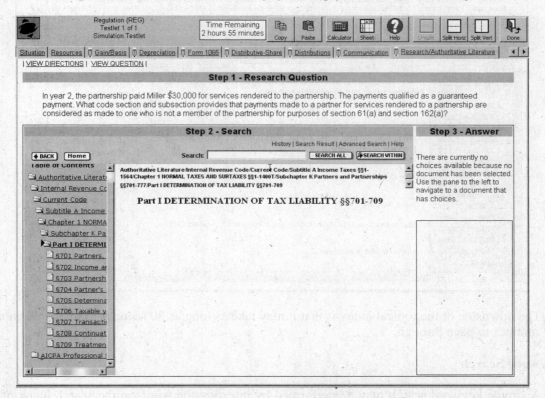

A table of contents search is usually efficient only when you have a good idea of the location of the relevant documents.  For example, assume that you are researching an issue regarding the impairment of a fixed asset.  If you know that FASB No. 144 deals with impairment of fixed assets, you can quickly get to the document using the table of contents of the original pronouncements. Then you can review the table of contents of the standard to get to the relevant paragraph.

## Topical Index Search

A topical index search is usually more efficient than a table of contents search.  The topical index will allow you to get directly to the relevant document, if you can find an appropriate entry in the index.

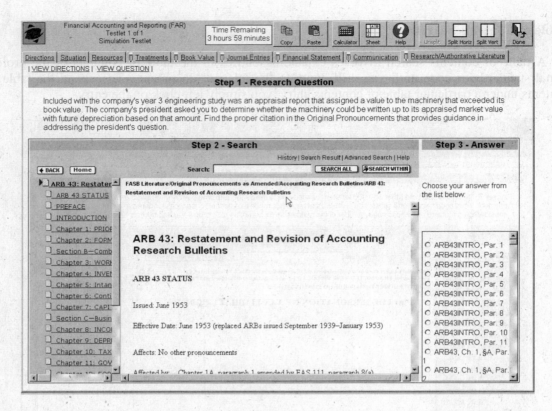

The downside of the topical index is that it may take as long as 30 seconds to load, and another few minutes to page through.

## Keyword Search

A simple keyword search may be performed by inserting the words in the search blank of the **Standards** or **Code** tab. To determine whether a simple keyword search will be efficient it is important to understand what documents are retrieved. Assume that you are looking for literature relevant to the costing of inventory. Accordingly, you input "inventory cost" in the search box. The software will retrieve a list of all of the documents that contain the word "inventory" and/or the word "cost." You can easily see that this could result in a large number of documents to review. Therefore, a more complex search is often more efficient.

## Natural Language Search

A natural language search operates much like a simple keyword search. You can type in a phrase or question and the software will search on the relevant literature. This involves returning all the literature that contains one or more of the keywords in the question or phrase. Therefore, a natural language search also will often return a large number of documents to review.

## Advanced Search

Advanced search provides a screen that offers more options to perform more focused searches.

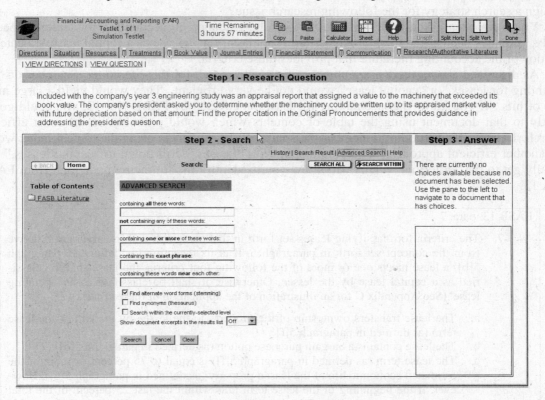

An advanced search may allow you to significantly restrict the number of documents you must consider, especially when you do not know where the particular guidance is located.  The advanced search allows you to

1. Retrieve only those documents containing all of the words listed.
2. Retrieve only those documents not containing any of the words listed.
3. Retrieve those documents containing one or more of the words listed.
4. Retrieve only those documents containing an exact phrase.
5. Retrieve only those documents containing the words listed when they are near each other.

In performing one of the above searches, you may also select certain other options, including

1. Find alternate word forms (stemming)—in performing the search the software will select alternative forms of the words.  For example, if "cost" was a listed word documents containing other forms of "cost" such as "costing" would also be retrieved.
2. Find synonyms—in performing the search the software will select documents that contain words that mean the same as a listed word.  For example, if "disbursement" was a listed word all documents that contain other words that mean the same as disbursement (e.g., expenditure) would be retrieved.
3. Search within the currently selected level—in performing the search the software will search only the documents in the currently selected level.

Generally, advanced search techniques are better than simple word searches or topical index searches.  The specific nature of the search means that a lesser number of documents will be retrieved.  This means less work for you when trying to identify the correct section.   On the other hand, if you are not very careful about how you construct the search, the relevant documents will not be retrieved at all.   This also could waste a significant amount of time.

## APPLYING THE SEARCH STRATEGIES

Now let's attempt to apply these search strategies to a couple of examples. How would you design a search strategy for the following research issue?

You have been asked by a client to provide the guidance on accounting for leases. Specifically, you have been asked to obtain the criteria for classifying a lease as a capital lease. Locate the section of the accounting literature that provides these criteria.

As discussed above, there are a number of ways to search for this literature. Searches on "accounting for leases" or "capital lease" would not be very efficient. They would yield a large number of hits. If you know that accounting for leases is covered by FASB No. 13, you could go directly to that document using the table of contents which would probably be the most efficient search strategy. If you do not remember the source of the guidance, using the topical index would be another efficient approach. You would start with "Leases," drill down to "capital leases," and finally get to the "criterion." This will allow you to identify the following paragraph from FASB No. 13.

---

FASB 13, para. 7

7. The criteria for classifying leases set forth in this paragraph and in paragraph 8 derive from the concept set forth in paragraph 6. If at its inception (as defined in paragraph 5[b]) a lease meets one or more of the following four criteria, the lease shall be classified as a capital lease by the lessee. Otherwise, it shall be classified as an operating lease. (See Appendix C for an illustration of the application of these criteria.)

    a. The lease transfers ownership of the property to the lessee by the end of the lease term (as defined in paragraph 5[f]).

    b. The lease contains a bargain purchase option (as defined in paragraph 5[d]).

    c. The lease term (as defined in paragraph 5[f]) is equal to 75 percent or more of the estimated economic life of the leased property (as defined in paragraph 5[g]). However, if the beginning of the lease term falls within the last 25 percent of the total estimated economic life of the leased property, including earlier years of use, this criterion shall not be used for purposes of classifying the lease.

    d. The present value at the beginning of the lease term of the minimum lease payments (as defined in paragraph 5[j]), excluding that portion of the payments representing executory costs such as insurance, maintenance, and taxes to be paid by the lessor, including any profit thereon, equals or exceeds 90 percent of the excess of the fair value of the leased property (as defined in paragraph 5[c]) to the lessor at the inception of the lease over any related investment tax credit retained by the lessor and expected to be realized by him. However, if the beginning of the lease term falls within the last 25 percent of the total estimated economic life of the leased property, including earlier years of use, this criterion shall not be used for purposes of classifying the lease. A lessor shall compute the present value of the minimum lease payments using the interest rate implicit in the lease (as defined in paragraph 5[k]). A lessee shall compute the present value of the minimum lease payments using his incremental borrowing rate (as defined in paragraph 5[1]), unless (i) it is practicable for him to learn the implicit rate computed by the lessor and (ii) the implicit rate computed by the lessor is less than the lessee's incremental borrowing rate. If both of those conditions are met, the lessee shall use the implicit rate.

---

Now, let's try to apply the strategies to a tax issue. How would you design a search strategy for the following issue?

A client has been paying a babysitter to watch his child while he works in 2007. He has heard from a friend that he can get a tax credit for the payments. Research the tax code and find the code section and subsection that provide the maximum amount of employment-related child care expenses that qualify for the tax credit.

This is a little more difficult because there is a child care credit for employers and employees. If you search on child care credit you will get a lot of hits related to the employer credit. Ideally, you would know that the employee credit is referred to as a dependent credit. Searching on "dependent credit" will get you to the appropriate section efficiently. Otherwise, a search on the topical index on credits would also get you to the appropriate literature fairly efficiently. The appropriate tax code citation is presented below.

> **21(c)** DOLLAR LIMIT ON AMOUNT CREDITABLE. --The amount of the employment-related expenses incurred during any taxable year which may be taken into account under subsection (a) shall not exceed –
>
> **21(c)(1)** $3,000 if there is 1 qualifying individual with respect to the taxpayer for such taxable year, or
>
> **21(c)(2)** $6,000 if there are 2 or more qualifying individuals with respect to the taxpayer for such taxable year.
>
> The amount determined under paragraph (1) or (2) (whichever is applicable) shall be reduced by the aggregate amount excludable from gross income under section 129 for the taxable year.

Finally, let's examine a research issue that might appear on the Auditing and Attestation section. How would you design a search strategy for the following issue?

Assume that you are performing the audit of a nonpublic company. You have completed the audit and are in the process of drafting the management representation letter to be signed by appropriate individuals in management positions. Search the professional literature for guidance on who should sign this letter.

For this issue it is fairly easy to develop an efficient search strategy. You might start with the phrase "management representations," but this will give you a fairly large number of hits. However, if you search within these documents and search on "signed," you will quickly get to the appropriate guidance. A topical index search would also result in a fairly efficient search. The appropriate guidance is contained in AU section 333.09, as illustrated below.

> **.09** The written representations should be addressed to the auditor. Because the auditor is concerned with events occurring through the date of his or her report that may require adjustment to or disclosure in the financial statements the representations should be made as of the date of the auditor's report. [If the auditor "dual dates" his or her report the auditor should consider whether obtaining additional representations relating to the subsequent event is appropriate. See section 530 *Dating of the Independent Auditor's Report* paragraph .05]. The letter should be signed by those members of management with overall responsibility for financial and operating matters that the auditor believes are responsible for and knowledgeable about directly or through others in the organization the matters covered by the representations. Such members of management normally include the chief executive officer and chief financial officer or others with equivalent positions in the entity. [As amended effective for audits of financial statements for periods ending on or after December 15, 2006 by Statement on Auditing Standards No. 113.]

There are numerous ways to approach a search. Some search strategies are more efficient than others. It is up to you to get proficient at searching the literature. The best way to do that is to practice with databases such as the AICPA accounting and auditing database. Once you have applied to sit for the exam and are deemed eligible by a state board of accountancy, you can receive a free six-month subscription to the accounting and auditing professional literature used on the CPA Exam. You can find out how to order your subscription at the AICPA Web site, www.cpa-exam.org. You should also practice with a tax database, such as RIA Checkpoint: Accounting or CCH Tax Research Network. There is no substitute for experience with these systems in improving the effectiveness and efficiency of your research searches.

# PROBLEMS

The following problems are designed to hone your research skills. In approaching the problems, use what you have learned to select the most efficient search strategy. If the first strategy is not efficient, try another. The key is to get practice in quickly deciding on and executing an efficient search strategy. The solutions to the problems are included in Appendix A.

1.  Assume that you are auditing the financial statements of Wagner Company. Management of the company has disclosed to you the existence of a lawsuit against the company by another company alleging patent infringement. Research the professional accounting literature to find the guidance on when an estimated liability for this lawsuit must be accrued.

2.  Assume that you are the CFO of Matrix Corp., a nonpublic company, and the company has recently established a pension plan. Research the professional accounting literature to obtain a list of the required financial statement disclosure for a pension plan of a nonpublic entity.

3.  Assume that you have a client that is considering obtaining a home equity loan and she has heard that the interest on the loan may be deductible. Research the federal income tax code to obtain the provisions that indicate the amount of home equity debt on which the taxpayer may deduct interest.

4.  Assume that a regular corporation has made a number of contributions to qualified charitable organizations. The corporation has a small amount of income in the current year. Research the federal income tax code to identify the provisions that indicate the income limitations on the deduction of the contributions by the corporation.

5.  Assume that you are performing a review of financial statements for Gordon Co., a nonpublic company. You are unsure of the specific inquiries and other procedures that must be performed. Research the auditing professional literature to identify the list of inquiries and other procedures that must be performed in the review of financial statements of a nonpublic company.

6.  Assume that you are auditing the financial statements of Howard Co., a nonpublic company. The company has inventory stored at a public warehouse in a remote location. Identify the auditing professional literature that describes the procedures that should be performed for such inventories.

# 3 COMMUNICATION REQUIREMENTS OF SIMULATIONS

As discussed in Chapter 1, every simulation includes a communication requirement. Typically, the requirement is to write a memorandum to management, the board of directors, or to the audit staff. Your communication will be scored based on the following criteria:

1. Organization: structure, ordering of ideas, and linking one idea to another

   - Overview/thesis statement
   - Unified paragraphs (topic and supporting sentences)
   - Transitions and connections

2. Development: supporting evidence/information to clarify thoughts

   - Details
   - Definitions
   - Examples
   - Rephrasing

3. Expression: use of standard business English

   - Grammar
   - Punctuation
   - Word usage
   - Capitalization
   - Spelling

Remember a communication response is not graded for technical accuracy. However, it must be on point to be graded at all. For example, if the requirement is to write a memorandum to describe the components of internal control, the response must describe a group of components although the group does not have to be complete or technically accurate. The information must be helpful to the intended user. In addition, you must demonstrate your writing ability. You should not convey information in the form of a table, bullet point list, or other abbreviated presentation.

## SUGGESTIONS FOR BETTER COMMUNICATION

### Idea Formation

You should develop coherent ideas from the material provided. Before beginning the communication, you should understand the purpose and the major information to be communicated. Thoughts should be organized in a logical fashion. Prepare an outline to organize your ideas.

### Coherent Organization

You should organize your responses in a manner that is logical and easy to follow. Jumbled paragraphs and disorderly sentences will only confuse the grader and make his/her job more difficult. The following techniques will help improve written coherence.[1]

---

[1] *Adapted from* **Writing for Accountants** *by Aletha S. Hendrickson (Cincinnati, OH: Southwestern Publishing Co., 1993) pp. 128-209.*

- Use short paragraphs composed of short sentences
- Indent paragraphs to set off lists, equations, key ideas, etc. when appropriate
- Maintain coherence within paragraphs

  - Use a topic sentence at the beginning of each paragraph
  - Develop and support this topic throughout the rest of the paragraph
  - Present old or given information before discussing new information
  - Discuss ideas in chronological order
  - Use parallel grammatical structure
  - Be consistent in person, verb tense, and number
  - Substitute pronouns or synonyms for previously used keywords
  - Use transitions (e.g., therefore, finally)

- Maintain coherence between paragraphs

  - Repeat keywords from previous paragraphs
  - Use transitions

As indicated above, you are strongly advised to keyword outline your responses **before** writing your communications. This technique helps you to focus on the flow of ideas you want to convey before starting the actual writing task.

## Conciseness

You should express yourself in as few words as possible. Complex, wordy sentences are hard to understand. Conciseness can be improved using the following guidelines.

- Write in short sentences
- Use a simple word instead of a long word if it serves the same purpose
- Avoid passive constructions (e.g., **was** evalua**ted**)
- Use words instead of phrases
- Combine sentences, if possible
- Avoid empty fillers (e.g., **it is** apparent; **there seems to be**)
- Avoid multiple negatives (e.g., **no** reason for **not** using)

## Clarity

Written responses should leave no doubt in the reader's mind as to the meaning intended. Clarity can be improved as follows:

- Do **not** use abbreviations
- Use correct terminology
- Use examples
- Use words with specific and precise meanings
- Write in short, well-constructed sentences
- Make sure subjects and verbs agree
- Make sure pronouns and their antecedents agree in number (e.g., the partnership must decide how **it** [not **they**] wants to split profits.)
- Avoid unclear references to a pronoun's antecedent (e.g., A should inform B that **he** must perform on the contract by January 1—Who does "he" refer to?)

## Use of Standard English

Spelling, punctuation, and word usage should follow the norm used in most books, newspapers, and magazines. Note the following common mistakes:

- Confusion of its/it's

  *The firm issued **its** stock.*
  ***It's** (it is) the stock of that firm.*

- Confusion of there/their/they're

  ***There** will be a dividend declaration.*
  ***Their** dividend was declared last week.*
  ***They're** (they are) declaring a dividend.*

- Spelling errors

  *Separate **not** seperate*
  *Receivable **not** recievable*

**The word processing software that you will use to write the communication on the exam has a spell check function.  Use it.**

## Appropriateness for the Reader

You will be asked to prepare a communication for a certain reader (e.g., a memorandum for a client).  Writing that is appropriate for the reader will take into account the reader's background, knowledge of the subject, interests, and concerns.  (When the intended reader is not specified, you should write for a knowledgeable CPA.)

Intended readers may include those who are unfamiliar with most terms and concepts, and who seek financial information because of self-interest (i.e., clients, stockholders).  Try the following techniques for these readers:

- Avoid jargon, if possible (i.e., GAAS, etc.)
- Use parenthetical definitions

  - *Limited partner (liable only to the extent of contributed capital)*
  - *Marketable equity securities (short-term investments in stock)*

- Set off definitions as appositives

  *A note, a two-party negotiable instrument, may become uncollectible.*

- Incorporate a "you" attitude

The requirement of a question may also specify that the response should be directed to professionals who are knowledgeable of most terms and concepts.  Employ the following techniques with these readers:

- Use jargon
- Refer to authoritative sources (i.e., Code section 543 or FASB 13)
- Incorporate a "we" attitude

Again, preparing a keyword outline will assist you in meeting many of these requirements. You should also reread each written communication in its entirety.  Writing errors are common during the exam, so take your time to proofread and edit your answers.  Again, make use of the spell check function of the word processing software.

## METHODS FOR IMPROVING YOUR WRITING SKILLS

### Organization

Logical organization is very important.  Again, this is where the keyword outline helps.

## Syntax, Grammar, and Style

By the time you sit for the CPA exam, you have at your disposal various grammatical constructs from which you may form sentences. Believe it or not, you know quite a bit of English grammar; if you did not, you would never have made it this far in your studies. So in terms of your grammar, relax! You already know it.

A frequent problem with writing occurs with the syntactic structure of sentences. Although the Board of Examiners does not expect the rhetoric of Cicero, it does expect to read and understand your answer. The way in which the graders will assess writing skills further indicates that they are looking more for writing skills at the micro level (sentence level) than at the macro level (organizational level).

1. Basic syntactic structure (transitive and intransitive action verbs)

   Most English sentences are based on this simple dynamic: that someone or something (the subject) does some action (the predicate). These sentences involve action verbs and are grouped in the following categories:

   a. Subject-Verb

      *The TAXPAYER WAITED for 3 weeks to get a refund.*

   b. Subject-Verb-Direct Object (The object receives the action of the verb.)

      *The TAXPAYER SIGNED the CONTRACT.*

   c. Subject-Verb-Indirect Object-Direct Object (The direct object receives the action of the verb, but the indirect object is also affected by this action, though not in the same way as the direct object.)

      *The IRS GAVE US a DEFINITE DECISION well beyond our expectations.*

2. Syntactic structure (linking verbs)

   Linking verbs are verbs which, rather than expressing action, say something about the subject's state of being. In sentences with linking verbs, the subject is linked to a work which describes it or renames it.

   a. Subject-Linking Verb-Nominative (The nominative renames the subject.)

      *In the field of Accounting, the FASB IS the standard-setting BOARD.*

   b. Subject-Linking Verb-Adjective (The adjective describes the subject.)

      *Evidence of SCIENTER IS always HELPFUL in proving fraud.*

3. Subordinate clauses

   a. Adverbial clauses (subordinating connector + sentence). These clauses modify the action of the main clause.

      *When amounts are not substantiated, a nondeductible expense is incurred.*

   b. Noun clauses (nominal connectors + sentence). These clauses function as nouns in the main sentence.

      *When a tax return is not signed, we know that the return is not filed.*

   c. Adjective clauses [relative pronoun + verb + (object/nominative/adjective)]. These clauses function as noun modifiers.

      *The court with the highest authority is the one that sets the precedent.*

The above are patterns which form basic clauses (both dependent and independent).  In addition, numerous phrases may function as modifiers of the basic sentence elements.

(1)  Prepositional (a preposition + an object)

> *of the FASB*
> *on the data*
> *about a new type of depreciation*

(2)  Verbal

(a)  Verb + ing + a modifier (noun, verb, adverb, prepositional phrase)

1]  Used as an adjective

> *the expense requiring substantiation*
> *the alternative minimizing taxes*

2]  Used as a noun (gerund)

> *Performing all of the duties required by a contract is necessary to avoid breach.*

(b)  Verb + ed + modifier (noun, adverb, prepositional phrase)

1]  Used as an adjective

> *The basis used when historical costs cannot be determined is estimated value.*

(c)  Infinitive (to + verb + object)

1]  Used as a noun

> *The company needs to respond by filing an amended tax return.*

## Sentence Clarity

When constructing your sentences, do not separate basic sentence elements with too many phrases.

> *The liability for partnership losses exceeding capital contributions is another characteristic of a general partnership.*

> **Better:**  *One characteristic of a general partnership is the liability for partnership losses which exceed capital contributions.*

Refrain from lumping prepositional and infinitive phrases together.

> *The delegation of authority by a corporate director of day-to-day or routine matters to officers and agents of that corporation is a power and a duty of the director.*

> **Better:**  *Delegating authority for routine matters to officers and agents is a power and a duty of corporation's directors.*

Make sure that your pronouns have a clear and obvious referent.

> *When an accountant contracts with a client for the primary benefit of a third party, they are in privity of contract.*

> **Better:**  *When known to be a primary beneficiary of an accountant-client contract, a third party is in privity of contract with the accountant.*

Make sure that any adjectival verbal phrase clearly modifies a noun stated in the sentence.

*To avoid incurring a penalty, each return was prepared exactly as required.*

**Better:** *To avoid incurring a penalty, we prepared each return exactly as required.*

## SOME COMMUNICATION EXAMPLES

In this section we will focus on how to use the suggestions above to construct actual written communications in the three sections of the CPA Exam that include simulations, Audit and Attestation, Financial Accounting and Reporting, and Regulation.

### Audit and Attestation Example

The following is a communication requirement from an Audit and Attestation simulation.

> Memorandum

> This is your firm's sixth audit of DietWeb. In a memorandum to the audit team (below) summarize your view of the audit committee's strengths, weaknesses, and any changes that have occurred relating to the audit committee this year.
> Remember: Your response will be graded for both technical relevance and writing skills. For writing skills you should demonstrate an ability to develop your ideas, organize them, and express them clearly. Do not convey information in the form of a table, bullet point list, or other abbreviated presentation.

> To:    Audit Team
> From:  CPA Candidate
> Re:    DietWeb Audit Committee

To complete this requirement you must review the data about the company in the Company Profile tab as shown below.

> Company Profile

> The company's mission is to provide solutions that help individuals to realize their full potential through better eating habits and lifestyles. Much of 20X1 and 20X2 was spent in developing a unique software platform that facilitates the production of individualized meal plans and shopping lists using a specific mathematical algorithm, which considers the user's physical condition, proclivity to exercise, food preferences, cooking preferences, desire to use prepackaged meals or dine out, among others. DietWeb sold its first online diet program in 20X2 and has continued to market memberships through increasing online advertising arrangements through the years. The company has continued to develop this program throughout the years and finally became profitable in 20X6.
> DietWeb is executing a strategy to be a leading online provider of services, information and products related to nutrition, fitness and motivation. In 20X8, the company derived approximately 86% of its total revenues from the sale of approximately 203,000 personalized subscription-based online nutrition plans related to weight management, to dietary regimens such as vegetarianism and to specific medical conditions such as Type 2 diabetes. Given the personal nature of dieting, DietWeb assures customers of complete privacy of the information they provide. To this point DietWeb's management is proud of its success in assuring the privacy of information supplied by its customers—this is a constant battle given the variety of intrusion attempts by various Internet hackers.

DietWeb nutrition plans are paid in advance by customers and offered in increments of thirteen weeks with the customers having the ability to cancel and receive a refund of the unused portion of the subscription—this results in a significant level of "deferred revenue" each period. Although some Diet-Web members are billed through use of the postal system, most DietWeb members currently purchase programs and products using credit cards, with renewals billed automatically, until cancellation. One week of a basic DietWeb membership costs less than one-half the cost of a weekly visit to the leading classroom-based diet program. The president, Mr. William Readings, suggests that in addition to its superior cost-effectiveness, the DietWeb online diet program is successful relative to classroom-based programs due to its customization, ease of use, expert support, privacy, constant availability, and breadth of choice. The basic DietWeb membership includes

- Customized meal plans and workout schedules and related tools such as shopping lists, journals, and weight and exercise tracking.
- Interactive online support and education including approximately 100 message boards on various topics of interest to members and a library of dozens of multimedia educational segments presented by experts including psychologists, mental health counselors, dietitians, fitness trainers, a spiritual advisor and a physician.
- 24/7/365 telephone support from a staff of approximately 30 customer service representatives, nutritionists and fitness personnel.

Throughout its nine-year history, Mr. William Readings has served as chief executive officer. The other three founders of the company are also officers. A fifth individual, Willingsley Williamson, also a founder, served as Chief Financial Officer until mid-20X8 when he left the company due to a difference of opinion with Mr. Readings. The four founders purchased Mr. Williamson's stock and invested an additional approximately $1.2 million in common stock during 20X8 so as to limit the use of long-term debt.

The company's board of directors is currently composed of the four individuals who remain active in the company; these four individuals also serve as the company's audit committee; Mr. Readings chairs both the board and the audit committee. Previously, Mr. Readings had also served on the board and the audit committee. With Mr. Williamson's departure, Ms. Jane Jennings, another of the founders, became the company's CFO.

In approaching this communication requirement, you should quickly review the relevant information. The requirement deals with the audit committee. So you should pull out all the information that is relevant to the makeup and activities of that committee. On your scratch paper you should outline the following information:

- Both the audit committee and the board of directors is made up of the four founders who remain active in the company
- Mr. Readings, the CEO, chairs both the board and the audit committee
- In mid-20X8, Willingsley Williamson, a founder, CFO and audit committee member, resigned and was bought out by the other four founders
- Ms. Jane Jennings, another of the founders, became the company's new CFO

In writing your response, remember that you must consider the purpose of the memorandum: to communicate the strengths and weaknesses of the audit committee and the related implications to the audit staff. You should start your communication with a statement of this objective or purpose. Next you should communicate the strengths and weaknesses noted and, finally, the related implications. A suggested communication is illustrated below.

> To:        Audit Team
> From:      CPA Candidate
> Re:        DietWeb audit committee
>
>      This memorandum is designed to describe the control implications of the makeup of DietWeb audit committee. Based on our understanding of the makeup of the audit committee of DietWeb, we have identified a weakness and a strength. The audit committee membership is identical to that of the board of directors. In addition, several of the members serve as officers of the company, including Mr. Readings who is the company's CEO, and chairman of both the board of directors and the audit committee. Accordingly, there are no independent members of the audit committee. This prevents the committee from performing one of its major functions, to oversee top management of the company.
>      On the other hand, the fact that the audit committee members are founders and officers means that the committee members should be interested and competent. This represents an internal control strength.
>      We will make a recommendation to the board of directors to correct this matter by bringing on independent board and audit committee members. In addition, we should consider the implications of this weakness in control environment on our audit.

## Financial Accounting and Reporting Example

The following is a communication requirement from a Financial Accounting and Reporting simulation.

### Memorandum

        Chris Green, CPA, is auditing Jasco Co.'s 20X5 financial statements. The controller, Dunn, has provided Green with the following information relating to income taxes:

- Dunn has prepared a schedule of all differences between financial statement and income tax return income. Dunn believes that as a result of pending legislation, the enacted tax rate at December 31, 20X5, will be increased for 20X5. Dunn is uncertain which differences to include and which rates to apply in computing deferred taxes under SFAS 109. Dunn has requested an overview of SFAS 109 from Green.

### Required:

Prepare a brief memo to Dunn from Green:

- Identifying the objectives of accounting for income taxes,
- Defining temporary differences,
- Explaining how to measure deferred tax assets and liabilities, and
- Explaining how to measure deferred income tax expense or benefit.

To:      Mr. Dunn
From:    Mr. Green, CPA
Re:      Accounting for income taxes

In this case the memorandum can be prepared from the information included solely in this tab. Let's again outline the major information that will be used in drafting our response:

- It is a memorandum from the CPA to the controller to explain the application of an accounting pronouncement

- The reader, the controller, should understand accounting terminology
- You need to consider what SFAS 109 says about measuring deferred tax assets, liabilities, expense and benefit

In completing a memorandum such as this one, remember that your answer does not have to be technically correct. For example, if you indicate that anticipated future tax rates should be used to measure deferred tax assets and liabilities, you would not affect your grade. Therefore, you should not spend a lot of time trying to remember the exact requirements of a professional standard. Just make your best guess and write the memorandum. Shown below is a suggested solution:

| | |
|---|---|
| To: | Mr. Dunn |
| From: | Mr. Green, CPA |
| Re: | Accounting for income taxes |

You have requested that I provide a brief overview of accounting for income taxes in accordance with SFAS 109. The objectives of accounting for income taxes are to recognize (1) the amount of taxes payable or refundable for the current year, and (2) deferred tax liabilities and assets for the estimated future tax consequences of temporary differences and carry-forwards. Temporary differences are differences between the tax basis of assets and liabilities and their reported amounts in the financial statements that will result in taxable or deductible amounts in future years.

Deferred tax assets and liabilities are measured based on the provisions of enacted tax law; the effects of future changes in the tax laws or rates are not anticipated. The measurement of deferred tax assets is reduced, if necessary, by a valuation allowance to reflect the net asset amount that is more likely than not to be realized. Deferred income tax expense or benefit is measured as the change during the year in the amount of the enterprise's deferred tax liabilities and assets.

If you have any other questions, please contact me.

## Regulation Example

The following is a communication requirement from a Regulation section of the CPA Examination.

| Memorandum |
|---|

Describe the results of your research in a memorandum to Mrs. Vick.

| | |
|---|---|
| To: | Mrs. Vick |
| From: | CPA Candidate |
| Re: | College savings plan |

In order to prepare this written communication you must examine the results of the related research requirement, which is illustrated below:

| Research |
|---|

Mrs. Vick is considering making contributions to a qualified tuition program to provide savings for her daughter's college education. However, Mrs. Vick is concerned that the contributions will be considered a gift of a future interest and result in a taxable gift. Which code section and subsection provide the gift tax treatment for contributions to a qualified tuition program? Indicate the reference to that citation in the shaded boxes below.

| Section | Subsection |
|---------|------------|
| §       | (        ) |

The answer to this research requirement is presented below:

> Internal Revenue Code Section 529, subsection (c) provides any contribution to a qualified tuition program on behalf of a beneficiary shall be treated as a completed gift and not a gift of a future interest in property.

| Section | Subsection |
|---------|------------|
| § 529   | ( c )      |

Let's again outline the major information that will be used in drafting our response:

- It is a memorandum from the CPA to an individual taxpayer
- The reader, the taxpayer, should not be expected to understand accounting and tax terminology

To:     Mrs. Vick
From:   CPA Candidate
Re:     College savings plan

As you requested, I have researched the gift tax implications of contributions that you are considering making to a qualified tuition program on behalf of your daughter. A contribution to these programs (often referred to as Sec. 529 plans) on behalf of a beneficiary is treated as a completed gift to such beneficiary and not a gift of a future interest. This means that the contributions are eligible for the annual gift tax exclusion, which is $12,000 for 2006. Furthermore, if the amount of contribution exceeds $12,000, an election can be made to treat the contribution as a gift made ratably over a five-year period which would permit you to make a contribution of $12,000 × 5 = $60,000 to your daughter's program without making a taxable gift.

In summary, your contributions to your daughter's 529 plan should result in minimal gift tax consequences. Please contact me if you have any additional questions.

## Software Tools

The AICPA software provides you with a couple of tools to help complete your communications. The first of these tools is the cut and paste function. You may cut and paste from anywhere in the simulation except for the professional standards or code material.

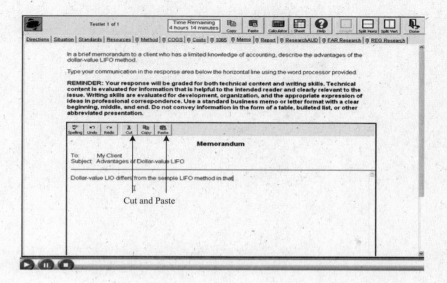

The software also has a spell-checker much like that available in other word processing packages.   **Be sure to use it.**

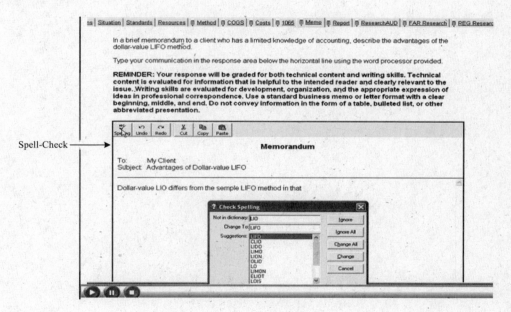

# 4 MASTERING FINANCIAL ACCOUNTING AND REPORTING SIMULATIONS

This chapter applies the principles described in Chapter 1 to the simulations in the Financial Accounting and Reporting (FAR) section of the CPA exam. Every FAR exam includes two simulations. As described in Chapter 1, the AICPA has identified the following skills required by CPAs to protect the public interest:

- Analysis—The ability to organize, process, and interpret data to develop options for decision making.
- Judgment—The ability to evaluate options for decision making and provide an appropriate conclusion.
- Communication—The ability to effectively elicit and/or express information through written or oral means.
- Research—The ability to locate and extract relevant information from available resource materials.
- Understanding—The ability to recognize and comprehend the meaning and application of a particular matter.

For the FAR section, the Board of Examiners has provided the following matrix to illustrate the interaction of content and skills:

| Content Specification Outline Areas | Skill Categories | | | | | Content Weights |
|---|---|---|---|---|---|---|
| | Communication | Research | Analysis | Judgment | Understanding | |
| I. Concepts and standards for financial statements | | | | | | 17-23% |
| II. Typical items in financial statements | | | | | | 27-33% |
| III. Specific types of transactions and events | | | | | | 27-33% |
| IV. Accounting and reporting for governmental entities | | | | | | 8-12% |
| V. Accounting and reporting for nongovernmental and not-for-profit organizations | | | | | | 8-12% |
| Skills Weights | 6-16% | 11-21% | 13-23% | 10-20% | 35-45% | |

You should keep these skills foremost in your mind as you prepare and sit for the FAR section.

## CONTENT OF THE FAR SECTION

To perform successfully on the FAR simulations, you must have an adequate knowledge of the content of the FAR exam. The AICPA Content Specification Outline of the coverage of the FAR section appears below. This outline was issued by the AICPA, and is effective for exams administered after 2005.

# AICPA CONTENT SPECIFICATION OUTLINE: FINANCIAL ACCOUNTING AND REPORTING

I. Concepts and Standards for Financial Statements (**17%-23%**)

   A. Financial Accounting Concepts

      1. Process by Which Standards Are Set and Roles of Standard-Setting Bodies
      2. Conceptual Basis for Accounting Standards

   B. Financial Accounting Standards for Presentation and Disclosure in General-Purpose Financial Statements

      1. Consolidated and Combined Financial Statements
      2. Balance Sheet
      3. Statement(s) of Income, Comprehensive Income, and Changes in Equity Accounts
      4. Statement of Cash Flows
      5. Accounting Policies and Other Notes to Financial Statements

   C. Other Presentations of Financial Data (Financial Statements Prepared in Conformity with Comprehensive Bases of Accounting other than GAAP)

   D. Financial Statement Analysis

II. Typical Items: Recognition, Measurement, Valuation, and Presentation in Financial Statements in Conformity with GAAP (**27%-33%**)

   A. Cash, Cash Equivalents, and Marketable Securities
   B. Receivables
   C. Inventories
   D. Property, Plant, and Equipment
   E. Investments
   F. Intangibles and Other Assets
   G. Payables and Accruals
   H. Deferred Revenues
   I. Notes and Bonds Payable
   J. Other Liabilities
   K. Equity Accounts
   L. Revenue, Cost, and Expense Accounts

III. Specific Types of Transactions and Events: Recognition, Measurement, Valuation, and Presentation in Financial Statements in Conformity with GAAP (**27%-33%**)

   A. Accounting Changes and Corrections of Errors
   B. Business Combinations
   C. Contingent Liabilities and Commitments
   D. Discontinued Operations
   E. Earnings Per Share

   F. Employee Benefits, Including Stock Options
   G. Extraordinary Items
   H. Financial Instruments, Including Derivatives
   I. Foreign Currency Transactions and Translation
   J. Income Taxes
   K. Interest Costs
   L. Interim Financial Reporting
   M. Leases
   N. Nonmonetary Transactions
   O. Related Parties
   P. Research and Development Costs
   Q. Segment Reporting
   R. Subsequent Events

IV. Accounting and Reporting for Governmental Entities (**8%-12%**)

   A. Governmental Accounting Concepts

      1. Measurement Focus and Basis of Accounting
      2. Fund Accounting Concepts and Application
      3. Budgetary Process

   B. Format and Content of Governmental Financial Statements

      1. Government-Wide Financial Statements
      2. Governmental Funds Financial Statements
      3. Conversion from Fund to Government-Wide Financial Statements
      4. Proprietary Fund Financial Statements
      5. Fiduciary Fund Financial Statements
      6. Notes to Financial Statements
      7. Required Supplementary Information, Including Management's Discussion and Analysis
      8. Comprehensive Annual Financial Report (CAFR)

   C. Financial Reporting Entity Including Blended and Discrete Component Units

   D. Typical Items and Specific Types of Transactions and Events: Recognition, Measurement, Valuation, and Presentation in Governmental Entity Financial Statements in Conformity with GAAP

      1. Net Assets
      2. Capital Assets and Infrastructure
      3. Transfers
      4. Other Financing Sources and Uses
      5. Fund Balance
      6. Nonexchange Revenues

7. Expenditures
8. Special Items
9. Encumbrances

E. Accounting and Financial Reporting for Governmental Not-for-Profit Organizations

V. Accounting and Reporting for Nongovernmental Not-for-Profit Organizations (8%-12%)

A. Objectives, Elements, and Formats of Financial Statements

1. Statement of Financial Position
2. Statement of Activities
3. Statement of Cash Flows
4. Statement of Functional Expenses

B. Typical Items and Specific Types of Transactions and Events: Recognition, Measurement, Valuation, and Presentation in the Financial Statements of Not-for-Profit Organizations in Conformity with GAAP

1. Revenues and Contributions
2. Restrictions on Resources
3. Expenses, Including Depreciation and Functional Expenses
4. Investments

**References—Financial Accounting and Reporting**

Financial Accounting Standards Board (FASB) Statements of Financial Accounting Standards and Interpretations, Accounting Principles Board Opinions, AICPA Accounting Research Bulletins, and FASB Technical Bulletins

- Codification of Statements on Auditing Standards

  AU Section 411, *The Meaning of Present Fairly in Conformity with Generally Accepted Accounting Principles*
  AU Section 560, *Subsequent Events*
  AU Section 623, *Special Reports*

- FASB Statements of Financial Accounting Concepts
- AICPA Statements of Position:

  93-7, Reporting on Advertising Costs
  94-6, Disclosure of Certain Significant Risks and Uncertainties
  96-1, Environmental Remediation Liabilities
  97-2, Software Revenue Recognition
  98-1, Accounting for the Costs of Computer Software Developed or Obtained for Internal Use
  98-2, Accounting for the Costs of Activities of Not-for-Profit Organizations and State and Local Governmental Entities That Include Fund Raising
  98-5, Reporting on the Costs of Start-Up Activities

- Governmental Accounting Standards Board (GASB) Statements, Interpretations, and Technical Bulletins

- AICPA Audit and Accounting Guides relating to governmental and not-for-profit organizations

- Current textbooks on accounting for business enterprises, not-for-profit organizations, and governmental entities

## COMMUNICATION REQUIREMENTS

As discussed in Chapter 1 every simulation requires you to prepare a written communication. In the FAR section this communication will usually involve preparing a memorandum that describes the accounting requirements for a transaction or financial account. The communication may be for someone who would be expected to understand accounting terminology, or someone who would not be expected to have such understanding. To get the maximum score, you should tailor your communication to the recipient. Remember that the communication must address the objectives that are set forth in the requirement. In other words, it must be helpful to the recipient. However, it does not have to be technically accurate. Therefore, you should not spend a lot of time thinking about the details of the financial standard. If you are not sure of specific rules, take a guess. If you do not have a clue, you might consider referring to the professional standards database and quickly reviewing the applicable professional standards. However, you do not have time to spare. Using an excessive amount of time on one written communication will decrease your overall score. Remember you should not quote from the standards, or construct your memorandum in the form of bullets. **You must demonstrate your own writing ability.** Chapter 3 is devoted to detailed suggestions on how to improve your writing ability to maximize your score on the communication requirements of simulations.

# RESEARCH REQUIREMENTS

Every simulation also contains a tab that requires you to perform research. Research components of simulations in the FAR section will require you to research authoritative financial accounting standards. In the research tab you will be presented with a research question or issue. For example, you may be asked to search the professional accounting standards to find the section that contains the criteria for classifying an equipment lease as a capital lease. In completing the requirement, you will be asked to select the section (paragraph or paragraphs) of professional standards that addresses the research question. The financial accounting database is organized as the Original Pronouncements (i.e., the original text of FASB Statements, APB Opinions, and Interpretations).

Since this is a fairly mechanical task, you want to complete it as quickly as possible, allowing you more time to spend on other parts of the simulation and the exam as a whole. Therefore, the key to effective performance on research requirements is to find the relevant section of the standards as quickly as possible.

When you are performing a research requirement of a FAR simulation you should approach it in a systematic fashion. As described in Chapter 2, a four-step approach that seems to work well for many candidates is presented below:

1. Define the issue. What is the research question to be answered?
2. Choose appropriate search technique. Select keywords that will locate the needed information or use the table of contents or index.
3. Execute the search. Enter the keyword(s), click on the topical index, or click on the table of contents or index item and complete the search.
4. Evaluate the results. Evaluate the research to see if an answer has been found. If not, try a new search.

## *Advanced Searches*

The advanced search screen allows you to use Boolean concepts to perform more precise searches. Examples of searches that can be performed in the advanced search mode include

1. Containing all these words—allows you to retrieve sections that contain two or more specified words.
2. Not containing any of these words—allows you to retrieve sections that do not contain specific words.
3. Containing one or more of these words—allows you to retrieve sections that contain any one or more of the specified words.
4. Containing these words near each other—allows you to retrieve sections that contain words near each other.

The advanced search also allows you to select options for the search. One alternative allows you to retrieve alternative word forms. For example, using this approach on a search on the word "cost" would also retrieve sections containing the word "costing." A synonyms option allows you to retrieve sections that contain words that mean the same as the specified word. You also have the option to only search on the selected sections of the literature.

# SOLVING FAR SIMULATIONS

To illustrate how to master the FAR simulations, this chapter will walk you through the process of solving two simulations. The chapter will conclude with two FAR simulations that you may use to apply the principles that you have learned. Recall from Chapter 1, the suggested steps to solving a simulation includes

1. **Review the entire problem.** Tab through the problem in order to get a feel for the topical area and related concepts that are being tested. Even though the format of the question may vary, the exam continues to test your understanding of applicable principles or con-

cepts.  Relax, take a deep breath, and determine your strategy for conquering the simulation.

2.  **Identify the requirements of the problem.**  This step will help you focus in more quickly on the solution(s) without wasting time reading irrelevant material.  Jot down the nature of the requirements on your scratch paper (which will be provided).

3.  **Study the items to be answered.**  As you do this and become familiar with the topical area being tested, you should think about the concepts of that area.  This will help you organize your thoughts so that you can relate logically the requirements of the simulation with the applicable concepts.

4.  **With the requirements in mind carefully review the information tabs.**  Make notes on your scratch paper of information from the tabs that will help you answer each requirement.

5.  **Answer each tab requirement one at a time.**  If the requirements do not build on one another, don't be afraid to answer the tab requirements out of order.  Also, if the scenario is long or complex, you may wish to use the split screen function to view the simulation data while answering a particular requirement.

6.  **Use the scratch paper and the spreadsheet and calculator tools to assist you in answering the simulation.**

Now let's apply this approach to some actual simulations.

## SIMULATION EXAMPLE 1

Applying steps 1, 2 and 3 in the solutions approach to the following simulation, you should first review all the tabs, focus on the requirements and concepts, and jot down the requirements.

(50 to 60 minutes)

| Directions | | | | |
|---|---|---|---|---|
| | Situation | Accounting Treatment | Communication | Research |

In the following simulation, you will be asked various questions regarding accounting and reporting for stockholders' equity.  You will use the content in the **Information Tabs** to complete the tasks in the **Work Tabs.**  (The following pictures are for illustration only; the actual tabs in your simulation may differ from these.)

**Information Tabs:**

| Directions | Situation | Standards | Resources |
|---|---|---|---|

Beginning with the **Directions** tab at the left side of the screen, go through each of the **Information Tabs** to familiarize yourself with the simulation content.  Note that the **Resources** tab will contain useful information, including formulas and definitions, to help you complete the tasks.  You may want to refer to this information while you are working.

**Work Tabs:**

| Cost Method | Amt to Report | COGS | Invent Costs | Form 1065 | Communication | Review Letter |
|---|---|---|---|---|---|---|

The **Work Tabs,** on the right side of the screen, contain the tasks for you to complete.

Once you complete any part of a task, the pencil for that tab will be shaded.  Note that a shaded pencil does NOT indicate that you have completed the entire task.

You must complete all of the tasks in the **Work Tabs** to receive full credit.

If you have difficulty answering a **Work Tab,** read the tab directions carefully.

*NOTE: If you believe you have encountered a software malfunction, report it to the test center staff immediately.*

| Directions | Situation | Accounting Treatment | Communication | Research |
|---|---|---|---|---|

Quonset, Inc. is a public company whose shares are actively traded in the over-the-counter market. The company's stockholders' equity account balances at December 31, year 1, were as follows:

| | |
|---|---|
| Common stock: $1 par value; 1,650,000 shares authorized; 850,000 shares issued and outstanding | $ 850,000 |
| Additional paid-in capital | 3,100,000 |
| Retained earnings | 3,700,000 |
| Total stockholders' equity | $7,650,000 |

During the year ended December 31, year 2, transactions and other information relating to Quonset's stockholders' equity were as follows:

- On February 1, year 2, Quonset issued 13,000 shares of common stock to Carson Co. in exchange for land. On the date issued, the stock had a market price of $13 per share. The land had a carrying value on Carson's books of $140,000 and an assessed value for property taxes of $95,000.
- On March 5, year 2, Quonset purchased 21,000 of its shares to hold as treasury stock at $12 per share. The shares were originally issued at $13 per share. Quonset uses the cost method to account for treasury stock. Treasury stock is permitted in Quonset's state of incorporation.
- On March 15, year 2, Quonset purchased a portfolio of marketable securities to be held as available-for-sale securities.
- On June 5, year 2, Quonset declared a property dividend of inventory. The inventory had a $65,000 carrying value and a $55,000 fair market value.
- On July 1, year 2, Quonset declared and issued a 15% stock dividend.
- On December 5, year 2, Quonset declared a cash dividend of $1 per share to all common stockholders of record on December 15, year 2. The dividend was paid on January 5, year 3.
- Net income for year 2 was $1,443,000.
- At December 31, year 2, unrealized gain on the portfolio of marketable securities purchased during the year was $95,000, net of tax.

Assume that Quonset does not elect the fair value option for reporting its financial assets.

| Directions | Situation | Accounting Treatment | Communication | Research |
|---|---|---|---|---|

Using the stockholders' equity balances as of December 31, year 1, and the transactions and other information relating to Quonset's stockholders' equity during year 2, complete the following worksheet analysis of stockholders' equity for year 2. Ignore the effect of income taxes.

For each item in column A:

- Enter in column B the effect (if any) on the number of Quonset shares issued and outstanding.
- Enter in columns C through G the dollar amount effect (if any) on the appropriate equity account(s).

Total stockholders' equity values at column H and ending balance in row 10 will automatically calculate based on your entries.

Enter increases to stockholders' equity as positive numbers and decreases to stockholders' equity as negative numbers. If there is no amount to enter in a particular shaded cell, enter a value of zero (0).

|   | A | B | C | D | E | F | G | H |
|---|---|---|---|---|---|---|---|---|
| 1 | Accounts | Number of shares issued and outstanding | Common stock | Additional paid-in capital | Retained earnings | Accumulated other comprehensive income (loss) | Treasury stock | Total stockholders' equity |
| 2 | Beginning balances | | | | | | | |
| 3 | Issuance of shares for property | | | | | | | |
| 4 | Purchase of treasury stock | | | | | | | |
| 5 | Property dividends distributed | | | | | | | |
| 6 | Stock dividend issued | | | | | | | |
| 7 | Cash dividend | | | | | | | |
| 8 | Net income for the year | | | | | | | |
| 9 | Unrealized gain (loss) on marketable securities available-for-sale | | | | | | | |
| 10 | Ending balances | | | | | | | |

| Directions | Situation | Accounting Treatment | Communication | | Research |
|---|---|---|---|---|---|

The management of Quonset, Inc. intends to issue stock options to key employees. Generally accepted accounting principles (GAAP) requires the fair value method of accounting for stock options. As the CFO of the company, write a memo to management discussing the fair value method of measuring and accounting for the cost of stock options. Include in your memo a discussion of when the cost is recognized for book purposes and the financial statement impacts of this recognition.

Type your communication in the response area below the horizontal line using the word processor provided.

*REMINDER: Your response will be graded for both technical content and writing skills. Technical content will be evaluated for information that is helpful to the intended reader and clearly relevant to the issue. Writing skills will be evaluated for development, organization, and the appropriate expression of ideas in professional correspondence. Use a standard business memo or letter format with a clear beginning, middle, and end. Do not convey information in the form of a table, bullet point list, or other abbreviated presentation.*

To:
From:

| Directions | Situation | Accounting Treatment | Communication | Research |
|---|---|---|---|---|

The company made open-market purchases of its own common stock with the intent to reissue the shares in the future. It is anticipated that the market price of the stock will be in excess of the purchase price when the stock is reissued. List the proper citation from the authoritative literature that provides guidance as to how the company should account for the excess of the market price at the time of reissuance over the purchase price of the common stock.

Find guidance in the FASB Standards that authoritatively addresses the situation above. To complete this task, use the search capabilities provided by the **Standards** tab to find the numbered paragraph in the Original Pronouncements that addresses the issue above. Select the appropriate paragraph(s) that answer the requirement.

## SOLVING THE SIMULATION

After you have reviewed the entire simulation and made notes of the requirements, you should have a list similar to the following:

1. Present the effects of each stockholders' equity transaction in the schedule.
2. Write a memorandum regarding the accounting for employee stock options.
3. Research the accounting standards for information on accounting for treasury stock transactions.

With these requirements in mind, you should carefully read the **Situation** tab. Then, you should begin the first work tab—the **Accounting Treatment** tab.

### Requirement 1

The **Accounting Treatment** tab requires you to complete a schedule that shows the effects of a number of stockholders' equity transactions. The first line of the schedule may be completed with the information about the beginning balances from the **Situation** tab as shown below.

| Common stock: $1 par value; 1,650,000 shares authorized; 850,000 shares issued and outstanding | $ 850,000 |
|---|---|
| Additional paid-in capital | 3,100,000 |
| Retained earnings | 3,700,000 |
| Total stockholders' equity | $7,650,000 |

|  | A | B | C | D | E | F | G | H |
|---|---|---|---|---|---|---|---|---|
| 1 | Accounts | Number of shares issued and outstanding | Common stock | Additional paid-in capital | Retained earnings | Accumulated other comprehensive income (loss) | Treasury stock | Total stockholders' equity |
| 2 | Beginning balances | 850,000 | $850,000 | $3,100,000 | $3,700,000 |  |  | $7,650,000 |

Now, let's analyze each transaction to determine its effect on the schedule. The first transaction is described as follows:

- On February 1, year 2, Quonset issued 13,000 shares of common stock to Carson Co. in exchange for land. On the date issued, the stock had a market price of $13 per share. The land had a carrying value on Carson's books of $140,000 and an assessed value for property taxes of $95,000.

Financial accounting requires such transactions to be recorded at the market value of the stock exchanged for the asset, or $169,000 (13,000 × $13). The transaction results in the issuance of 13,000 shares with a par value of $13,000. Therefore, additional paid-in capital for the transaction is equal to $156,000 ($169,000 − $13,000), and the effect on total stockholders' equity is an increase of $169,000.

| | A | B | C | D | E | F | G | H |
|---|---|---|---|---|---|---|---|---|
| 1 | Accounts | Number of shares issued and outstanding | Common stock | Additional paid-in capital | Retained earnings | Accumulated other comprehensive income (loss) | Treasury stock | Total stockholders' equity |
| 2 | Beginning balances | 850,000 | $850,000 | $3,100,000 | $3,700,000 | | | $7,650,000 |
| 3 | Issuance shares property | 13,000 | 13,000 | 156,000 | | | | 169,000 |

The second transaction is described below.

- On March 5, year 2, Quonset purchased 21,000 of its shares to hold as treasury stock at $12 per share. The shares were originally issued at $13 per share. Quonset uses the cost method to account for treasury stock. Treasury stock is permitted in Quonset's state of incorporation.

Using the cost method to account for the treasury stock, this transaction would be recorded as follows:

| | | |
|---|---|---|
| Treasury stock | 252,000 | |
| Cash | | 252,000 |

The transaction also would reduce the number of shares outstanding by 21,000 and stockholders' equity by the total cost of $252,000.

| | A | B | C | D | E | F | G | H |
|---|---|---|---|---|---|---|---|---|
| 1 | Accounts | Number of shares issued and outstanding | Common stock | Additional paid-in capital | Retained earnings | Accumulated other comprehensive income (loss) | Treasury stock | Total stockholders' equity |
| 2 | Beginning balances | 850,000 | $850,000 | $3,100,000 | $3,700,000 | | | $7,650,000 |
| 3 | Issuance of shares for property | 13,000 | 13,000 | 156,000 | | | | 169,000 |
| 4 | Purchase of treasury stock | (21,000) | | | | | 252,000 | (252,000) |

The next transaction, as described below, has no effect on stockholders' equity at the time of the purchase of the securities.

- On March 15, year 2, Quonset purchased a portfolio of marketable securities to be held as available-for-sale securities.

The fourth transaction, as described below, involves the issuance of a property dividend.

- On June 5, year 2, Quonset declared a property dividend of inventory. The inventory had a $65,000 carrying value and a $55,000 fair market value.

Property dividends are recorded at the fair value of the property distributed as illustrated below:

| | |
|---|---|
| Retained earnings | 55,000 |
| Inventory | 55,000 |

Therefore, this transaction would reduce retained earnings and total stockholders' equity by $55,000. The $10,000 ($65,000 − $55,000) loss on inventory would be included as a loss in net income.

| | A | B | C | D | E | F | G | H |
|---|---|---|---|---|---|---|---|---|
| 1 | **Accounts** | **Number of shares issued and outstanding** | **Common stock** | **Additional paid-in capital** | **Retained earnings** | **Accumulated other comprehensive income (loss)** | **Treasury stock** | **Total stockholders' equity** |
| 2 | Beginning balances | 850,000 | $850,000 | $3,100,000 | $3,700,000 | | | $7,650,000 |
| 3 | Issuance of shares for property | 13,000 | 13,000 | 156,000 | | | | 169,000 |
| 4 | Purchase of treasury stock | (21,000) | | | | | (252,000) | (252,000) |
| 5 | Property dividends distributed | | | | (55,000) | | | (55,000) |

The fifth transaction involves the declaration and issuance of a stock dividend:

- On July 1, year 2, Quonset declared and issued a 15% stock dividend when the market price of the common stock is $10.

A stock dividend of less than 20 to 25% of the outstanding shares should be valued at fair value. The number of shares outstanding at the time of the declaration is 842,000 (850,000 + 13,000 − 21,000). Therefore, the number of shares issued is equal to 126,300 (842,000 × 15%). The market value of this number of shares is equal to $1,263,000 ($10 × 126,300) and the transaction would be recorded as follows:

| | |
|---|---|
| Retained earnings | 1,263,000 |
| Common stock | 126,300 |
| Additional paid-in capital | 1,136,700 |

| | A | B | C | D | E | F | G | H |
|---|---|---|---|---|---|---|---|---|
| 1 | **Accounts** | **Number of shares issued and outstanding** | **Common stock** | **Additional paid-in capital** | **Retained earnings** | **Accumulated other comprehensive income (loss)** | **Treasury stock** | **Total stockholders' equity** |
| 2 | Beginning balances | 850,000 | $850,000 | $3,100,000 | $3,700,000 | | | $7,650,000 |
| 3 | Issuance of shares for property | 13,000 | 13,000 | 156,000 | | | | 169,000 |
| 4 | Purchase of treasury stock | (21,000) | | | | | (252,000) | (252,000) |
| 5 | Property dividends distributed | | | | (55,000) | | | (55,000) |
| 6 | Stock dividend issued | 126,300 | 126,300 | 1,136,700 | (1,263,000) | | | 0 |

The sixth transaction involves the declaration of a cash dividend, as described below:

- On December 5, year 2, Quonset declared a cash dividend of $1 per share to all common stockholders of record on December 15, year 2.  The dividend was paid on January 5, year 3.

The total cash dividend would be calculated by multiplying $1 by the number of shares outstanding.  The number of shares outstanding is equal to 968,300 (850,000 + 13,000 − 21,000 + 126,300).  The cash dividend would be recorded as follows:

| Retained earnings | 968,300 | |
|---|---|---|
| Cash | | 968,300 |

| | A | B | C | D | E | F | G | H |
|---|---|---|---|---|---|---|---|---|
| 1 | Accounts | Number of shares issued and outstanding | Common stock | Additional paid-in capital | Retained earnings | Accumulated other comprehensive income (loss) | Treasury stock | Total stockholders' equity |
| 2 | Beginning balances | 850,000 | $850,000 | $3,100,000 | $3,700,000 | | | $7,650,000 |
| 3 | Issuance of shares for property | 13,000 | 13,000 | 156,000 | | | | 169,000 |
| 4 | Purchase of treasury stock | (12,000) | | | | | (252,000) | (252,000) |
| 5 | Property dividends distributed | | | | (55,000) | | | (55,000) |
| 6 | Stock dividend issued | 126,300 | 126,300 | 1,136,700 | (1,263,000) | | | 0 |
| 7 | Cash dividend | | | | (968,300) | | | (968,300) |

Next, we must make the spreadsheet entry to recognize net income as described below:

- Net income for year 2 was $1,443,000.

Net income increases retained earnings and total stockholders' equity.

| | A | B | C | D | E | F | G | H |
|---|---|---|---|---|---|---|---|---|
| 1 | Accounts | Number of shares issued and outstanding | Common stock | Additional paid-in capital | Retained earnings | Accumulated other comprehensive income (loss) | Treasury stock | Total stockholders' equity |
| 2 | Beginning balances | 850,000 | $850,000 | $3,100,000 | $3,700,000 | | | $7,650,000 |
| 3 | Issuance of shares for property | 13,000 | 13,000 | 156,000 | | | | 169,000 |
| 4 | Purchase of treasury stock | (21,000) | | | | | (252,000) | (252,000) |
| 5 | Property dividends distributed | | | | (55,000) | | | (55,000) |
| 6 | Stock dividend issued | 126,300 | 126,300 | 1,136,700 | (1,263,000) | | | 0 |
| 7 | Cash dividend | | | | (968,300) | | | (968,300) |
| 8 | Net income for the year | | | | 1,443,000 | | | 1,443,000 |

The final entry is one to record the unrecognized gain on the portfolio of available-for-sale securities. The details are described below:

- At December 31, year 2, unrealized gain on the portfolio of marketable securities purchased during the year was $95,000, net of tax.

The unrealized gain increases other comprehensive income and, therefore, increases total stockholders' equity.

| | A | B | C | D | E | F | G | H |
|---|---|---|---|---|---|---|---|---|
| 1 | Accounts | Number of shares issued and outstanding | Common stock | Additional paid-in capital | Retained earnings | Accumulated other comprehensive income (loss) | Treasury stock | Total stockholders' equity |
| 2 | Beginning balances | 850,000 | $850,000 | $3,100,000 | $3,700,000 | | | $7,650,000 |
| 3 | Issuance of shares for property | 13,000 | 13,000 | 156,000 | | | | 169,000 |
| 4 | Purchase of treasury stock | (21,000) | | | | | (252,000) | (252,000) |
| 5 | Property dividends distributed | | | | (55,000) | | | (55,000) |
| 6 | Stock dividend issued | 126,300 | 126,300 | 1,136,700 | (1,263,000) | | | 0 |
| 7 | Cash dividend | | | | (968,300) | | | (968,300) |
| 8 | Net income for the year | | | | 1,443,000 | | | 1,443,000 |
| 9 | Unrealized gain (loss) on marketable securities available-for-sale | | | | | 95,000 | | 95,000 |
| 10 | Ending balances | 968,300 | 989,300 | 4,392,700 | 2,856,700 | 95,000 | (252,000) | 8,081,700 |

On the examination, the spreadsheet would automatically sum the total stockholders' equity row and each of the columns. However, when completing this part you should be sure to review each set of entries to make sure they make sense. Also, be sure to use the calculator tool to calculate amounts for the individual transactions. Don't make careless mistakes.

## Requirement 2

The **Communication** tab requires you to develop a memorandum to management regarding the financial effects of employee stock options. Specifically it requires the following:

*The management of Quonset, Inc. intends to issue stock options to key employees. Generally accepted accounting principles (GAAP) requires the fair value method of accounting for stock options. As the CFO of the company, write a memo to management discussing the fair value method of measuring and accounting for the cost of stock options. Include in your memo a discussion of when the cost is recognized for book purposes and the financial statement impacts of this recognition.*

In this case, the memorandum can be prepared from the information included in this tab. In approaching the requirement, begin by outlining the major observations that should be used in drafting the memorandum:

- It is a memorandum from the CFO to management explaining the application of an accounting standard.
- The readers, management of the company, should have an understanding of business terminology but not accounting terminology.
- You need to consider what SFAS 123(R) says about measuring and reporting employee stock options.

With these observations in mind, you can develop your memorandum. In doing so remember the guidance from Chapter 3:

1. Start the memorandum with an introduction indicating its purpose.
2. Use simple sentences.
3. Since you are communicating with management, you should avoid accounting jargon.
4. Use the spelling checker in the exam software.
5. Don't worry that much about getting the requirements of the standard exactly correct. Remember your response will not be graded for technical accuracy.

Review the following memorandum, noting how it applies to the principles described above.

---

To:        Management, Quonset, Inc.
From:   CPA candidate, CFO
Re:        Accounting for stock compensation

You have requested information about the rules of accounting for employee stock options. Accounting for stock compensation to employees is governed by the accounting rules in Statement of Financial Accounting Standards No. 123(R). This accounting standard applies to all share-based payments issued in the form of stock shares, share options, or other equity instruments.

When stock options are issued to an employee, they are recorded at the fair value of the options granted. The fair value of an option is ideally measured based on the observable market price of an option with the same or similar terms and conditions. If no market for similar options exists, the fair value of the options can be estimated using an options pricing model, such as the Black-Scholes model.

In recording the options, employee compensation cost is recognized in the financial statements at the fair value of the options granted. Since the compensation is a payment for future services, it is recorded initially as deferred (prepaid) compensation cost, and amortized (written off) on a straight-line basis to compensation expense over the service period. The service period is the time over which the employee is required to provide the services in order to receive the stock options.

No compensation cost is recognized if an employee forfeits the shares because a service or performance condition is not met. However, if an employee renders the requisite service and the options expire or are not exercised, previously recognized compensation expense is not reversed.

If you would like additional information regarding the accounting for stock options, please contact me.

[*Signature*]

[*Date*]

---

## Requirement 3

The **Research** tab requires you to search the financial literature to identify the section that describes the accounting for treasury stock. Specifically, the Research tab states:

*The company made open-market purchases of its own common stock with the intent to reissue the shares in the future. It is anticipated that the market price of the stock will be in excess of the purchase price when the stock is reissued. List the proper citation from the authoritative literature that provides guidance as to how the company should account for the excess of the market price at the time of reissuance over the purchase price of the common stock.*

The guidance regarding the accounting for treasury stock transactions is contained in ARB 43, Chapter 1b as amended by Accounting Principles Board Opinion (APB) No. 6. If you recall that from your studies, you could narrow your search. One search strategy for this tab would be to search on the term "treasury stock." However, the term "treasury stock" will yield a large number of hits. A more efficient search would result from using the phrase "sales of treasury stock." This will require the use of the advanced search for items "containing the exact phrase." This will lead you quickly to the guidance in APB No. 6, paragraph 12(b), as quoted below.

> 12. b. When a corporation's stock is acquired for purposes other than retirement (formal or constructive), or when ultimate disposition has not yet been decided, the cost of acquired stock may be shown separately as a deduction from the total of capital stock, capital surplus, and retained earnings, or may be accorded the accounting treatment appropriate for retired stock, or in some circumstances may be shown as an asset in accordance with paragraph 4 of Chapter 1A of ARB 43. "Gains" on sales of treasury stock not previously accounted for as constructively retired should be credited to capital surplus; "losses" may be charged to capital surplus to the extent that previous net "gains" from sales or retirements of the same class of stock are included therein, otherwise to retained earnings.

When you select the answer, your results should look similar to the following:

• APB 6, par. 12(b)

### SIMULATION EXAMPLE 2

Let's attempt another simulation. Begin by reviewing the tabs to get a feel for what you are asked to do and to recall the applicable concepts. On your scratch paper write down a list of the major requirements.

In the following simulation, you will be asked various questions regarding accounting and reporting for stockholders' equity. You will use the content in the **Information Tabs** to complete the tasks in the **Work Tabs**. (The following pictures are for illustration only; the actual tabs in your simulation may differ from these.)

**Information Tabs:**

| Directions | Situation | Standards | Resources |
|---|---|---|---|

Beginning with the **Directions** tab at the left side of the screen, go through each of the **Information Tabs** to familiarize yourself with the simulation content. Note that the **Resources** tab will contain useful information, including formulas and definitions, to help you complete the tasks. You may want to refer to this information while you are working.

**Work Tabs:**

| Cost Method | Amt to Report | COGS | Invent Costs | Form 1065 | Communication | Review Letter |
|---|---|---|---|---|---|---|

The **Work Tabs,** on the right side of the screen, contain the tasks for you to complete.

Once you complete any part of a task, the pencil for that tab will be shaded. Note that a shaded pencil does NOT indicate that you have completed the entire task.

You must complete all of the tasks in the **Work Tabs** to receive full credit.

If you have difficulty answering a **Work Tab,** read the tab directions carefully.

*NOTE: If you believe you have encountered a software malfunction, report it to the test center staff immediately.*

(50 to 60 minutes)

| Situation | | | | | |
|---|---|---|---|---|---|
| | Concepts | Journal Entries | Calculations | Research | Communication |

A client, Blaedon Co., sells lawn mowers and garden tillers. The garden tillers are purchased from Bestbuilt Tillers and sold to customers without modification. The lawn mowers, however, are purchased from several contractors. Blaedon then makes ongoing design refinements to the mowers before selling them to customers.

The lawn mowers cost $200. Blaedon then makes the design refinements at a cost of $85 per lawn mower. Blaedon stores the lawn mowers in its own warehouse and sells them directly to retailers at a list price of $500. Blaedon uses the FIFO inventory method. Approximately two-thirds of new lawn mower sales involve trade-ins. For each used lawn mower traded in and returned to Blaedon, retailers receive a $40 allowance regardless of whether the trade-in was associated with a sale of a 2007 or 2008 model. Blaedon's net realizable value on a used lawn mower averages $25.

At December 31, 2007, Blaedon's inventory of new lawn mowers includes both 2007 and 2008 models. When the 2008 model was introduced in September 2007, the list price of the remaining 2007 model lawn mowers was reduced below cost. Blaedon is experiencing rising inventory costs.

Blaedon has contacted your firm for advice on how to report the carrying value of inventory, the impact of the decline in value on the 2007 models, and the effects of using the FIFO method on their December 31, 2007 financial statements.

| | | Concepts | | | |
|---|---|---|---|---|---|
| Situation | | | Journal Entries | Calculations | Research | Communication |

Indicate whether each of the following is included in the cost of inventory.

| | | *Included* | *Not included* |
|---|---|---|---|
| 1. | Merchandise purchased for resale | O | O |
| 2. | Freight out | O | O |
| 3. | Direct materials | O | O |
| 4. | Sales returns | O | O |
| 5. | Packaging for shipment to customer | O | O |
| 6. | Normal factory overhead | O | O |
| 7. | Interest on inventory loan | O | O |
| 8. | Purchase discounts not taken | O | O |
| 9. | Freight-in | O | O |
| 10. | Direct labor | O | O |

| | | Journal Entries | | | |
|---|---|---|---|---|---|
| Situation | Concepts | | Calculations | Research | Communication |

Assume that Blaedon uses the periodic inventory method for inventories. Prepare the journal entries for each of the following transactions. Blaedon uses the gross method for recording inventory transactions.

1. On January 5, 2007, purchased $17,000 of garden tillers on account from Bestbuilt Tillers, terms 2/10, n/30, FOB destination. Freight charges were $200.
2. On January 10, 2007, returned garden tillers worth $2,000 to Bestbuilt Tillers due to defects.
3. On January 14, 2007, paid for the remaining tillers purchased in **1.**
4. On January 28, 2007, purchased $30,000 of lawn mowers from Lawn Giant, terms 3/10, n/30, FOB shipping point. The freight charges were $820.
5. On February 6, 2007, paid for the lawn mowers purchased in part **4.** from Lawn Giant.

| Situation | Concepts | Journal Entries | **Calculations** | | Research | Communication |
|-----------|----------|-----------------|------------------|---|----------|---------------|

Assume that Blaedon had the following information regarding the garden tiller inventory:

| | |
|---|---|
| Purchases | $210,000 |
| Purchase discounts | 38,000 |
| Purchase returns | 17,500 |
| Freight-in | 12,100 |
| Freight out | 18,000 |
| Beginning inventory | 42,900 |
| Ending inventory | 34,250 |

Calculate the following items:

1. Goods available for sale
2. Cost of goods sold

| Situation | Concepts | Journal Entries | Calculations | **Research** | | Communication |
|-----------|----------|-----------------|--------------|--------------|---|---------------|

During the course of the audit two research issues arose.

1. What costs should be included in Blaedon's inventory?
2. How should Blaedon report the 2007 inventory that has declined in value below its cost?

Find guidance in the FASB Standards that authoritatively address the issues above. To complete this task, use the search capabilities provided by the **Standards** tab to find the numbered paragraph or paragraphs in the Original Pronouncements that address each of the issues above. Click (highlight) the appropriate literature and then select the appropriate paragraph(s) that answers the requirement.

| Situation | Concepts | Journal Entries | Calculations | Research | **Communication** |
|-----------|----------|-----------------|--------------|----------|-------------------|

Prepare a memo to the CEO of Blaedon Corp. explaining:

- How Blaedon should determine the carrying amounts assigned to its lawn mower inventory for the 2007 and 2008 models.
- Considering only the 2008 model lawn mower, explain in your memo the impact of the FIFO cost flow assumptions in Blaedon's 2007 income statement and balance sheet amounts.

*REMINDER: Your response will be graded for both technical content and writing skills. Technical content will be evaluated for information that is helpful to the intended reader and clearly relevant to the issue. Writing skills will be evaluated for development, organization, and the appropriate expression of ideas in professional correspondence. Use a standard business memo or letter format with a clear beginning, middle, and end. Do not convey information in the form of a table, bullet point list, or other abbreviated presentation.*

To:     CEO, Blaedon Corp.
From:   CPA Candidate
Re:     Inventory valuation

**Solving the Simulation**

After performing your review and identifying the requirements, you should have a list similar to the following:

1. Identify the items that should be included as part of inventory costs.
2. Prepare journal entries for transactions involving inventory.
3. Calculate goods available for sale and cost of goods sold.
4. Research the items that should be included inventory and how to report a decline in market value of inventory.
5. Write a memorandum to the CEO explaining how inventory costs should be determined and the effects of the FIFO cost flow assumption.

Because the research requirement (Requirement 4) is to determine the items to be included in inventory costs, you should consider performing that requirement before you work on the others. The research may provide you with information that will help you answer the **Concepts** tab and the **Communication** tab.

*Requirement 4*

The **Research** tab requires you to obtain the professional standards sections that provide the answers to two research questions. The key to performing well on this requirement is to identify the appropriate sections as quickly as possible.

Research the following issues in the authoritative literature.

**1.** What types of costs should be included in Blaedon's inventory?
**2.** How should Blaedon report the 2007 inventory that has declined in value below its costs?

How would you approach the search for the appropriate professional standards sections? The first research question is "What types of inventory should be included in inventory?" If you remember from your studies that the guidance regarding inventory costing was originally set forth in Accounting Research Bulletin (ARB) No. 43, you will be able to save significant time in your search. If you also remember that the guidance in ARB No. 43 was amended by FASB No. 151, you will be even further ahead. This knowledge will limit the number of hits that you will get in your keyword search.

The logical keywords for your search in this case would be "inventory costs." However, you should go to the advanced search screen and use the command to search for sections "containing the exact phrase." Otherwise, you will get a large number of hits that contain the individual words *inventory* and *costs* that are not on point.

If you do not remember the authoritative sources, a search of the entire database using the phrase "inventory costs" would be effective. Then, you can look through the results to find ARB 43 and FASB No. 151. You could also use the topical index to find discussions of inventory costs in the professional literature. See Chapter 2 for a description of advanced search techniques. In the end, you will get the following standard paragraphs that address the issue.

1. What types of costs should be included in Blaedon's inventories?

**ARB 43, Ch. 4, Para 5 (amended by FAS 151, para 2)**

5. Inventories are presumed to be stated at cost. The definition of cost as applied to inventories is understood to
mean acquisition and production cost,[2] and its determination involves many considerations. Although principles for
the determination of inventory costs may be easily stated,
their application, particularly to such inventory items as
work in process and finished goods, is difficult because of
the variety of considerations in the allocation of costs and
charges. For example, variable production overheads are
allocated to each unit of production on the basis of the actual use of the production facilities. However, the allocation
of fixed production overheads to the costs of conversion is
based on the normal capacity of the production facilities.
Normal capacity refers to a range of production levels.
Normal capacity is the production expected to be achieved
over a number of periods or seasons under normal circumstances, taking into account the loss of capacity resulting
from planned maintenance. Some variation in production
levels from period to period is expected and establishes the
range of normal capacity. The range of normal capacity will
vary based on business- and industry-specific factors.
Judgment is required to determine when a production level
is abnormally low (that is, outside the range of expected
variation in production). Examples of factors that might be
anticipated to cause an abnormally low production level
include significantly reduced demand, labor and materials
shortages, and unplanned facility or equipment downtime.
The actual level of production may be used if it approxi-
mates normal capacity. In periods of abnormally high production, the amount of fixed overhead allocated to each unit
of production is decreased so that inventories are not measured above cost. The amount of fixed overhead allocated
to each unit of production is not increased as a consequence
of abnormally low production or idle plant.

5A. Unallocated overheads are recognized as an expense in
the period in which they are incurred. Other items such as
abnormal freight, handling costs, and amounts of wasted
materials (spoilage) require treatment as current period
charges rather than as a portion of the inventory cost. Also,
under most circumstances, general and administrative expenses[2a] should be included as period charges, except for
the portion of such expenses that may be clearly related to
production and thus constitute a part of inventory costs
(product charges). Selling expenses constitute no part of
inventory costs. The exclusion of all overheads from inventory costs does not constitute an accepted accounting
procedure. The exercise of judgment in an individual situation involves a consideration of the adequacy of the procedures of the cost accounting system in use, the soundness of
the principles thereof, and their consistent application.

The second research question is "How should Blaedon report the 2007 inventory that has declined in value below its cost?" This research question is also addressed by ARB No. 43. Again,
if you remember this from your studies, you can save a great deal of time in your search by only
searching this professional literature. A logical way to search for the appropriate guidance would
be to use an advanced search using the command search for sections "containing the exact phrase."
From your studies you should remember that this issue is referred to as valuation of inventory at

lower of cost or market. Therefore, you should search on the exact phrase "lower of cost or market." Other search strategies, such as searches on "inventory" or searches on "decline in value of inventory" will be less efficient. The relevant paragraphs that address this issue are shown below.

**2.** How should Blaedon report the 2007 inventory that has declined in value below its cost?

### ARB 43, Ch. 4, Para 9

As used in the phrase lower of cost or market, the term market means current replacement cost (by purchase or by reproduction, as the case may be) except that

(1) Market should not exceed the net realizable value (i.e., estimated selling price in the ordinary course of business less reasonably predictable costs of completion and disposal); and

(2) Market should not be less than net realizable value reduced by an allowance for an approximately normal profit margin.

### ARB 43, Ch. 4, Para 9

9. The rule of cost or market, whichever is lower is intended to provide a means of measuring the residual usefulness of an inventory expenditure. The term market is therefore to be interpreted as indicating utility on the inventory date and may be thought of in terms of the equivalent expenditure which would have to be made in the ordinary course at that date to procure corresponding utility. As a general guide, utility is indicated primarily by the current cost of replacement of the goods as they would be obtained by purchase or reproduction. In applying the rule, however, judgment must always be exercised and no loss should be recognized unless the evidence indicates clearly that a loss has been sustained. There are therefore exceptions to such a standard. Replacement or reproduction prices would not be appropriate as a measure of utility when the estimated sales value reduced by the costs of completion and disposal, is lower, in which case the realizable value so determined more appropriately measures utility. Furthermore, where the evidence indicates that cost will be recovered with an approximately normal profit upon sale in the ordinary course of business, no loss should be recognized even though replacement or reproduction costs are lower. This might be true, for example, in the case of production under firm sales contracts at fixed prices, or when a reasonable volume of future orders is assured at stable selling prices.

With this information about inventory pricing it is easier to answer the first requirement in the **Concepts** tab.

### *Requirement 1*

The **Concepts** tab requires you to indicate the items that should be included in the cost of inventory. As indicated in ARB No. 43, inventory cost should include "acquisition and production costs." It also states that "under most circumstances, general and administrative expenses should be included as period charges..." Using this information as guidance, we can complete the **Concepts** tab. The first item, merchandise purchased for resale, would obviously be included in inventory. The second item, freight out, is the cost of shipping goods to customers. Therefore, it is a sales expense that is not included in the cost of inventory. Direct materials, item three, is a part of the cost of manufacturing a product. Accordingly, it is included in the cost of inventory. Sales returns, the fourth category of costs, is obviously not included because it is not part of the cost of producing the inventory. Packaging for shipment to customer, item five, is a part of selling expenses and not included as a part of inventory cost. Item six, normal factory overhead, is part of the costs required to produce the inventory and included in inventory cost. Interest on inventory loan is a financing cost and not included in cost of inventory. Purchase discounts not taken, item eight, are part of financing costs and not included in inventory cost. Item nine, freight-in, is included in inventory cost because it is a cost necessary to produce the inventory. Finally, direct labor is a cost necessary to produce the inventory and, therefore, included in the cost of inventory. The accurately completed tab is presented below.

|  |  | *Included* | *Not included* |
|---|---|:---:|:---:|
| 1. | Merchandise purchased for resale | ● | ○ |
| 2. | Freight out | ○ | ● |
| 3. | Direct materials | ● | ○ |
| 4. | Sales returns | ○ | ● |
| 5. | Packaging for shipment to customer | ○ | ● |
| 6. | Normal factory overhead | ● | ○ |
| 7. | Interest on inventory loan | ○ | ● |
| 8. | Purchase discounts not taken | ○ | ● |
| 9. | Freight-in | ● | ○ |
| 10. | Direct labor | ● | ○ |

## Requirement 2

The **Journal Entries** tab requires you to journalize a series of inventory transactions. Let's illustrate how you could complete this requirement effective and efficiently. The first transaction is described below:

1. On January 5, 2007, purchased $17,000 of garden tillers on account from Bestbuilt Tillers, terms 2/10, n/30, FOB destination. Freight charges were $200.

The entry to record this transaction simply involves a debit to Purchases and a credit to Accounts payable, because the goods were purchased on credit. The debit is to Purchases and not Inventory because we are told that the company uses a periodic inventory system. There is no entry necessary to record the freight because the terms are FOB destination, meaning that the supplier pays for the freight costs.

| | | |
|---|---|---|
| Purchases | 17,000 | |
| Accounts payable | | 17,000 |

The second transaction involves the return of goods as described below.

2. On January 10, 2007, returned garden tillers worth $2,000 to Bestbuilt Tillers due to defects.

The return of goods involves a debit to accounts payable and credit to purchase returns, as illustrated below.

| | | |
|---|---|---|
| Accounts payable | 2,000 | |
| Purchase returns | | 2,000 |

The third transaction involves the payment for the remaining tillers purchased in transaction one, as described below.

3. On January 14, 2007, paid for the remaining tillers purchased in 1.

Since $2,000 in goods were returned in transaction two, Blaedon owes Bestbuilt only $15,000 ($17,000 – $2,000). In addition, since Blaedon is paying the account within the discount period, it would be entitled to a 2% discount on the outstanding balance, or $300 ($15,000 × 2%). Therefore, the transaction would be recorded as follows:

| | | |
|---|---|---|
| Accounts payable | 15,000 | |
|   Purchase discounts | | 300* |
|   Cash | | 14,700 |

*15,000 × .02 = 300*

The fourth transaction involves the purchase of lawn mowers, as shown below:

4.  On January 28, 2007, purchased $30,000 of lawn mowers from Lawn Giant, terms 3/10, n/30, FOB shipping point. The freight charges were $820.

This purchase is somewhat different than the one described in number 1, because the shipping terms or FOB shipping point. This means that Blaedon must pay the shipping charges. Therefore, the transaction involves a debit to Purchases for $30,000, a debit to Freight-in for $820 and a credit to Accounts payable for the total of $30,820. The journal entry is presented below.

| | | |
|---|---|---|
| Purchases | 30,000 | |
| Freight-in | 820 | |
|   Accounts payable | | 30,820 |

The last transaction involves payment for the mowers purchased in transaction 4, as shown below.

5.  On February 6, 2007, paid for the lawn mowers purchased in part 4 from Lawn Giant.

The journal entry to record this transaction includes a debit to Accounts payable for the amount of the liability, $30,000, a credit to Purchases discounts in the amount of $900 ($30,000 × 3%), and a credit to cash for the amount that must be paid, $29,100 ($30,000 − $900). The entry is illustrated below.

| | | |
|---|---|---|
| Accounts payable | 30,000 | |
|   Purchase discounts | | 900 |
|   Cash | | 29,100 |
| (This assumes the freight bill is paid separately | | |
|   to the freight company) | | |

## *Requirement 3*

The Calculations tab requires you to compute two amounts, the goods available for sale and the cost of goods sold, from the following information.

| | |
|---|---|
| Purchases | $210,000 |
| Purchase discounts | 38,000 |
| Purchase returns | 17,500 |
| Freight-in | 12,100 |
| Freight out | 18,000 |
| Beginning inventory | 42,900 |
| Ending inventory | 34,250 |

All of these items are used in the computations except for Freight out; recall that it is a selling expense. The easiest way to make these computations is to use the spreadsheet function. Since it does not become part of the answer, you should use abbreviations on your spreadsheet as shown below.

| | A | B | C | D |
|---|---|---|---|---|
| 1 | Beg inv | | 42,900 | |
| 2 | Plus Pur | | 210,000 | |
| 3 | Less Pur disc | | (38,000) | |
| 4 | Less Pur ret | | (17,500) | |
| 5 | Plus Freight-in | | 12,100 | |
| 6 | Equal Goods avail | | 209,500 | |
| 7 | Less End inv | | (34,250) | |
| 8 | Equal Cost of sales | | 175,250 | |

The information from the spreadsheet allows you to complete the schedule below. When you use the spreadsheet of calculator functions, you should use the copy and paste function to transfer the answer to prevent transposition errors.

1. Goods available for sale      $209,500
2. Cost of goods sold           $175,250

## Requirement 5

The Communication tab requires you to write a memorandum to the CEO of Blaedon that explains the following:

- How Blaedon should determine the carrying amounts assigned to its lawn mower inventory for the 2007 and 2008 models.
- Considering only the 2008 model lawn mower, explain in your memo the impact of the FIFO cost flow assumptions in Blaedon's 2007 income statement and balance sheet amounts.

As discussed in Chapter 3, you should begin by outlining the major observations that should be used in drafting the memorandum:

- It is a memorandum to the CEO explaining the application of an accounting standard.
- The CEO should have an understanding of business terminology but not accounting terminology.
- You need to consider what ARB No. 43 says about measuring and reporting inventories.

As discussed in Chapter 3, there are several things that you should remember in developing a memorandum including

1. Start the memorandum with an introduction indicating its purpose.
2. Use simple sentences.
3. Since you are communicating with management, you should avoid accounting jargon.
4. Use the spelling checker in the exam software.
5. Don't worry that much about getting the requirements of the standard exactly correct. Remember your response will not be graded for technical accuracy.

Now, read the following memorandum carefully to see how it incorporates the characteristics listed above.

---

To:     CEO, Blaedon Corp.
From:   CPA Candidate
Re:     Inventory valuation

In our last meeting, you inquired as to the valuation methods used for Blaedon's lawn mower inventory. Normally, inventory is valued by accumulating all necessary and reasonable costs to get the inventory in place for sale to customers. These costs may include design costs, purchase price from contractors, freight-in, and warehousing costs. For its 2008 models, Blaedon should include all these costs in valuing the lawn mower inventory.

However, when the value of inventory is less than its historical cost, the inventory must be written down to the amount for which it can be sold, or net realizable value. For the 2007 model inventory, net realizable value is the current list price or the mowers reduced by both disposition costs and the loss on the trade ins.

Regarding the 2008 models, the use of the first-in-first-out (FIFO) method of valuing inventory requires Blaedon to assign the costs of the earliest purchased items to cost of goods sold. With rising costs, this will result in matching old, relatively low, inventory costs to current revenues. Therefore, net income and retained earnings will be higher than reported using certain other inventory methods.

The FIFO method assigns the costs of items most recently purchased to ending inventory. Therefore, the carrying amount of Blaedon's FIFO ending inventory would normally approximate replacement cost.

If you have any additional questions, please contact me.

# PROBLEMS

The following two simulations are for you to attempt. As you complete them be sure to apply the principles that you have learned in this text.

## FAR Simulation Problem 1

| Directions | | | | | | | | |
|---|---|---|---|---|---|---|---|---|
| | Situation | Temporary and Permanent Differences | Deferred Tax Schedule | Calculate Taxable Income | Journal Entries | Disclosures | Communication | Research |

In the following simulation, you will be asked various questions regarding accounting and reporting for stockholders' equity. You will use the content in the **Information Tabs** to complete the tasks in the **Work Tabs**. (The following pictures are for illustration only; the actual tabs in your simulation may differ from these.)

## Information Tabs:

| Directions | Situation | Standards | Resources |
|---|---|---|---|

Beginning with the **Directions** tab at the left side of the screen, go through each of the **Information Tabs** to familiarize yourself with the simulation content. Note that the **Resources** tab will contain useful information, including formulas and definitions, to help you complete the tasks. You may want to refer to this information while you are working.

## Work Tabs:

| ✏ Cost Method | ✏ Amt to Report | ✏ COGS | ✏ Invent Costs | ✏ Form 1065 | ✏ Communication | ✏ Review Letter |
|---|---|---|---|---|---|---|

The **Work Tabs** on the right side of the screen contain the tasks for you to complete.

Once you complete any part of a task, the pencil for that tab will be shaded. ✏ Note that a shaded pencil does NOT indicate that you have completed the entire task.

You must complete all of the tasks in the **Work Tabs** to receive full credit.

If you have difficulty answering a **Work Tab,** read the tab directions carefully.

*NOTE: If you believe you have encountered a software malfunction, report it to the test center staff immediately.*

| | Situation | | | | | | | |
|---|---|---|---|---|---|---|---|---|
| Directions | | Temporary and Permanent Differences | Deferred Tax Schedule | Calculate Taxable Income | Journal Entries | Disclosures | Communication | Research |

Jasco Corporation is in its first year of operations. The company has pretax income of $400,000. The company has the following items recorded in its records. No estimated tax payments were made during 2007.

| | |
|---|---:|
| Premiums on life insurance of key officer | $10,000 |
| Depreciation on tax return in excess of book depreciation | 12,000 |
| Interest on municipal bonds | 5,300 |
| Warranty expense | 4,000 |
| Actual warranty repairs | 3,250 |
| Bad debt expense | 1,400 |
| Beginning balance in allowance for uncollectible accounts | 0 |
| End balance for allowance for uncollectible accounts | 800 |
| Rent received in advance from clients that will be recognized evenly over the next three years | 24,000 |
| Tax rate for 2007 and future years | 40% |

| Directions | Situation | Temporary and Permanent Differences | Deferred Tax Schedule | Calculate Taxable Income | Journal Entries | Disclosures | Communication | Research |
|---|---|---|---|---|---|---|---|---|

Identify for Jasco which of the following items create temporary differences and which create permanent differences.

| | *Temporary* | *Permanent* |
|---|:---:|:---:|
| Premiums on life insurance of key officer | ○ | ○ |
| Depreciation | ○ | ○ |
| Interest on municipal bonds | ○ | ○ |
| Warranties | ○ | ○ |
| Bad debts | ○ | ○ |
| Rent received in advance from clients | ○ | ○ |

| Directions | Situation | Temporary and Permanent Differences | Deferred Tax Schedule | Calculate Taxable Income | Journal Entries | Disclosures | Communication | Research |
|---|---|---|---|---|---|---|---|---|

Prepare the following schedule for the deferred tax amounts for the year.  Choose items from the following list:

*Items*

| | |
|---|---|
| Premium on life insurance | Warranties |
| Depreciation | Bad debts |
| Interest on municipal bonds | Rent received |

| Item | Difference between taxable amount and income statement amount | Classification: Deferred tax asset Deferred tax liability | Current or noncurrent | Deferred tax amount |
|---|---|---|---|---|
| | | | | |
| | | | | |
| | | | | |
| | | | | |
| | | | | |

| Directions | Situation | Temporary and Permanent Differences | Deferred Tax Schedule | Calculate Taxable Income | Journal Entries | Disclosures | Communication | Research |
|---|---|---|---|---|---|---|---|---|

Complete the following table to calculate taxable income. If no adjustment is needed for a particular item enter 0 as your calculation.

| | |
|---|---|
| Pretax financial income | |
| Premiums on life insurance of key officer | |
| Interest on municipal bonds | |
| Depreciation for tax in excess of book depreciation | |
| Adjustment for warranties | |
| Adjustment for bad debts | |
| Adjustment for rent received in advance | |
| | |
| Taxable income | |

| Directions | Situation | Temporary and Permanent Differences | Deferred Tax Schedule | Calculate Taxable Income | Journal Entries | Disclosures | Communication | Research |
|---|---|---|---|---|---|---|---|---|

Prepare the journal entries to record tax expense for 2007. Select your account titles from the following list:

       Deferred tax asset—Current
       Deferred tax asset—Noncurrent
       Deferred tax liability—Current
       Deferred tax liability—Noncurrent
       Income tax expense
       Income taxes payable
       Prepaid income taxes

| Account title | Debit | Credit |
|---|---|---|
| | | |
| | | |
| | | |
| | | |
| | | |
| | | |
| | | |

| Directions | Situation | Temporary and Permanent Differences | Deferred Tax Schedule | Calculate Taxable Income | Journal Entries | Disclosures | Communication | Research |
|---|---|---|---|---|---|---|---|---|

Using the appropriate netting procedures, indicate the amounts that will be shown in which of the following classifications on the balance sheet.

| | |
|---|---|
| Deferred tax asset—Current | |
| Deferred tax asset—Noncurrent | |
| Deferred tax liability—Current | |
| Deferred tax liability—Noncurrent | |

| | | Temporary and Permanent Differences | Deferred Tax Schedule | Calculate Taxable Income | Journal Entries | | | Communication | | |
|---|---|---|---|---|---|---|---|---|---|---|
| Directions | Situation | | | | | Disclosures | | | | Research |

Chris Green, CPA, is auditing Jasco Co.'s 2007 financial statements.  The controller, Dunn, has provided Green with the following information relating to income taxes:

- Dunn has prepared a schedule of all differences between financial statement and income tax return income.  Dunn believes that as a result of pending legislation the enacted tax rate at December 31, 2007, will be increased for 2007.  Dunn is uncertain which differences to include and which rates to apply in computing deferred taxes under FASB No. 109.  Dunn has requested an overview of FASB No. 109 from Green.

**Required:**

Prepare a brief memo to Dunn from Green

- Identifying the objectives of accounting for income taxes,
- Defining temporary differences,
- Explaining how to measure deferred tax assets and liabilities, and
- Explaining how to measure deferred income tax expense or benefit.

*REMINDER: Your response will be graded for both technical content and writing skills.  Technical content will be evaluated for information that is helpful to the intended reader and clearly relevant to the issue. Writing skills will be evaluated for development, organization, and the appropriate expression of ideas in professional correspondence.  Use a standard business memo or letter format with a clear beginning, middle, and end.  Do not convey information in the form of a table, bullet point list, or other abbreviated presentation.*

To:      Mr. Dunn
From:   Mr. Green, CPA
Re:      Accounting for income taxes

<br><br><br><br><br>

| | | Temporary and Permanent Differences | Deferred Tax Schedule | Calculate Taxable Income | Journal Entries | | | | Research |
|---|---|---|---|---|---|---|---|---|---|
| Directions | Situation | | | | | Disclosures | Communication | | |

Management of Jasco has asked you to provide the authoritative definition of "deferred tax expense."

Find guidance in the FASB Standards that authoritatively addresses the definition.  To complete this task, use the search capabilities provided by the **Standards** tab to find the numbered paragraph in the Original Pronouncements that addresses the issue above.  Select the appropriate paragraph(s) that answer the requirement.

**FAR Simulation Problem 2**

In the following simulation, you will be asked various questions regarding accounting and reporting for stockholders' equity.  You will use the content in the **Information Tabs** to complete the tasks in the **Work Tabs**. (The following pictures are for illustration only; the actual tabs in your simulation may differ from these.)

**Information Tabs:**

| Directions | Situation | Standards | Resources |
|------------|-----------|-----------|-----------|

Beginning with the **Directions** tab at the left side of the screen, go through each of the **Information Tabs** to familiarize yourself with the simulation content. Note that the **Resources** tab will contain useful information, including formulas and definitions, to help you complete the tasks. You may want to refer to this information while you are working.

**Work Tabs:**

| Cost Method | Amt to Report | COGS | Invent Costs | Form 1065 | Communication | Review Letter |
|-------------|---------------|------|--------------|-----------|---------------|---------------|

The **Work Tabs** on the right side of the screen contain the tasks for you to complete.

Once you complete any part of a task, the pencil for that tab will be shaded. Note that a shaded pencil does NOT indicate that you have completed the entire task.

You must complete all of the tasks in the **Work Tabs** to receive full credit.

If you have difficulty answering a **Work Tab,** read the tab directions carefully.

*NOTE: If you believe you have encountered a software malfunction, report it to the test center staff immediately.*

| Situation | | | | | | | |
|-----------|----------|----------------------|----------------------------------------|-----------------|------------------------|---------------|----------|
| | Concepts | Uncollectible Accounts | Provision for Uncollectible Accounts Expense | Journal Entries | Transfer of Receivables | Communication | Research |

Sigma Co. began operations on January 1, 2006. On December 31, 2006, Sigma provided for uncollectible accounts based on 1% of annual credit sales. On January 1, 2007, Sigma changed its method of determining its allowance for uncollectible accounts by applying certain percentages to the accounts receivable aging as follows:

| Days past invoice date | Percent deemed to be uncollectible |
|:----------------------:|:----------------------------------:|
| 0–30 | 1 |
| 31–90 | 5 |
| 91–180 | 20 |
| Over 180 | 80 |

In addition, Sigma wrote off all accounts receivable that were over one year old. The following additional information relates to the years ended December 31, 2007, and 2006:

| | 2007 | 2006 |
|---|---|---|
| Credit sales | $3,000,000 | $2,800,000 |
| Collections | 2,915,000 | 2,400,000 |
| Accounts written off | 27,000 | None |
| Recovery of accounts previously written off | 7,000 | None |

| *Days past invoice date at 12/31* | | |
|---|---|---|
| 0–30 | 300,000 | 250,000 |
| 31–90 | 80,000 | 90,000 |
| 91–180 | 60,000 | 45,000 |
| Over 180 | 25,000 | 15,000 |

| Situation | Concepts | Uncollectible Accounts | Provision for Uncollectible Accounts Expense | Journal Entries | Transfer of Receivables | Communication | Research |
|---|---|---|---|---|---|---|---|
| | | | | | | | |

Identify which of the following items are disclosed as cash or cash equivalents on the balance sheet.

| | | *Cash* | *Not cash* |
|---|---|---|---|
| **1.** | Checking accounts | ○ | ○ |
| **2.** | Treasury stock | ○ | ○ |
| **3.** | Treasury bills | ○ | ○ |
| **4.** | Money market funds | ○ | ○ |
| **5.** | Petty cash | ○ | ○ |
| **6.** | Trading securities | ○ | ○ |
| **7.** | Savings accounts | ○ | ○ |
| **8.** | Sinking fund cash | ○ | ○ |
| **9.** | Compensating balances against long-term borrowings | ○ | ○ |
| **10.** | Cash restricted for new building | ○ | ○ |
| **11.** | Postdated check for customers | ○ | ○ |
| **12.** | Available-for-sale securities | ○ | ○ |

| Situation | Concepts | Uncollectible Accounts | Provision for Uncollectible Accounts Expense | Journal Entries | Transfer of Receivables | Communication | Research |
|---|---|---|---|---|---|---|---|
| | | | | | | | |

Complete the following schedule showing the calculation of the allowance for uncollectible accounts at December 31, 2007.

**Sigma Company**
## SCHEDULE OF CALCULATION OF ALLOWANCE FOR UNCOLLECTIBLE ACCOUNTS
*December 31, 2007*

| | *Amounts of accounts receivable* | *Percentage of uncollectible accounts* | *Estimate of uncollectible accounts* |
|---|---|---|---|
| 0 to 30 days | | | |
| 31 to 90 days | | | |
| 91 to 180 days | | | |
| Over 180 days | | | |
| Total accounts receivable | | | |
| Total allowance for uncollectible accounts | | | |

| Situation | Concepts | Uncollectible Accounts | Provision for Uncollectible Accounts Expense | Journal Entries | Transfer of Receivables | Communication | Research |
|---|---|---|---|---|---|---|---|

Complete the following table and calculate the provision for uncollectible accounts expense for 2007.

Computation of 2007 provision.

| Balance December 31, 2006 | |
|---|---|
| Write-offs during 2007 | |
| Recoveries during 2007 | |
| Balance before 2007 provision | |
| Required allowance at December 31, 2007 | |
| 2007 Provision | |

| Situation | Concepts | Uncollectible Accounts | Provision for Uncollectible Accounts Expense | Journal Entries | Transfer of Receivables | Communication | Research |
|---|---|---|---|---|---|---|---|

Prepare the journal entries for the write-offs and recoveries for 2007, and for the provision for uncollectible accounts expense at December 31, 2007.

**Write-offs**

| | | |
|---|---|---|
| | | |
| | | |
| | | |

**Recoveries**

| | | |
|---|---|---|
| | | |
| | | |
| | | |

**Provision for uncollectible accounts expense at December 31, 2007**

| | | |
|---|---|---|
| | | |
| | | |
| | | |

| Situation | Concepts | Uncollectible Accounts | Provision for Uncollectible Accounts Expense | Journal Entries | Transfer of Receivables | Communication | Research |
|---|---|---|---|---|---|---|---|

Sigma enters into an agreement with First Finance Corporation to sell a group of receivables without recourse. The total face value of the receivables is $150,000. First Finance Corp. will charge 15% interest on the weighted-average time to maturity of the receivables of 45 days plus a 2% fee.

Prepare the journal entry to record the transfer of the receivables.

| | | |
|---|---|---|
| | | |
| | | |
| | | |

| Situation | Concepts | Uncollectible Accounts | Provision for Uncollectible Accounts Expense | Journal Entries | Transfer of Receivables | Communication | Research |
|---|---|---|---|---|---|---|---|

Write a memo to the CEO of Sigma Company explaining the two methods for estimating uncollectible accounts.

*REMINDER: Your response will be graded for both technical content and writing skills. Technical content will be evaluated for information that is helpful to the intended reader and clearly relevant to the issue. Writing skills will be evaluated for development, organization, and the appropriate expression of ideas in professional correspondence. Use a standard business memo or letter format with a clear beginning, middle, and end. Do not convey information in the form of a table, bullet point list, or other abbreviated presentation.*

To:     CEO, Sigma Company
From:   CPA Candidate
Re:     Estimating uncollectible accounts

| Situation | Concepts | Uncollectible Accounts | Provision for Uncollectible Accounts Expense | Journal Entries | Transfer of Receivables | Communication | Research |
|---|---|---|---|---|---|---|---|

Sigma is planning to obtain cash by transferring some of its accounts receivable to a factor and they want a copy of the authoritative literature that addresses each of the following issues.

1.  With regard to transfers of financial assets, what is the financial components approach?
2.  Describe the criteria for determining when control has been surrendered in a transfer of receivables.
3.  How are transfers of receivables accounted for if one or more of the criteria for determining whether control has been surrendered are not met?

Find guidance in the FASB Standards that authoritatively address the issues above. To complete this task, use the search capabilities provided by the **Standards** tab to find the numbered paragraph in the Original Pronouncements that addresses each of the issues above. Select the appropriate paragraph(s) that the answer the requirement.

# 5 MASTERING REGULATION SIMULATIONS

This chapter applies the principles described in Chapter 1 to the simulations in the Regulation (REG) section of the CPA exam. Every REG examination includes two simulations. As discussed in Chapter 1, the AICPA has identified the following skills required by CPAs to protect the public interest:

- Analysis—The ability to organize, process, and interpret data to develop options for decision making.
- Judgment—The ability to evaluate options for decision making and provide an appropriate conclusion.
- Communication—The ability to effectively elicit and/or express information through written or oral means.
- Research—The ability to locate and extract relevant information from available resource materials.
- Understanding—The ability to recognize and comprehend the meaning and application of a particular matter.

For the Regulation section the Board of Examiners have provided the following matrix to illustrate the interaction of content and skills:

| Content Specification Outline Areas | Skill Categories | | | | | Content Weights |
|---|---|---|---|---|---|---|
| | Communication | Research | Analysis | Judgment | Understanding | |
| I. Ethics and professional responsibility | | | | | | 15-20% |
| II. Business law | | | | | | 20-25% |
| III. Federal tax procedures and accounting issues | | | | | | 8-12% |
| IV. Federal taxation of property transactions | | | | | | 8-12% |
| V. Federal taxation—individuals | | | | | | 12-18% |
| VI. Federal taxation—entities | | | | | | 22-28% |
| **Skills Weights** | 0-14% | 9-19% | 9-19% | 8-18% | 45-55% | |

You should keep these skills foremost in your mind as you prepare and sit for the Regulation section.

## CONTENT OF THE REGULATION SECTION

To perform successfully on the REG simulations, you must have an adequate knowledge of the content of the REG exam. The AICPA Content Specification Outline of the coverage of the REG section appears below. This outline was issued by the AICPA, and is effective for exams administered after 2005.

# AICPA CONTENT SPECIFICATION OUTLINE:  REGULATION

I. Ethics and Professional and Legal Responsibilities (**15%-20%**)

    A.  Code of Professional Conduct
    B.  Proficiency, Independence, and Due Care
    C.  Ethics and Responsibilities in Tax Practice
    D.  Licensing and Disciplinary Systems Imposed by the Profession and State Regulatory Bodies
    E.  Legal Responsibilities and Liabilities

        1.  Common Law Liability to Clients and Third Parties
        2.  Federal Statutory Liability

    F.  Privileged Communications and Confidentiality

II. Business Law (**20%-25%**)

    A.  Agency

        1.  Formation and Termination
        2.  Duties and Authority of Agents and Principals
        3.  Liabilities and Authority of Agents and Principals

    B.  Contracts

        1.  Formation
        2.  Performance
        3.  Third-Party Assignments
        4.  Discharge, Breach, and Remedies

    C.  Debtor-Creditor Relationships

        1.  Rights, Duties, and Liabilities of Debtors, Creditors, and Guarantors
        2.  Bankruptcy

    D.  Government Regulation of Business

        1.  Federal Securities Acts
        2.  Other Government Regulation (Antitrust, Pension, and Retirement Plans, Union and Employee Relations, and Legal Liability for Payroll and Social Security Taxes)

    E.  Uniform Commercial Code

        1.  Negotiable Instruments and Letters of Credit
        2.  Sales
        3.  Secured Transactions
        4.  Documents of Title and Title Transfer

    F.  Real Property, Including Insurance

III. Federal Tax Procedures and Accounting Issues (**8%-12%**)

    A.  Federal Tax Procedures
    B.  Accounting Periods

    C.  Accounting Methods Including Cash, Accrual, Percentage-of-Completion, Completed-Contract, and Installment Sales
    D.  Inventory Methods, Including Uniform Capitalization Rules

IV. Federal Taxation of Property Transactions (**8%-12%**)

    A.  Types of Assets
    B.  Basis of Assets
    C.  Depreciation and Amortization
    D.  Taxable and Nontaxable Sales and Exchanges
    E.  Income, Deductions, Capital Gains and Capital Losses, Including Sales and Exchanges of Business Property and Depreciation Recapture

V. Federal Taxation—Individuals (**12%-18%**)

    A.  Gross Income—Inclusions and Exclusions
    B.  Reporting of Items from Pass-Through Entities, Including Passive Activity Losses
    C.  Adjustments and Deductions to Arrive at Taxable Income
    D.  Filing Status and Exemptions
    E.  Tax Computations, Credits, and Penalties
    F.  Alternative Minimum Tax
    G.  Retirement Plans
    H.  Estate and Gift Taxation, Including Transfers Subject to the Gift Tax, Annual Exclusion, and Items Includible and Deductible from Gross Estate

VI. Federal Taxation—Entities (**22%-28%**)

    A.  Similarities and Distinctions in Tax Reporting among Such Entities as Sole Proprietorships, General and Limited Partnerships, Subchapter C Corporations, Subchapter S Corporations, Limited Liability Companies, and Limited Liability Partnerships
    B.  Subchapter C Corporations

        1.  Determination of Taxable Income and Loss, and Reconciliation of Book Income to Taxable Income
        2.  Tax Computations, Credits, and Penalties, Including Alternative Minimum Tax
        3.  Net Operating Losses
        4.  Consolidated Returns
        5.  Entity/Owner Transactions, Including Contributions and Distributions

    C.  Subchapter S Corporations

        1.  Eligibility and Election

2. Determination of Ordinary Income, Separately Stated Items, and Reconciliation of Book Income to Taxable Income
3. Basis of Shareholder's Interest
4. Entity/Owner Transactions, Including Contributions and Liquidating and Nonliquidating Distributions
5. Built-In Gains Tax

D. Partnerships

1. Determination of Ordinary Income, Separately State Items, and Reconciliation of Book Income to Taxable Income
2. Basis of Partner's Interest and Basis of Assets Contributed to the Partnership
3. Partnership and Partner Elections
4. Partner Dealing with Own Partnership
5. Treatment of Partnership Liabilities
6. Distribution of Partnership Assets
7. Ownership Changes and Liquidation and Termination of Partnership

E. Trusts

1. Types of Trusts
2. Income and Deductions
3. Determination of Beneficiary's Share of Taxable Income

**References—Regulation**

*Ethics, Professional and Legal Responsibilities, and Business Law*

- AICPA Professional Standards: Code of Professional Conduct and Bylaws
- AICPA Statements on Auditing Standards dealing explicitly with proficiency, confidentiality, independence, and due care
- AICPA Statements on Standards for Consulting Services
- AICPA Statements on Responsibilities in Personal Financial Planning Practice
- Pronouncements of the Independence Standards Board
- Current textbooks covering business law, auditing, and accounting
- Sarbanes-Oxley Act of 2002
- Public Company Accounting Oversight Board (PCAOB) Auditing, Attestation and Quality Control Standards
- Securities Exchange Act of 1933
- Securities Exchange Act of 1934 *Federal Taxation*
- Internal Revenue Code and Income Tax Regulations
- Internal Revenue Service Circular 230
- AICPA Statements on Standards for Tax Services
- US Master Tax Guide
- Current federal income tax textbooks

## COMMUNICATION REQUIREMENTS

As discussed in Chapter 1, every simulation requires you to prepare a written communication. In the REG section this communication will usually involve preparing a memorandum that describes the tax treatment of a proposed transaction or other tax situation. The communication may be for someone who would be expected to understand tax and accounting terminology, or someone who would not be expected to have such understanding. To get the maximum score, you should tailor your communication to the recipient. Remember that the communication must address the objectives that are set forth in the requirement. In other words it must be helpful to the recipient. However, it does not have to be technically accurate. Therefore, you should not spend a lot of time thinking about the details of the tax rules. If you are not sure of specific rules, take a guess. If you do not have a clue, you might consider referring to the code database and quickly reviewing the applicable rules. However, you do not have time to spare. Using an excessive amount of time on one written communication will decrease your overall score. Remember you should not quote from the code, or construct your memorandum in the form of bullets. **You must demonstrate your own writing ability.** Chapter 3 is devoted to suggestions on how to improve your writing ability to maximize your score on the communication requirements of simulations.

## RESEARCH REQUIREMENTS

Every simulation also contains a tab that requires you to perform research. Research components of simulations in the REG section will require you to research the tax code. In the **Research** tab you will be presented with a research question or issue. For example, you may be asked to search the tax code to find the section that contains the rules for a Roth IRA. In completing the requirement, you will be asked to transfer to the answer area the section (paragraph or paragraphs) of code that addresses the research question.

When you are performing a research requirement of a REG simulation you should approach it in a systematic fashion. A five-step approach that seems to work well for many candidates is presented below:

1. Define the issue. What is the research question to be answered?
2. Select the database to search.
3. Choose appropriate search technique. Select keywords that will locate the needed information, use the topical index, or use the table of contents.
4. Execute the search. Enter the keyword(s) or click on the table of contents item and complete the search.
5. Evaluate the results. Evaluate the research to see if an answer has been found. If not, try a new search.

## SOLVING REGULATION SIMULATIONS

The remainder of this chapter will illustrate how to approach and solve simulations in the REG section of the CPA examination. As you attempt to solve any simulation, keep in mind the five-step suggested approach presented in Chapter 1:

1. Review **the entire problem**. Tab through the problem in order to get a feel for the topical area and related concepts that are being tested. Even though the format of the question may vary, the exam continues to test your understanding of applicable principles or concepts. Relax, take a deep breath, and determine your strategy for conquering the simulation.
2. Identify **the requirements of the problem**. This step will help you focus more quickly on the solution(s) without wasting time reading irrelevant material. Jot down the nature of the requirements on your scratch paper.
3. With **the requirements in mind carefully review the information tabs**. Make notes of information from the tabs that will help you answer each requirement.
4. Answer **each tab requirement one at a time**. If the requirements don't build on one another, don't be afraid to answer the tab requirements out of order. Also, if the scenario is long or complex, you may wish to use the split screen function to view the simulation data while answering a particular requirement.
5. **Use the scratch paper (which will be provided) and the spreadsheet and calculator tools to assist you in answering the simulation.**

Now let's apply this approach to some actual regulation simulations.

## SIMULATION EXAMPLE 1

First, you should take a very few minutes to review the information, requirements and concepts. Write down on your scratch paper what you are asked to do.

(35 to 40 minutes)

| Directions | | | | | | | |
|---|---|---|---|---|---|---|---|
| | Situation | Gain/Basis | Depreciation Expense | Distributive Share | Liquidating Distributions | Written Communication | Research |

In the following simulation, you will be asked to respond to various questions regarding the tax treatment of partnerships. You will use the content in the **Information Tabs** to complete the tasks in the **Work Tabs**. (The following pictures are for illustration only; the actual tabs in your simulation may differ from these.)

**Information Tabs:**

| Directions | Situation | Standards | Resources |
|---|---|---|---|

Beginning with the **Directions** tab at the left side of the screen, go through each of the **Information Tabs** to familiarize yourself with the simulation content.  Note that the **Resources** tab will contain useful information, including formulas and definitions, to help you complete the tasks. You may want to refer to this information while you are working.

**Work Tabs:**

| Cost Method | Amt to Report | COGS | Invent Costs | Form 1065 | Communication | Review Letter |
|---|---|---|---|---|---|---|

The **Work Tabs,** on the right side of the screen, contain the tasks for you to complete.

Once you complete any part of a task, the pencil for that tab will be shaded.

Note that a shaded pencil does NOT indicate that you have completed the entire task.

You must complete all of the tasks in the **Work Tabs** to receive full credit.

If you have difficulty answering a **Work Tab,** read the tab directions carefully.

*NOTE:  If you believe you have encountered a software malfunction, report it to the test center staff immediately.*

| Directions | Situation | | Gain/Basis | Depreciation Expense | Distributive Share | Liquidating Distributions | Written Communication | Research |
|---|---|---|---|---|---|---|---|---|

Miller, Smith, and Tucker decided to form a partnership to perform engineering services.  All of the partners have extensive experience in the engineering field and now wish to pool their resources and client contacts to begin their own firm.  The new entity, Sabre Consulting, will begin operations on April 1, 2007, and will use the calendar year for reporting purposes.

All of the partners expect to work full time for Sabre and each will contribute cash and other property to the company sufficient to commence operations.  The partners have agreed to share all income and losses of the partnership equally.  A written partnership agreement, duly executed by the partners, memorializes this agreement among the partners.

The table below shows the estimated values for assets contributed to Sabre by each partner. None of the contributed assets' costs have been previously recovered for tax purposes.

| Partner | Cash contribution | Estimated FMV of noncash property contributed | Basis in noncash property contributed |
|---|---|---|---|
| Miller | $15,000 | $11,000 | $10,000 |
| Smith | 10,000 | 17,000 | 15,000 |
| Tucker | 20,000 | 6,500 | 5,000 |
| Totals | 45,000 | 34,500 | 30,000 |

| Directions | Situation | Gain/Basis | Depreciation Expense | Distributive Share | Liquidating Distributions | Written Communication | Research |
|---|---|---|---|---|---|---|---|

Complete the shaded cells in the following table by entering the gain or loss recognized by each partner on the property contributed to Sabre Consulting, the partner's basis in the partnership interest, and Sabre's basis in the contributed property. Loss amounts should be recorded as a negative number.

*NOTE: To use a formula in the spreadsheet, it must be preceded by an equal sign (e.g., = B1 + B2).*

| E16 | • | *fx* | | |
|---|---|---|---|---|
| | A | B | C | D |
| 1 | | Partner's gain or loss on property transferred | Partner's basis in partnership interest | Partnership's basis in property contributed |
| 2 | Miller | | | |
| 3 | Smith | | | |
| 4 | Tucker | | | |

| Directions | Situation | Gain/Basis | Depreciation Expense | Distributive Share | Liquidating Distributions | Written Communication | Research |
|---|---|---|---|---|---|---|---|

Using the MACRS table (which can be found by clicking the Resources tab) and the partnership basis in the contributed assets calculated on the prior tab, complete the following table to determine Sabre's tax depreciation expense for 2007. Assume that none of the original cost of any asset was expensed by the partnership under the provisions of Section 179.

*NOTE: To use a formula in the spreadsheet, it must be preceded by an equal sign (e.g., = B1 + B2).*

| D15 | • | *fx* | | |
|---|---|---|---|---|
| | A | B | C | D |
| 1 | Partner | Asset type | Depreciable basis | 2007 Depreciation expense |
| 2 | Miller | Office furniture | | |
| 3 | Smith | Pickup truck used 100% for business purposes | | |
| 4 | Tucker | Computers and printers | | |

| Directions | Situation | Gain/Basis | Depreciation Expense | Distributive Share | Liquidating Distributions | Written Communication | Research |
|---|---|---|---|---|---|---|---|

Assume that Sabre had only the items of income and expenses shown in the following table for the 2007 tax year. Complete the remainder of the table by properly classifying each item of income and expense as ordinary business income that is reportable on page 1, Form 1065, or as a separately stated item that is reportable on Schedule K, Form 1065. Some entries may appear in both columns.

*NOTE: To use a formula in the spreadsheet, it must be preceded by an equal sign (e.g., = B1 + B2).*

| G15 | • | *fx* | | | |
|---|---|---|---|---|---|
| | A | | B | C | D |
| 1 | | | | **Ordinary Income** | **Separately stated items** |
| 2 | Sales revenue | | $500,000 | | |
| 3 | Interest income | | $4,000 | | |
| 4 | Depreciation expenses | | $(7,500) | | |
| 5 | Operating expenses | | $(426,000) | | |
| 6 | Charitable contributions | | $(3,000) | | |
| 7 | | | | | |
| 8 | Total net ordinary income | | | | |

| Directions | Situation | Gain/Basis | Depreciation Expense | Distributive Share | Liquidating Distributions | Written Communication | Research |
|---|---|---|---|---|---|---|---|

The partners have decided to liquidate Sabre Consulting at December 31, 2007. On that date, Tucker received the following asset as a liquidating distribution in exchange for his entire partnership interest. There were no partnership liabilities at the date of liquidation. Tucker's basis in the partnership interest at the date of liquidation was $3,000.

| | Cost | Accumulated depreciation | Estimated FMV |
|---|---|---|---|
| Drafting equipment | $12,000 | $8,000 | $6,000 |

Based on the foregoing information, complete the following table. Loss amounts should be recorded as a negative number.

*NOTE: To use a formula in the spreadsheet, it must be preceded by an equal sign (e.g., = B1 + B2).*

| D15 | • | *fx* | | |
|---|---|---|---|---|
| | A | | | B |
| 1 | Gain or loss recognized by partnership on the liquidating distribution | | | |
| 2 | Gain or loss recognized by Tucker on the liquidating distribution | | | |
| 3 | Tucker's basis in the asset received as part of the liquidating distribution | | | |

| Directions | Situation | Gain/Basis | Depreciation Expense | Distributive Share | Liquidating Distributions | Written Communication | Research |
|---|---|---|---|---|---|---|---|

You also handle Mr. Smith's personal taxes. He received dividends from foreign stocks during the year from which foreign taxes of $50 were withheld. He has requested your help in determining whether it would be more advantageous to claim these foreign taxes paid as an itemized deduction or as a credit against income taxes. For the current year, Mr. Smith is single, has adjusted gross income of $85,000, total itemized deductions of $8,000, and taxable income of $74,000. His marginal tax rate is 30%. Write a letter to Mr. Smith explaining which option would be more advantageous for the tax year based on the above information.

REMINDER:  *Your response will be graded for both technical content and writing skills.  Technical content will be evaluated for information that is helpful to the intended reader and clearly relevant to the issue. Writing skills will be evaluated for development, organization, and the appropriate expression of ideas in professional correspondence.  Use a standard business memo or letter format with a clear beginning, middle, and end.  Do not convey information in the form of a table, bullet point list, or other abbreviated presentation.*

| Directions | Situation | Gain/Basis | Depreciation Expense | Distributive Share | Liquidating Distributions | Written Communication | Research |
|---|---|---|---|---|---|---|---|

During its initial tax year, Sabre Consulting incurred $2,000 of legal fees and $750 of accounting fees to organize the partnership.  What code section and subsection permits the partnership to elect to deduct these expenses for federal tax purposes?

To complete this task, use the search capabilities provided by the **Code** tab to find the section and subsection in the IRS Code that addresses the issue above.  Select the appropriate paragraph(s) that answer the requirement.

## Solving the Simulation

Now, let's apply the approach we suggest to solving this simulation.  The list of requirements that you developed should be something like the following:

1. Calculate the gain or loss recognized by each partner on the property contributed.
2. Using the MACRS table and the partnership basis, compute the depreciation expense for 2007.
3. Classify revenue and expense items as being either part of ordinary income of a separately reported item.
4. Determine the gain or loss recognized by the partnership and a partner on a liquidating distribution.
5. Write a memorandum explaining to a taxpayer the alternative that is more advantageous, claiming foreign taxes paid as an itemized deduction or as a credit against income taxes.
6. Research the code section that allows the deduction for organization costs.

Because these first three requirements are sequential in that you need information from an earlier requirement to do the next one, you should complete the requirements in order.   So let's start with the first requirement.

## Requirement 1

| Directions | Situation | Gain/Basis | Depreciation Expense | Distributive Share | Liquidating Distributions | Written Communication | Research |
|---|---|---|---|---|---|---|---|

Complete the shaded cells in the following table by entering the gain or loss recognized by each partner on the property contributed to Sabre Consulting, the partner's basis in the partnership interest, and Sabre's basis in the contributed property.  Loss amounts should be recorded as a negative number.

*NOTE:  To use a formula in the spreadsheet, it must be preceded by an equal sign (e.g., = B1 + B2).*

| E16 | ▼ | *fx* | | |
|-----|---|------|---|---|
| | A | B | C | D |
| 1 | | **Partner's gain or loss on property transferred** | **Partner's basis in partnership interest** | **Partnership's basis in property contributed** |
| 2 | Miller | | | |
| 3 | Smith | | | |
| 4 | Tucker | | | |

To complete this table, we need the information from the contribution table in the **Situation** tab as shown below:

| Partner | Cash contribution | Estimated FMV of noncash property contributed | Basis in noncash property contributed |
|---------|-------------------|-----------------------------------------------|----------------------------------------|
| Miller | $15,000 | $11,000 | $10,000 |
| Smith | 10,000 | 17,000 | 15,000 |
| Tucker | 20,000 | 6,500 | 5,000 |
| Totals | 45,000 | 34,500 | 30,000 |

In beginning this requirement, you must remember the tax rules regarding contributions of assets to a partnership for a partnership interest. Generally, no gain or loss is recognized on the contribution of property in exchange for a partnership interest. The partner's initial basis for the partnership interest is equal to the amount of cash plus the adjusted basis of any noncash property contributed. Similarly, the partnership's basis in the transferred property is equal to the partner's basis prior to the transfer. Miller's initial partnership basis consists of the $15,000 plus the $10,000 adjusted basis of noncash property contributed, or $25,000. Smith's partnership basis consists of $10,000 cash plus the $15,000 basis of noncash property contributed, or $25,000. Finally, Tucker's partnership basis is equal to $20,000 cash plus the $5,000 basis of noncash property contributed, or $25,000.

| E16 | ▼ | *fx* | | |
|-----|---|------|---|---|
| | A | B | C | D |
| 1 | | **Partner's gain or loss on property transferred** | **Partner's basis in partnership interest** | **Partnership's basis in property contributed** |
| 2 | Miller | $0 | $25,000 | $10,000 |
| 3 | Smith | $0 | $25,000 | $15,000 |
| 4 | Tucker | $0 | $25,000 | $5,000 |

## Requirement 2

The **Depreciation Expense** tab requires you to compute the depreciation for 2007 on each of the assets contributed by the partners, as shown below:

| D15 | ▼ | *fx* | | |
|-----|---|------|---|---|
| | A | B | C | D |
| 1 | **Partner** | **Asset type** | **Depreciable basis** | **2007 Depreciation expense** |
| 2 | Miller | Office furniture | | |
| 3 | Smith | Pickup truck used 100% for business purposes | | |
| 4 | Tucker | Computers and printers | | |

You need the MACRS table in the **Resource** tab to complete this requirement.  The tab would have provided you with the following table:

General Depreciation System
Applicable Depreciation Method: 200 or 150%
Declining Balance Switching to Straight Line
Applicable Recovery Period: 3, 5, 7, 10, 15, 20 years
Applicable Convention: Half-year

| If the Recovery Year is: | and the Recovery Period is: | | | | | |
|---|---|---|---|---|---|---|
| | 3-year | 5-year | 7-year | 10-year | 15-year | 20-year |
| 1 | 33.33 | 20.00 | 14.29 | 10.00 | 5.00 | 3.75 |
| 2 | 44.45 | 32.00 | 24.49 | 18.00 | 9.50 | 7.219 |
| 3 | 14.81 | 19.20 | 17.49 | 14.40 | 8.55 | 6.677 |
| 4 | 7.41 | 11.52 | 12.49 | 11.52 | 7.70 | 6.177 |
| 5 | | 11.52 | 8.93 | 9.22 | 6.93 | 5.713 |
| 6 | | 5.76 | 8.92 | 7.37 | 6.23 | 5.285 |
| 7 | | | 8.93 | 6.55 | 5.90 | 4.888 |
| 8 | | | 4.46 | 6.55 | 5.90 | 4.522 |
| 9 | | | | 6.56 | 5.91 | 4.462 |
| 10 | | | | 6.55 | 5.90 | 4.461 |
| 11 | | | | 3.28 | 5.91 | 4.462 |
| 12 | | | | | 5.90 | 4.461 |
| 13 | | | | | 5.91 | 4.462 |
| 14 | | | | | 5.90 | 4.461 |
| 15 | | | | | 5.91 | 4.462 |
| 16 | | | | | 2.95 | 4.461 |
| 17 | | | | | | 4.462 |
| 18 | | | | | | 4.461 |
| 19 | | | | | | 4.462 |
| 20 | | | | | | 4.461 |
| 21 | | | | | | 2.231 |

Since this **Resource** tab only has the depreciation percentages and not the descriptions of classes of property, you would need to be familiar with the classification of assets.  The office furniture has a 7-year recovery period, while the pickup truck and the computers and printers have 5-year recovery periods.  The MACRS depreciation table that is provided is based on the 200% declining-balance method and already incorporates the half-year convention, which permits just a half-year of depreciation for the year that the property is placed in service.  The depreciation expense for the office furniture is its basis multiplied by 14.29%, and the depreciation expense amounts for the other two assets are equal to their bases multiplied by 20%.  The depreciable basis of the property is simply taken from the table in the **Gain/Basis** tab.  After inputting the basis amounts, the easiest and safest way to compute depreciation is to use spreadsheet formulas as shown below.

| D15 | ▼ | fx |  |  |
|---|---|---|---|---|
|  | A | B | C | D |
| 1 | **Partner** | **Asset type** | **Depreciable basis** | **2007 Depreciation expense** |
| 2 | Miller | Office furniture | $10,000 | = C2*.1429 |
| 3 | Smith | Pickup truck used 100% for business purposes | $15,000 | = C3*.2 |
| 4 | Tucker | Computers and printers | $5,000 | = C4*.2 |

The completed table would then appear as follows:

| D15 | ▼ | fx |  |  |
|---|---|---|---|---|
|  | A | B | C | D |
| 1 | **Partner** | **Asset type** | **Depreciable basis** | **2007 Depreciation expense** |
| 2 | Miller | Office furniture | $10,000 | $1,429 |
| 3 | Smith | Pickup truck used 100% for business purposes | $15,000 | $3,000 |
| 4 | Tucker | Computers and printers | $5,000 | $1,000 |

## Requirement 3

The **Distributive Share** tab requires you to complete the following table that classifies revenue and expenses as to whether they are part of the computation of ordinary income or separately reported on the partnership tax return.   Recall from your knowledge of partnership taxation, that partnership items having special tax characteristics must be reported separately so that their special characteristics are preserved when reported on the partners' tax returns.   In contrast, partnership ordinary income and deduction items having no special tax characteristics can be netted together in the computation of a partnership's ordinary income and deductions from trade or business activities on page 1 of Form 1065.  In this case, assuming that the $4,000 of interest income is from investments, it represents portfolio income and must be separately stated on Schedule K of the partnership return.  Similarly, the charitable contributions of $3,000 must be separately stated so that the appropriate percentage limitations can be applied when passed through to partners.  Sales revenue, depreciation, and operating expenses are ordinary items. You should use the SUM function to calculate the operating income of $66,500.

| G15 | ▼ | fx |  |  |
|---|---|---|---|---|
|  | A | B | C | D |
| 1 |  |  | **Ordinary Income** | **Separately stated items** |
| 2 | Sales revenue | $500,000 | 500,000 |  |
| 3 | Interest income | $4,000 |  | 4,000 |
| 4 | Depreciation expense | $(7,500) | (7,500) |  |
| 5 | Operating expenses | $(426,000) | (426,000) |  |
| 6 | Charitable contributions | $(3,000) |  | (3,000) |
| 7 |  |  |  |  |
| 8 | Total net ordinary income |  | SUM (C2:C6) |  |

Your final answer should appear as follows:

| G15 | ▼ | fx | | | |
|---|---|---|---|---|---|
| | A | B | C | D |
| 1 | | | **Ordinary Income** | **Separately stated items** |
| 2 | Sales revenue | $500,000 | $500,000 | |
| 3 | Interest income | $4,000 | | $4,000 |
| 4 | Depreciation expense | $(7,500) | $(7,500) | |
| 5 | Operating expenses | $(426,000) | $(426,000) | |
| 6 | Charitable contributions | $(3,000) | | $(3,000) |
| 7 | | | | |
| 8 | Total net ordinary income | | $66,500 | |

## Requirement 4

The **Liquidating Distributions** tab requires you to complete a table regarding a liquidating distribution to Tucker. Tucker received drafting equipment for his entire partnership interest, which had a basis to Tucker of $3,000. Information about the drafting equipment is shown below.

| | Cost | Accumulated depreciation | Estimated FMV |
|---|---|---|---|
| Drafting equipment | $12,000 | $8,000 | $6,000 |

Again, you must recall your knowledge of partnership taxation. Remember, generally no gain or loss is recognized by a partnership on the distribution of noncash property in complete liquidation of the partnership. Similarly, generally no gain or loss is recognized by the partner when noncash property is received in complete liquidation of the partner's partnership interest. In this situation, Sabre recognizes no gain when it distributes the drafting equipment with a fair market value of $6,000 and an adjusted basis of $4,000, and Tucker recognizes no gain when he receives the drafting equipment in liquidation of his partnership interest. Although distributed property generally has a transferred basis, the basis of the drafting equipment to Tucker is limited to his $3,000 basis for his partnership interest before the distribution. Therefore, the table should be completed as follows:

| D15 | ▼ | fx | | |
|---|---|---|---|---|
| | A | | B |
| 1 | Gain or loss recognized by partnership on the liquidating distribution | | $0 |
| 2 | Gain or loss recognized by Tucker on the liquidating distribution | | $0 |
| 3 | Tucker's basis in the asset received as part of the liquidating distribution | | $3,000 |

## Requirement 5

The **Written Communication** tab requires you to draft a memorandum to a tax client regarding whether it is more advantageous to take an itemized deduction or a credit for foreign taxes paid. The taxpayer has income of $85,000, total itemized deductions of $8,000, and taxable income of $74,000. His marginal tax rate is 30%. In completing communication requirements such as these, you should remember that the memorandum will not be graded for technical accuracy. As long as it is on point, your score will be determined based the quality of the communication, including its organization. Chapter 3 describes how you can improve your writing skills. Before you start writing the memorandum, you should develop a very short outline. It may be as simple as the one shown below.

1.   Introduction and objective of the memorandum
2.   Difference between a credit and a deduction
3.   Recommendation and rationale
4.   Closing

With these observations in mind, you can develop your memorandum. In doing so remember the guidance from Chapter 3:

1.   Start the memorandum with an introduction indicating its purpose.
2.   Use simple sentences.
3.   Since you are communicating with management, you should avoid accounting jargon.
4.   Use the spelling checker in the exam software.
5.   Don't worry that much about getting the requirements of the standard exactly correct. Remember your response will not be graded for technical accuracy.

Review the following memorandum, noting how it applies the principles described above.

---

Mr. Harold Smith
232 Pine Street
Anytown, NB

Dear Mr. Smith:

As we discussed, you have had $50 in foreign taxes withheld from the dividends that you have received on foreign investments. You have asked me to evaluate whether it is preferable to include the amount of taxes withheld in your itemized deductions or to take the foreign tax credit for the taxes withheld. While an itemized deduction decreases your taxable income, a tax credit directly reduces the amount of taxes you owe.

If you elect to take the taxes as a deduction, you will reduce your taxable income by $50. At a marginal tax rate of 30%, this would reduce your tax liability by $15 ($50 × 30%). Alternatively, if you elect to take the tax credit, your tax liability is reduced by $50. Therefore, you will save $35 in taxes by electing to take the foreign tax credit.

If you would like to discuss this option further, please contact me.

Sincerely,

CPA Candidate

---

## Requirement 6

The **Research** tab requires you to identify the code section and subsection that allows the deduction of organizational expenditures by a partnership. You could perform a search on "organization expenditures" but that would lead to a number of irrelevant hits. A more efficient search strategy would be an advanced search that retrieves only those documents containing all of the words listed, using the terms "organization, expenditures, and partnership."

| | | | | | | | Research |
|---|---|---|---|---|---|---|---|
| Directions | Situation | Gain/Basis | Depreciation Expense | Distributive Share | Liquidating Distributions | Written Communication | |

§709 (b)

Code Sec. 709(b) allows a partnership to elect to deduct up to $5,000 of organizational expenditures for the tax year in which the partnership begins business. The $5,000 amount must be reduced by the amount by which organizational expenditures exceed $50,000. Remaining expenditures are deducted ratably over the 180-month period beginning with the month in which the partnership begins business.

# SIMULATION EXAMPLE 2

Now, let's walk through the solution of another regulation simulation. Review the requirements and concepts of the simulation presented below and as you proceed, write them down on your scratch paper.

| Directions | | | | | | | |
|---|---|---|---|---|---|---|---|
| | Situation | Income & Expense | Depreciation | Self-Employment Tax | Communication | Research | Resources |

In the following simulation, you will be asked various questions regarding business income or loss generated by a farm operated as a sole proprietorship and reported on Schedule F, Farm Income and Expenses, of Form 1040, US Individual Income Tax Return. You will use the content in the **Information Tabs** to complete the tasks in the **Work Tabs**. (The following pictures are for illustration only; the actual tabs in your simulation may differ from these.)

## Information Tabs:

| Directions | Situation | Standards | Resources |
|---|---|---|---|

Beginning with the **Directions** tab at the left side of the screen, go through each of the **Information Tabs** to familiarize yourself with the simulation content. Note that the **Resources** tab will contain useful information, including formulas and definitions, to help you complete the tasks. You may want to refer to this information while you are working.

## Work Tabs:

| Cost Method | Amt to Report | COGS | Invent Costs | Form 1065 | Communication | Review Letter |
|---|---|---|---|---|---|---|

The **Work Tabs,** on the right side of the screen, contain the tasks for you to complete.

Once you complete any part of a task, the pencil for that tab will be shaded.

Note that a shaded pencil does NOT indicate that you have completed the entire task.

You must complete all of the tasks in the **Work Tabs** to receive full credit.

If you have difficulty answering a **Work Tab,** read the tab directions carefully.

*NOTE: If you believe you have encountered a software malfunction, report it to the test center staff immediately.*

| | Situation | | | | | | |
|---|---|---|---|---|---|---|---|
| Directions | | Income & Expense | Depreciation | Self-Employment Tax | Communication | Research | Resources |

Richard Norton recently purchased a farm. The farm is being operated as a sole proprietorship. Farm operations began on January 1, year 1, and became profitable in year 2. Richard uses the cash basis of accounting for book and tax purposes.

During year 2, Richard employed as many as 20 part-time workers, including Richard's spouse, Lucy, and children, Edward and Darla, ages 19 and 14, respectively. Lucy was unemployed during year 1, and Richard had no other earned income for year 1, except from the farm. Richard and Lucy filed a joint income tax return for year 2 and year 1.

Richard is not yet providing the farm employees with life insurance, medical and dental coverage, or retirement benefits.  Richard is paying the life and medical insurance premiums for the family from personal funds.

| Directions | Situation | Income & Expense | Depreciation | Self-Employment Tax | Communication | Research | Resources |
|---|---|---|---|---|---|---|---|

The following table includes a partial listing of the income and expense items that Richard recorded on the farm's books for **year 2**.  For each item of income and expense, select the appropriate cell to indicate whether the item should be reported on Richard's Schedule F, shown elsewhere on the joint income tax return, or not included or deducted anywhere on the joint income tax return.  Richard Norton and Lucy have consistently itemized deductions on their joint income tax return.

| A | B | C Reported on Richard's Schedule F | D Shown elsewhere on the joint return | E Not included or deducted on the joint return | |
|---|---|---|---|---|---|
| | | | | | 1 |
| **Revenues and Receipts** | | | | | 2 |
| Cash receipts from sale of cattle bought for resale | $201,300 | | | | 3 |
| Proceeds from farm line of credit | 31,100 | | | | 4 |
| Bank interest on Edward's personal bank account | 300 | | | | 5 |
| Bank interest on Richard's farm account | 600 | | | | 6 |
| | | | | | 7 |
| **Expenses and Disbursements** | | | | | 8 |
| Cost of cattle sold this year | 113,800 | | | | 9 |
| Interest on farm line of credit loan | 8,600 | | | | 10 |
| Principal repayments on farm line of credit | 1,200 | | | | 11 |
| Chemicals and pesticides | 8,100 | | | | 12 |
| Contribution to Richard's Roth IRA account | 2,000 | | | | 13 |
| State estimated tax payments on farm earnings | 2,300 | | | | 14 |
| Property taxes on the Norton home | 1,700 | | | | 15 |
| Fertilizer costs | 2,300 | | | | 16 |
| Farm travel expenses | 1,200 | | | | 17 |
| Late payment penalties on farm payroll taxes | 200 | | | | 18 |
| Livestock feed expenses | 1,400 | | | | 19 |
| Repairs and maintenance on farm equipment | 900 | | | | 20 |

| Directions | Situation | Income & Expense | Depreciation | Self-Employment Tax | Communication | Research | Resources |
|---|---|---|---|---|---|---|---|

Richard Norton had a net loss before MACRS depreciation and Section 179 deduction on the farm operations for year 1.

Calculate the depreciation on Richard's farm assets for year 1 using the information in the table below and the 150% MACRS tables found by clicking the tab marked **Resources**. Note that any property used in a farming business cannot be depreciated using the 200% declining balance method under MACRS for tax purposes.

- In cells F2 and F3, enter the appropriate MACRS basis for each of the assets listed.
- In cells G2 and G3, calculate and enter the year 1 MACRS depreciation for each asset.
- The total year 1 MACRS depreciation will automatically calculate in cell G4.

*NOTE: To use a formula in the spreadsheet, it must be preceded by an equal sign (e.g., = B1 + B2).*

| | A | B | C | D | E | F | G |
|---|---|---|---|---|---|---|---|
| 1 | Date placed in service | Asset | Cost | Life | Section 179 elected | MACRS basis | Year 1 MACRS depreciation |
| 2 | January 1, year 1 | Truck | 44,000 | 5 years | -- | | |
| 3 | January 1, year 1 | Combine | 60,000 | 7 years | 25,000 | | |
| 4 | Total year 1 MACRS depreciation | | | | | | |
| 5 | Note: Richard Norton elected out of all applicable bonus depreciation allowances, if any, for year 1 and did not elect the straight-line method of depreciation. | | | | | | |

On November 1, year 2, Richard purchased a new truck, and on November 30, year 2, Richard sold an old truck. The new truck was the only asset purchased during the year. Richard did not elect any Section 179 deduction for year 2.

Calculate the depreciation on Richard's farm assets shown below for year 2 using the information provided and the 150% MACRS tables found by clicking the tab marked **Resources**. Enter your answers in the shaded spaces provided. The total year 2 MACRS depreciation will automatically calculate in cell G5.

For purposes of this tab (Depreciation) only, assume that Richard had net farm income for year 2 of $200,000 before MACRS depreciation and Section 179 deduction.

| | A | B | C | D | E | F | G |
|---|---|---|---|---|---|---|---|
| 1 | Date placed in service | Asset | Cost | Life | Section 179 elected in year 1 | Section 179 elected in year 2 | Year 2 MACRS depreciation |
| 2 | January 1, year 1 | Old truck | 44,000 | 5 years | -- | -- | |
| 3 | January 1, year 1 | Combine | 60,000 | 7 years | 25,000 | -- | |
| 4 | November 1, year 2 | New truck | 65,000 | 5 years | -- | -- | |
| 5 | Total year 2 MACRS depreciation | | | | | | |
| 6 | Note: Richard Norton elected out of all applicable bonus depreciation allowances, if any, for year 2 and did not elect the straight-line method of depreciation. | | | | | | |

In the shaded cells below, answer the following questions related to the $25,000 Section 179 deduction elected in year 1.

| | A | G |
|---|---|---|
| 1 | How much is allowed in year 1 for tax purposes? | |
| 2 | How much is allowed in year 2 for tax purposes? | |

| Directions | Situation | Income & Expense | Depreciation | Self-Employment Tax | | Communication | Research | Resources |
|---|---|---|---|---|---|---|---|---|

Richard Norton is required to pay a self-employment tax based on the net profits of the farm business. For purposes of this tab (Self-Employment Tax), assume that Richard had a net profit of $105,000 from the farm business for year 3 and $10,000 of Section 1231 gain.

Complete Section A of the Form 1040, Schedule SE, for year 3 below by entering the appropriate values in the shaded cells. Round values to the nearest dollar. If a cell should be left empty, enter a zero.

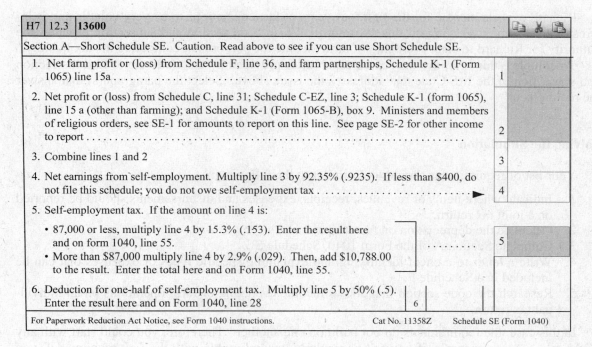

| H7 | 12.3 | 13600 |
|---|---|---|

Section A—Short Schedule SE. Caution. Read above to see if you can use Short Schedule SE.

1. Net farm profit or (loss) from Schedule F, line 36, and farm partnerships, Schedule K-1 (Form 1065) line 15a . . . . . . . . . . . . . . . . . . . . . . . . . . . . . . . . . . . . . . . . . . . . . . . . . . . . . . .  **1**

2. Net profit or (loss) from Schedule C, line 31; Schedule C-EZ, line 3; Schedule K-1 (form 1065), line 15 a (other than farming); and Schedule K-1 (Form 1065-B), box 9. Ministers and members of religious orders, see SE-1 for amounts to report on this line. See page SE-2 for other income to report . . . . . . . . . . . . . . . . .  **2**

3. Combine lines 1 and 2     **3**

4. Net earnings from self-employment. Multiply line 3 by 92.35% (.9235). If less than $400, do not file this schedule; you do not owe self-employment tax . . . . . . . . . . . . . . . . . . . . . . . ▶  **4**

5. Self-employment tax. If the amount on line 4 is:
   - 87,000 or less, multiply line 4 by 15.3% (.153). Enter the result here and on form 1040, line 55.
   - More than $87,000 multiply line 4 by 2.9% (.029). Then, add $10,788.00 to the result. Enter the total here and on Form 1040, line 55.  . . . . . . . .  **5**

6. Deduction for one-half of self-employment tax. Multiply line 5 by 50% (.5). Enter the result here and on Form 1040, line 28     **6**

For Paperwork Reduction Act Notice, see Form 1040 instructions.         Cat No. 11358Z         Schedule SE (Form 1040)

| Directions | Situation | Income & Expense | Depreciation | Self-Employment Tax | Communication | | Research | Resources |
|---|---|---|---|---|---|---|---|---|

Brown, another of your clients, plans to start a farming business as a sole proprietor. Write Brown a letter identifying and explaining specific types of expenses that can be included on Brown's Schedule F. In your letter, you should discuss at least two of the following topics:

- Cash or accrual method of accounting
- Personal income and deductions reported elsewhere on the return
- Payroll tax return filings necessary for businesses with employees
- Self-employment tax for Brown

Type your communication in the response area below the horizontal line using the word processor provided.

To:
From:

*REMINDER:  Your response will be graded for both technical content and writing skills.  Technical content will be evaluated for information that is helpful to the intended reader and clearly relevant to the issue. Writing skills will be evaluated for development, organization, and the appropriate expression of ideas in professional correspondence.  Use a standard business memo or letter format with a clear beginning, middle, and end.  Do not convey information in the form of a table, bullet point list, or other abbreviated presentation.*

| Directions | Situation | Income & Expense | Depreciation | Self-Employment Tax | Communication | Research | Resources |
|---|---|---|---|---|---|---|---|

Richard expects income for the first four years of farm operations to be very volatile and is interested in income averaging on this tax return.  Which code section and subsection provides the authority for Richard to elect averaging of farm income for purposes of computing his tax liability?

To complete this task, use the search capabilities provided by the **Code** tab to find the section and subsection in the IRS Code that addresses the issue above.  Select the paragraph(s) that answer the requirement.

## Solving the Simulation

Your list of requirements should look similar to the following:

1. Indicate where items of revenues, receipts, expenses and disbursements should be reported on a joint tax return.
2. Calculate the depreciation on farm assets.
3. Complete Section A of the Form 1040, Schedule SE.
4. Write a letter to a client identifying and explaining specific types of expenses that can be included in a Schedule F.
5. Research the code section that allows income averaging of farm operations on an individual tax return.

In this case, the requirements do not build on one another.  Therefore, you could start with any of the tabs.  As an example, if you felt particularly uncomfortable with the first requirement, you could start with the second and come back to requirement 1 if you have time.  For our purposes, let's work the requirements in order.

### Requirement 1

The **Income and Expense** tab requires you to classify revenues, receipts, expenses, and disbursements as to where they are reported on a tax return.  Farm operations are much like other businesses.  The items that make up revenues and expenses from operations are included on Schedule F.  Other items are shown elsewhere on the tax return or not reported at all.  Now let's consider the list of items.

### Revenues and Receipts

- Cash receipts from sale of cattle bought for resale is business income and would be reported on Schedule F—Profit or Loss from Farming.
- Proceeds from the farm line of credit are not revenue or expenses.  The proceeds of a loan would not be included at all on the joint return.
- Bank interest on Edward's personal bank account is income that must be reported on Edward's tax return, not on Richard's joint return.
- Bank interest on Richard's farm account would be reported on Schedule B—Interest and Dividend Income.

## Expenses and Disbursements

- Cost of cattle sold this year is a business expense that would be deducted on Schedule F.
- Interest on farm line of credit loan is related to farming and would be deducted on Schedule F.
- Principal repayments on farm line of credit represent repayments of a loan and would not be deductible on the joint return.
- Chemicals and pesticides used in farming are business expenses that would be deducted on Schedule F.
- Contributions to Richard's Roth IRA account are not deductible and not included on the joint return.
- State estimated income tax payments on farm earnings would be deductible as an itemized deduction on Schedule A of Form 1040.
- Property taxes on the Norton home are unrelated to farming and would be deductible as an itemized deduction on Schedule A of Form 1040.
- Fertilizer cost would be deductible as a business expense on Schedule F.
- Farm travel expenses would be deductible on Schedule F.
- Late payment penalties on farm payroll taxes are not deductible for federal tax purposes.
- Livestock feed expenses are deductible on Schedule F.
- Repairs and maintenance on farm equipment are deductible as business expenses on Schedule F.

The completed schedule is shown below.

| A | B | C | D | E | |
|---|---|---|---|---|---|
| | | Reported on Richard's Schedule F | Shown elsewhere on the joint return | Not included or deducted on the joint return | 1 |
| **Revenues and Receipts** | | | | | 2 |
| Cash receipts from sale of cattle bought for resale | $201,300 | X | | | 3 |
| Proceeds from farm line of credit | 31,100 | | | X | 4 |
| Bank interest on Edward's personal bank account | 300 | | | X | 5 |
| Bank interest on Richard's farm account | 600 | | X | | 6 |
| | | | | | 7 |
| **Expenses and Disbursements** | | | | | 8 |
| Cost of cattle sold this year | 113,800 | X | | | 9 |
| Interest on farm line of credit loan | 8,600 | X | | | 10 |
| Principal repayments on farm line of credit | 1,200 | | | X | 11 |
| Chemicals and pesticides | 8,100 | X | | | 12 |
| Contribution to Richard's Roth IRA account | 2,000 | | | X | 13 |
| State estimated tax payments on farm earnings | 2,300 | | X | | 14 |
| Property taxes on the Norton home | 1,700 | | X | | 15 |
| Fertilizer costs | 2,300 | X | | | 16 |
| Farm travel expenses | 1,200 | X | | | 17 |
| Late payment penalties on farm payroll taxes | 200 | | | X | 18 |
| Livestock feed expenses | 1,400 | X | | | 19 |
| Repairs and maintenance on farm equipment | 900 | X | | | 20 |

## *Requirement 2*

The **Depreciation** tab requires you to compute income tax depreciation for year 1 and year 2 using MACRS tables. Generally, tangible personal property used in a farming business is depreciated using the 150% declining-balance method. The MACRS depreciation table that was provided is based on the 150% declining-balance method and already incorporates the half-year convention, which permits just a half-year of depreciation for the year that depreciable personal property is placed in service. This table obtained by clicking on the **Resource** tab is shown below.

MACRS table (half-year convention, 150% declining balance method)

| Year | Depreciation rate for recovery period | | | |
|---|---|---|---|---|
|  | 3 years | 5 years | 7 years | 10 years |
| 1 | 25.00% | 15.00% | 10.71% | 7.5% |
| 2 | 37.50% | 25.50% | 19.13% | 13.88% |
| 3 | 25.00% | 17.85% | 15.03% | 11.79% |
| 4 | 12.50% | 16.66% | 12.25% | 10.02% |
| 5 |  | 16.66% | 12.25% | 8.74% |
| 6 |  | 8.33% | 12.25% | 8.74% |
| 7 |  |  | 12.25% | 8.74% |
| 8 |  |  | 6.13% | 8.74% |
| 9 |  |  |  | 8.74% |
| 10 |  |  |  | 8.74% |
| 11 |  |  |  | 4.37% |
| 12 |  |  |  |  |
| 13 |  |  |  |  |
| 14 |  |  |  |  |
| 15 |  |  |  |  |
| 16 |  |  |  |  |

The truck is 5-year property and its MACRS basis is $44,000, so the year 1 depreciation determined from the table would be $44,000 × 15% = $6,600. The combine is 7-year property and Richard elected to expense $25,000 of its cost under Sec. 179 which reduces its MACRS basis to $60,000 − $25,000 = $35,000. The year 1 MACRS depreciation determined from the table would be $35,000 × 10.71% = $3,749.

|  | A | B | C | D | E | F | G |
|---|---|---|---|---|---|---|---|
| 1 | Date placed in service | Asset | Cost | Life | Section 179 elected | MACRS basis | Year 1 MACRS depreciation |
| 2 | January 1, year 1 | Truck | 44,000 | 5 years | -- | 44,000 | 6,600 |
| 3 | January 1, year 1 | Combine | 60,000 | 7 years | 25,000 | 35,000 | 3,749 |
| 4 | Total year 1 MACRS depreciation | | | | | | 10,349 |
| 5 | Note: Richard Norton elected out of all applicable bonus depreciation allowances, if any, for year 1 and did not elect the straight-line method of depreciation. | | | | | | |

For year 2, you must calculate depreciation for Richard's old truck, combine, and new truck using the information provided and the MACRS tables found by clicking on the **Resources** tab. Since the old truck was tangible personal property and was sold during year 1, only a half-year of depreciation would be allowed for year 2. However, this half-year of depreciation for the year of sale is not built into the table and must be separately calculated. As a result, the year 2 depreciation for the old truck which is 5-year property would be $44,000 × 25.50% × ½ = $5,610. The year 2 depreciation for the combine which is 7-year property would be $35,000 × 19.13% = $6,696. Richard is presumably a calendar-year taxpayer and purchased a new truck for $65,000 on November 1 of year 2. Since this was the only asset that he purchased during the year and it was placed in service during the last quarter of Richard's tax year, he is required to use the midquarter convention for the new truck. The mid quarter convention must be used if more than 40% of a taxpayer's tangible personal property is placed in service during the last quarter of the year. The year 2 depreciation on the new truck which is 5-year property would be $65,000 × 3.75% = $2,438.

| | A | B | C | D | E | F | G |
|---|---|---|---|---|---|---|---|
| 1 | Date placed in service | Asset | Cost | Life | Section 179 elected in year 1 | Section 179 elected in year 2 | Year 2 MACRS depreciation |
| 2 | January 1, year 1 | Old truck | 44,000 | 5 years | -- | -- | 5,610 |
| 3 | January 1, year 1 | Combine | 60,000 | 7 years | 25,000 | -- | 6,696 |
| 4 | November 1, year 2 | New truck | 65,000 | 5 years | -- | -- | 2,438 |
| 5 | Total year 1 MACRS depreciation | | | | | | 14,744 |
| 6 | *Note: Richard Norton elected out of all applicable bonus depreciation allowances, if any, for year 2 and did not elect the straight-line method of depreciation.* | | | | | | |

You must also determine the amount of Richard's Sec. 179 expense deduction for years 1 and 2. Section 179 permits a taxpayer to elect to treat the cost of qualifying depreciable personal property as an expense rather than a capital expenditure. However, the amount of expense election that is allowed as a deduction is limited to the taxpayer's aggregate taxable income derived from any trade of business before the expense election. Any expense election that is not currently deductible because of the taxable income limitation is carried forward and is deductible subject to the taxable income limitation in carryforward years. Here the farm operations resulted in a net loss before the Sec. 179 deduction in year 1, and resulted in $200,000 of net farm income before the Sec. 179 deduction in year 2. As a result, the $25,000 of Sec. 179 expense elected for year 1 cannot be deducted in year 1, but instead is carried over to year 2 where it is allowed as a deduction.

| | A | G |
|---|---|---|
| 1 | How much is allowed in year 1 for tax purposes? | -- |
| 2 | How much is allowed in year 2 for tax purposes? | 25,000 |

## Requirement 3

The Self-Employment Tax tab requires you to complete Richard's self-employment tax by completing Section 1 of Form 1040, Schedule SE. The self-employment tax is imposed on self-employment income to provide social security and Medicare benefits for self-employed individuals. Self-employment income includes an individual's net earnings from a trade or business carried on as a sole proprietor or as an independent contractor. Self-employment income *excludes* personal interest, dividends, rents, capital gains and losses, and gains from the disposition of business property. Here, Richard's self-employment income consists of the $105,000 net profit from his farming business carried on as a sole proprietor, but excludes the $10,000 of Sec. 1231 gain from the disposition of farm property.

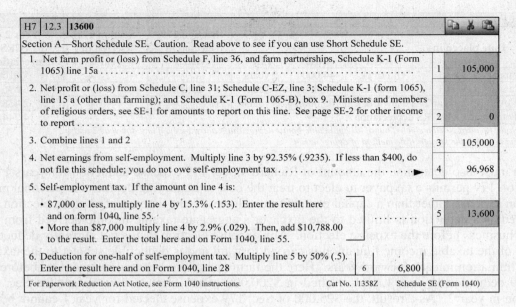

| H7 | 12.3 | **13600** | | | |
| --- | --- | --- | --- | --- | --- |

Section A—Short Schedule SE.  Caution.  Read above to see if you can use Short Schedule SE.

| | | |
| --- | --- | --- |
| 1. Net farm profit or (loss) from Schedule F, line 36, and farm partnerships, Schedule K-1 (Form 1065) line 15a . . . . . . . . . . . . . . . . . . . . . . . . . . . . . . . . . . . . . . . . . . . . . . . . . . . . . . . . . . . . . . . | 1 | 105,000 |
| 2. Net profit or (loss) from Schedule C, line 31; Schedule C-EZ, line 3; Schedule K-1 (form 1065), line 15 a (other than farming); and Schedule K-1 (Form 1065-B), box 9.  Ministers and members of religious orders, see SE-1 for amounts to report on this line.  See page SE-2 for other income to report . . . . . . . . . . . . . . . . . . . . . . . . . . . . . . . . . . . . . . . . . . . . . . . . . . . . . . . . . . . . . . . . . | 2 | 0 |
| 3. Combine lines 1 and 2 | 3 | 105,000 |
| 4. Net earnings from self-employment.  Multiply line 3 by 92.35% (.9235).  If less than $400, do not file this schedule; you do not owe self-employment tax . . . . . . . . . . . . . . . . . . . . . . . . ▶ | 4 | 96,968 |
| 5. Self-employment tax.  If the amount on line 4 is:  <br> • 87,000 or less, multiply line 4 by 15.3% (.153).  Enter the result here and on form 1040, line 55.  <br> • More than $87,000 multiply line 4 by 2.9% (.029).  Then, add $10,788.00 to the result.  Enter the total here and on Form 1040, line 55. | 5 | 13,600 |
| 6. Deduction for one-half of self-employment tax.  Multiply line 5 by 50% (.5). Enter the result here and on Form 1040, line 28      6    6,800 | | |

For Paperwork Reduction Act Notice, see Form 1040 instructions.      Cat No. 11358Z     Schedule SE (Form 1040)

## Requirement 4

The **Communication** tab requires you to draft a letter to Brown, a client, explaining the cash and accrual method of accounting, personal income and deductions reported elsewhere on the return, payroll tax return filings necessary for businesses with employees, and self-employment tax. Before you start writing the memorandum, you should develop a very short outline.  It may be as simple as the one shown below.

1. Introduction and objective of the memorandum
2. Explain the option of cash or accrual basis
3. Describe personal income and deductions
4. Explain payroll tax return filing and self-employment tax
5. Closing

With these observations in mind, you can develop your memorandum. In doing so remember the guidance from Chapter 3:

1. Start the memorandum with an introduction indicating its purpose.
2. Use simple sentences.
3. Since you are communicating with management, you should avoid accounting jargon.
4. Use the spelling checker in the exam software.
5. Don't worry that much about getting the requirements of the standard exactly correct.  Remember your response will not be graded for technical accuracy.

Review the following memorandum, noting how it applies the principles described above.

Dear Mr. Brown,

I understand that you plan to start a farming business as a sole proprietor. As such you will be reporting all of your farming income and expenses on Schedule F of Form 1040. Additionally, I would like to point out several things that you will need to consider in conjunction with your farming business, including the selection of a method of tax accounting, the proper reporting of personal income and deductions, payroll tax filings for any farm employees, and the self-employment tax.

You must choose an accounting method for your farm business when you file an income tax return that includes a Schedule F. Most farmers use the cash method because it is easier to keep cash method records. Under the cash method, you include in gross income items of income that you actually or constructively receive during the year. You generally can deduct expenses in the tax year in which you actually pay them.

Reporting farm income and expenses on Schedule F will not change where you report your personal income and deductions. For example, the mortgage interest and taxes on your principal residence and the contributions that you make to charitable organizations will still be deducted on Schedule A when you itemize deductions. Similarly, your interest and dividend income that you receive from your personal investments will be reported on Schedule B.

If you hire any employees to work in your farming business, you may have to withhold federal income, social security, and Medicare taxes. You will also have to pay the employer's share (7.65%) of social security and Medicare taxes, and will report withheld federal income tax and social security and Medicare taxes on Form 943. Additionally, you may have to pay federal unemployment tax on your employees' wages. This tax is imposed on you as the employer and will be reported on Form 940.

As a sole proprietor, you will have to pay self-employment taxes on your net farm profit. This tax is designed to provide self-employed individuals with social security and Medicare benefits and is generally imposed at a rate of 15.3%. The self-employment tax is computed on Schedule SE and is paid along with your federal income tax.

It is important that we meet to discuss the above considerations as well as others in order to minimize the tax liability from your farming business. Please call me at your earliest convenience so that we can schedule a time to meet.

Sincerely,

CPA Candidate

## Requirement 5

The **Research** tab requires you to research the code provisions that allow a taxpayer engaged in farming to make an election to determine their tax liability by averaging. An efficient search strategy for this situation would be an advanced search that retrieves only those documents containing all of the words listed, using the terms "farm and averaging"

§1301(a)

Code Sec. 1301 (a) permits individuals engaged in farming to make an election to determine their tax liability by averaging, over the previous three years, all or part of their current year's taxable income from farming. Making the election will result in a lower tax if an individual's current year farming income is high, and taxable income for one or more of the three prior years was low.

# RESOURCES

MACRS tables (midquarter convention, 150% declining balance method)

## Property placed in service in First Quarter

| Year | Depreciation rate for recovery period | | | |
|---|---|---|---|---|
| | 3 years | 5 years | 7 years | 10 years |
| 1 | 43.75% | 26.25% | 18.75% | 13.13% |
| 2 | 28.13% | 22.13% | 17.41% | 13.03% |
| 3 | 25.00% | 16.52% | 13.68% | 11.08% |
| 4 | 3.12% | 16.52% | 12.16% | 9.41% |
| 5 | | 16.52% | 12.16% | 8.71% |
| 6 | | 2.06% | 12.16% | 8.71% |
| 7 | | | 12.16% | 8.71% |
| 8 | | | 1.52% | 8.71% |
| 9 | | | | 8.71% |
| 10 | | | | 8.71% |
| 11 | | | | 1.09% |
| 12 | | | | |
| 13 | | | | |
| 14 | | | | |
| 15 | | | | |
| 16 | | | | |

MACRS table (midquarter convention, 150% declining balance method)

## Property placed in service in Second Quarter

| Year | Depreciation rate for recovery period | | | |
|---|---|---|---|---|
| | 3 years | 5 years | 7 years | 10 years |
| 1 | 31.25% | 18.75% | 13.39% | 9.38% |
| 2 | 34.38% | 24.38% | 18.56% | 13.59% |
| 3 | 25.00% | 17.06% | 14.58% | 11.55% |
| 4 | 9.37% | 16.76% | 12.22% | 9.82% |
| 5 | | 16.76% | 12.22% | 8.73% |
| 6 | | 6.29% | 12.22% | 8.73% |
| 7 | | | 12.23% | 8.73% |
| 8 | | | 4.58% | 8.73% |
| 9 | | | | 8.73% |
| 10 | | | | 8.73% |
| 11 | | | | 3.28% |
| 12 | | | | |
| 13 | | | | |
| 14 | | | | |
| 15 | | | | |
| 16 | | | | |

MACRS table (midquarter convention, 150% declining balance method)

Property placed in service in Third Quarter

| Year | Depreciation rate for recovery period | | | |
|---|---|---|---|---|
| | 3 years | 5 years | 7 years | 10 years |
| 1 | 18.75% | 11.25% | 8.04% | 5.63% |
| 2 | 40.63% | 26.63% | 19.71% | 14.16% |
| 3 | 25.00% | 18.64% | 15.48% | 12.03% |
| 4 | 15.62% | 16.56% | 12.27% | 10.23% |
| 5 | | 16.57% | 12.28% | 8.75% |
| 6 | | 10.35% | 12.27% | 8.75% |
| 7 | | | 12.28% | 8.75% |
| 8 | | | 7.67% | 8.74% |
| 9 | | | | 8.75% |
| 10 | | | | 8.74% |
| 11 | | | | 5.47% |
| 12 | | | | |
| 13 | | | | |
| 14 | | | | |
| 15 | | | | |
| 16 | | | | |

MACRS table (midquarter convention, 150% declining balance method)

Property placed in service in Fourth Quarter

| Year | Depreciation rate for recovery period | | | |
|---|---|---|---|---|
| | 3 years | 5 years | 7 years | 10 years |
| 1 | 6.25% | 3.75% | 2.68% | 1.88% |
| 2 | 46.88% | 28.88% | 20.85% | 14.72% |
| 3 | 25.00% | 20.21% | 16.39% | 12.51% |
| 4 | 21.87% | 16.40% | 12.87% | 10.63% |
| 5 | | 16.41% | 12.18% | 9.04% |
| 6 | | 14.35% | 12.18% | 8.72% |
| 7 | | | 12.19% | 8.72% |
| 8 | | | 10.66% | 8.72% |
| 9 | | | | 8.72% |
| 10 | | | | 8.71% |
| 11 | | | | 7.63% |
| 12 | | | | |
| 13 | | | | |
| 14 | | | | |
| 15 | | | | |
| 16 | | | | |

## PROBLEMS

The following two simulations are for you to attempt. As you complete them be sure to apply the principles that you have learned in this text.

### REG Simulation Problem 1

| Introduction | | | | | | |
|---|---|---|---|---|---|---|
| | Schedule M-1 Adjustments | Deductibility | Taxability | Alternative Minimum Tax | Communication | Research |

In the following simulation, you will be asked to respond to various questions regarding the tax treatment of corporations. You will use the content in the **Information Tabs** to complete the tasks in the **Work Tabs**. (The following pictures are for illustration only; the actual tabs in your simulation may differ from these.)

### Information Tabs:

| Directions | Situation | Standards | Resources |
|---|---|---|---|

Beginning with the **Directions** tab at the left side of the screen, go through each of the **Information Tabs** to familiarize yourself with the simulation content. Note that the **Resources** tab will contain useful information, including formulas and definitions, to help you complete the tasks. You may want to refer to this information while you are working.

### Work Tabs:

| Cost Method | Amt to Report | COGS | Invent Costs | Form 1065 | Communication | Review Letter |
|---|---|---|---|---|---|---|

The **Work Tabs,** on the right side of the screen, contain the tasks for you to complete.

Once you complete any part of a task, the pencil for that tab will be shaded.

Note that a shaded pencil does NOT indicate that you have completed the entire task.

You must complete all of the tasks in the **Work Tabs** to receive full credit.

If you have difficulty answering a **Work Tab,** read the tab directions carefully.

*NOTE: If you believe you have encountered a software malfunction, report it to the test center staff immediately.*

| | Schedule M-1 Adjustments | | | | | |
|---|---|---|---|---|---|---|
| Introduction | | Deductibility | Taxability | Alternative Minimum Tax | Communication | Research |

Reliant Corp., an accrual-basis calendar-year C corporation, filed its 2007 federal income tax return on March 15, 2008.

The following **two** responses are required for each of the **items 1 through 6**.

- Determine the amount of Reliant's 2007 Schedule M-1 adjustment.
- Indicate if the adjustment increases, decreases, or has no effect, on Reliant's 2007 taxable income.

## Selections

I.   Increases Reliant's 2007 taxable income.
D.   Decreases Reliant's 2007 taxable income.
N.   Has no effect on Reliant's 2007 taxable income.

| | Schedule M-1 Adjustment | (I) | (D) | (N) |
|---|---|---|---|---|
| **1.** Reliant's disbursements included reimbursed employees' expenses in 2007 for travel of $100,000, and business meals of $30,000.  The reimbursed expenses met the conditions of deductibility and were properly substantiated under an accountable plan.  The reimbursement was not treated as employee compensation. | _____ | ○ | ○ | ○ |
| **2.** Reliant's books expensed $7,000 in 2007 for the term life insurance premiums on the corporate officers.  Reliant was the policy owner and beneficiary. | _____ | ○ | ○ | ○ |
| **3.** Reliant's books indicated an $18,000 state franchise tax expense for 2007.  Estimated state tax payments for 2007 were $15,000. | _____ | ○ | ○ | ○ |
| **4.** Book depreciation on computers for 2007 was $10,000.  These computers, which cost $50,000, were placed in service on January 2, 2006.  Tax depreciation used MACRS with the half-year convention.  No election was made to expense part of the computer cost or to use a straight-line method. | _____ | ○ | ○ | ○ |
| **5.** For 2007, Reliant's books showed a $4,000 short-term capital gain distribution from a mutual fund corporation and a $5,000 loss on the sale of Retro stock that was purchased in 2005.  The stock was an investment in an unrelated corporation.  There were no other 2007 gains or losses and no loss carryovers from prior years. | _____ | ○ | ○ | ○ |
| **6.** Reliant's 2007 taxable income before the charitable contribution and the dividends received deductions was $500,000.  Reliant's books expensed $15,000 in board of director-authorized charitable contributions that were paid on January 5, 2008.  Charitable contributions paid and expensed during 2007 were $35,000.  All charitable contributions were properly substantiated.  There were no net operating losses or charitable contributions that were carried forward. | _____ | ○ | ○ | ○ |

| Introduction | Schedule M-1 Adjustments | Deductibility | Taxability | Alternative Minimum Tax | Communication | Research |
|---|---|---|---|---|---|---|

For the following, indicate if the expenses are fully deductible, partially deductible, or nondeductible for regular tax purposes on Reliant's 2007 federal income tax return.

## Selections

F.   Fully taxable for regular tax purposes on Reliant's 2007 federal income tax return.
P.   Partially taxable for regular tax purposes on Reliant's 2007 federal income tax return.
N.   Nontaxable for regular tax purposes on Reliant's 2007 federal income tax return.

|  | (F) | (P) | (N) |
|---|---|---|---|
| 1. Reliant purchased theater tickets for it's out of town clients. The performances took place after Reliant's substantial and bona fide business negotiations with its clients. | O | O | O |
| 2. Reliant accrued advertising expenses to promote a new product line. Ten percent of the new product line remained in ending inventory. | O | O | O |
| 3. Reliant incurred interest expense on a loan to purchase municipal bonds. | O | O | O |
| 4. Reliant paid a penalty for the underpayment of 2006 estimated taxes. | O | O | O |
| 5. On December 9, 2007, Reliant's board of directors voted to pay a $500 bonus to each nonstockholder employee for 2007. The bonuses were paid on February 3, 2008. | O | O | O |

| Introduction | Schedule M-1 Adjustments | Deductibility | Taxability | Alternative Minimum Tax | Communication | Research |
|---|---|---|---|---|---|---|

For the following, indicate if the items are fully taxable, partially taxable, or nontaxable for regular tax purposes on Reliant's 2007 federal income tax return. All transactions occurred during 2007.

### *Selections*

F.    Fully taxable for regular tax purposes on Reliant's 2007 federal income tax return.
P.    Partially taxable for regular tax purposes on Reliant's 2007 federal income tax return.
N.    Nontaxable for regular tax purposes on Reliant's 2007 federal income tax return.

Items are based on the following:

Reliant filed an amended federal income tax return for 2005 and received a refund that included both the overpayment of the federal taxes and interest.

|  | (F) | (P) | (N) |
|---|---|---|---|
| 1. The portion of Reliant's refund that represented the overpayment of the 2005 federal taxes. | O | O | O |
| 2. The portion of Reliant's refund that is attributable to the interest on the overpayment of federal taxes. | O | O | O |
| 3. Reliant received dividend income from a mutual fund that solely invests in municipal bonds. | O | O | O |
| 4. Reliant, the lessor, benefited from the capital improvements made to its property by the lessee in 2007. The lease agreement is for one year ending December 31, 2007, and provides for a reduction in rental payments by the lessee in exchange for the improvements. | O | O | O |
| 5. Reliant collected the proceeds on the term life insurance policy on the life of a debtor who was not a shareholder. The policy was assigned to Reliant as collateral security for the debt. The proceeds exceeded the amount of the debt. | O | O | O |

| Introduction | Schedule M-1 Adjustments | Deductibility | Taxability | Alternative Minimum Tax | Communication | Research |
|---|---|---|---|---|---|---|

Indicate if the following items increase, decrease, or have no effect on Reliant's 2007 alternative minimum taxable income (AMTI) **prior to** the adjusted current earnings adjustment (ACE).

*Selections*

I.   Increases Reliant's 2007 AMTI.
D.   Decreases Reliant's 2007 AMTI.
N.   Has no effect on Reliant's 2007 AMTI.

|  |  | (I) | (D) | (N) |
|---|---|---|---|---|
| **1.** | Reliant used the 70% dividends received deduction for regular tax purposes. | ○ | ○ | ○ |
| **2.** | Reliant received interest from a state's general obligation bonds. | ○ | ○ | ○ |
| **3.** | Reliant used MACRS depreciation on seven-year personal property placed into service January 3, 2007, for regular tax purposes. No expense or depreciation election was made. | ○ | ○ | ○ |
| **4.** | Depreciation on nonresidential real property placed into service on January 3, 2007, was under the general MACRS depreciation system for regular tax purposes. | ○ | ○ | ○ |
| **5.** | Reliant had only cash charitable contributions for 2007. | ○ | ○ | ○ |

| Introduction | Schedule M-1 Adjustments | Deductibility | Taxability | Alternative Minimum Tax | Communication | Research |
|---|---|---|---|---|---|---|

The owner of Reliant Corporation, Mary Evans, contacts you and indicates that Reliant expects to form a wholly owned subsidiary, Surety Corporation, to conduct business unrelated to Reliant's current operations. Mary wants to have Surety expense the costs of formation, including the amounts paid for legal fees and the cost of issuing stock. Write a letter to Mary Evans explaining the appropriate tax treatment of the costs of forming Surety Corporation.

Dear Ms. Evans:

*REMINDER: Your response will be graded for both technical content and writing skills. Technical content will be evaluated for information that is helpful to the intended reader and clearly relevant to the issue. Writing skills will be evaluated for development, organization, and the appropriate expression of ideas in professional correspondence. Use a standard business memo or letter format with a clear beginning, middle, and end. Do not convey information in the form of a table, bullet point list, or other abbreviated presentation.*

| Introduction | Schedule M-1 Adjustments | Deductibility | Taxability | Alternative Minimum Tax | Communication | Research |
|---|---|---|---|---|---|---|

What Internal Revenue Code section, subsection, and paragraph limits a corporation's deduction for charitable contributions to a percentage of its taxable income before specified deductions?

To complete this task, use the search capabilities provided by the Code tab to find the section and subsection in the IRS Code that addressed the issue above. Select the appropriate paragraph(s) that answer the requirement.

## REG Simulation Problem 2

| Situation | | | |
|---|---|---|---|
| | Schedule D | Communication | Research |

In the following simulation, you will be asked to respond to various questions regarding the tax treatment of individual taxpayers. You will use the content in the **Information Tabs** to complete the tasks in the **Work Tabs**. (The following pictures are for illustration only; the actual tabs in your simulation may differ from these.)

**Information Tabs:**

| Directions | Situation | Standards | Resources |
|---|---|---|---|

Beginning with the **Directions** tab at the left side of the screen, go through each of the **Information Tabs** to familiarize yourself with the simulation content. Note that the **Resources** tab will contain useful information, including formulas and definitions, to help you complete the tasks. You may want to refer to this information while you are working.

**Work Tabs:**

| Cost Method | Amt to Report | COGS | Invent Costs | Form 1065 | Communication | Review Letter |
|---|---|---|---|---|---|---|

The **Work Tabs,** on the right side of the screen, contain the tasks for you to complete.

Once you complete any part of a task, the pencil for that tab will be shaded.

Note that a shaded pencil does NOT indicate that you have completed the entire task.

You must complete all of the tasks in the **Work Tabs** to receive full credit.

If you have difficulty answering a **Work Tab,** read the tab directions carefully.

*NOTE: If you believe you have encountered a software malfunction, report it to the test center staff immediately.*

Lou Tomsik (social security #324-65-7037) reported the following transactions for calendar year 2006:

- Lou sold 100 shares of Copperleaf Industries on October 20, 2006, for $4,200. Lou had acquired the stock for $2,500 on March 1, 2005.
- Lou sold 200 shares of King Corporation stock for $5,000 on November 15, 2006. He had purchased the stock on February 24, 2006, for $4,000.
- Tomsik had a net short-term capital loss carryforward from 2005 of $7,300, and during December 2006 received a $1,500 capital gain distribution from the Brooks Mutual fund.

| | Schedule D | | |
|---|---|---|---|
| Situation | | Communication | Research |

Use the above information to complete the following 2006 Form 1040 Schedule D for Tomsik.

**SCHEDULE D**
**(Form 1040)**

Department of the Treasury
Internal Revenue Service    (99)

# Capital Gains and Losses

▶ Attach to Form 1040 or Form 1040NR.    ▶ See Instructions for Schedule D (Form 1040).

▶ Use Schedule D-1 to list additional transactions for lines 1 and 8.

OMB No. 1545-0074

**2006**

Attachment
Sequence No. **12**

Name(s) shown on return

Your social security number

## Part I    Short-Term Capital Gains and Losses—Assets Held One Year or Less

| (a) Description of property (Example: 100 sh. XYZ Co.) | (b) Date acquired (Mo., day, yr.) | (c) Date sold (Mo., day, yr.) | (d) Sales price (see page D-6 of the instructions) | (e) Cost or other basis (see page D-7 of the instructions) | (f) Gain or (loss) Subtract (e) from (d) |
|---|---|---|---|---|---|
| **1** | | | | | |
| | | | | | |
| | | | | | |
| | | | | | |
| | | | | | |
| | | | | | |

**2** Enter your short-term totals, if any, from Schedule D-1, line 2 . . . . . . . . . . . . . . . . . . . . . . | **2** | | | | |

**3** Total short-term sales price amounts. Add lines 1 and 2 in column (d) . . . . . . . . . . . . . . . . . | **3** | | | | |

**4** Short-term gain from Form 6252 and short-term gain or (loss) from Forms 4684, 6781, and 8824 | **4** |

**5** Net short-term gain or (loss) from partnerships, S corporations, estates, and trusts from Schedule(s) K-1 . . . . . . . . . . . . . . . . . . . . . . | **5** |

**6** Short-term capital loss carryover. Enter the amount, if any, from line 10 of your **Capital Loss Carryover Worksheet** on page D-7 of the instructions . . . . . . . . . . | **6** ( )

**7** **Net short-term capital gain or (loss).** Combine lines 1 through 6 in column (f) . . . . . . | **7** |

## Part II    Long-Term Capital Gains and Losses—Assets Held More Than One Year

| (a) Description of property (Example: 100 sh. XYZ Co.) | (b) Date acquired (Mo., day, yr.) | (c) Date sold (Mo., day, yr.) | (d) Sales price (see page D-6 of the instructions) | (e) Cost or other basis (see page D-7 of the instructions) | (f) Gain or (loss) Subtract (e) from (d) |
|---|---|---|---|---|---|
| **8** | | | | | |
| | | | | | |
| | | | | | |
| | | | | | |
| | | | | | |
| | | | | | |

**9** Enter your long-term totals, if any, from Schedule D-1, line 9 . . . . . . . . . . . . . . . . . . . . . . | **9** | | | | |

**10** Total long-term sales price amounts. Add lines 8 and 9 in column (d) . . . . . . . . . . . . . . . . . | **10** | | | | |

**11** Gain from Form 4797, Part I; long-term gain from Forms 2439 and 6252; and long-term gain or (loss) from Forms 4684, 6781, and 8824 . . . . . . . . . . . . . . . . | **11** |

**12** Net long-term gain or (loss) from partnerships, S corporations, estates, and trusts from Schedule(s) K-1 . . . . . . . . . . . . . . . . . . . . . . | **12** |

**13** Capital gain distributions. See page D-2 of the instructions . . . . . . . . . . . . | **13** |

**14** Long-term capital loss carryover. Enter the amount, if any, from line 15 of your **Capital Loss Carryover Worksheet** on page D-7 of the instructions . . . . . . . . . . | **14** ( )

**15** **Net long-term capital gain or (loss).** Combine lines 8 through 14 in column (f). Then go to Part III on the back . . . . . . . . . . . . . . . . . . . . . . | **15** |

For Paperwork Reduction Act Notice, see Form 1040 or Form 1040NR instructions.          Cat. No. 11338H          **Schedule D (Form 1040) 2006**

Schedule D (Form 1040) 2006        Page **2**

**Part III**    **Summary**

16   Combine lines 7 and 15 and enter the result. If line 16 is a loss, skip lines 17 through 20, and go to line 21. If a gain, enter the gain on Form 1040, line 13, or Form 1040NR, line 14. Then go to line 17 below . . . . . . . . . . . . . . . . . . . . . .    **16**

17   Are lines 15 and 16 **both** gains?
☐ **Yes.** Go to line 18.
☐ **No.** Skip lines 18 through 21, and go to line 22.

18   Enter the amount, if any, from line 7 of the **28% Rate Gain Worksheet** on page D-8 of the instructions . . . . . . . . . . . . . ▶    **18**

19   Enter the amount, if any, from line 18 of the **Unrecaptured Section 1250 Gain Worksheet** on page D-9 of the instructions . . . . . . . . . . . . . ▶    **19**

20   Are lines 18 and 19 **both** zero or blank?
☐ **Yes.** Complete Form 1040 through line 43, or Form 1040NR through line 40. Then complete the **Qualified Dividends and Capital Gain Tax Worksheet** on page 38 of the Instructions for Form 1040 (or in the Instructions for Form 1040NR). **Do not** complete lines 21 and 22 below.
☐ **No.** Complete Form 1040 through line 43, or Form 1040NR through line 40. Then complete the **Schedule D Tax Worksheet** on page D-10 of the instructions. **Do not** complete lines 21 and 22 below.

21   If line 16 is a loss, enter here and on Form 1040, line 13, or Form 1040NR, line 14, the **smaller** of:

● The loss on line 16 or     } . . . . . . . . . . . . . . . . .    **21**   (           )
● ($3,000), or if married filing separately, ($1,500)

**Note.** When figuring which amount is smaller, treat both amounts as positive numbers.

22   Do you have qualified dividends on Form 1040, line 9b, or Form 1040NR, line 10b?
☐ **Yes.** Complete Form 1040 through line 43, or Form 1040NR through line 40. Then complete the **Qualified Dividends and Capital Gain Tax Worksheet** on page 38 of the Instructions for Form 1040 (or in the Instructions for Form 1040NR).
☐ **No.** Complete the rest of Form 1040 or Form 1040NR.

Schedule D (Form 1040) 2006

| Situation | Schedule D | Communication | Research |
|---|---|---|---|

Tomsik contacts you and indicates that he expects to incur a substantial net capital loss for calendar-year 2007 and wonders what the treatment of the carryforwards will be in future years. Write a letter to Tomsik explaining the treatment of an individual's capital loss carryforwards.

Dear Mr. Tomsik:

*REMINDER: Your response will be graded for both technical content and writing skills. Technical content will be evaluated for information that is helpful to the intended reader and clearly relevant to the issue. Writing skills will be evaluated for development, organization, and the appropriate expression of ideas in professional correspondence. Use a standard business memo or letter format with a clear beginning, middle, and end. Do not convey information in the form of a table, bullet point list, or other abbreviated presentation.*

| Situation | Schedule D | Communication | Research |
|-----------|-----------|---------------|----------|

Special rules apply to the gains and losses from capital assets.  What Internal Revenue Code section defines "capital assets"?

To complete this task, use the search capabilities provided by the **Code** tab to find the section and subsection in the IRS Code that addresses the issue above.  Select the appropriate paragraph(s) that answer the requirement.

# 6 MASTERING AUDITING AND ATTESTATION SIMULATIONS

This chapter applies the principles described in Chapter 1 to the simulations in the Auditing and Attestation (AUD) section of the CPA exam. Every AUD exam includes two simulations. As discussed in Chapter 1, the AICPA has identified the following skills required by CPAs to protect the public interest.

- Analysis—the ability to organize, process, and interpret data to develop options for decision making.
- Judgment—the ability to evaluate options for decision-making and provide an appropriate conclusion.
- Communication—the ability to effectively elicit and/or express information through written or oral means.
- Research—the ability to locate and extract relevant information from available resource materials.
- Understanding—the ability to recognize and comprehend the meaning and application of a particular matter.

For the AUD section, the Board of Examiners has provided the following matrix to illustrate the interaction of content and skills:

| Content Specification Outline Areas | Skill Categories | | | | | Content Weights |
| --- | --- | --- | --- | --- | --- | --- |
| | Communication | Research | Analysis | Judgment | Understanding | |
| I. Planning the engagement | | | | | | 22-28% |
| II. Internal controls | | | | | | 12-18% |
| III. Obtain and document information | | | | | | 32-38% |
| IV. Review engagement and evaluate information | | | | | | 8-12% |
| V. Prepare communications | | | | | | 12-18% |
| Skills Weights | 10-20% | 6-16% | 12-22% | 12-22% | 35-45% | |

You should keep these skills foremost in your mind as you prepare and sit for the AUD section.

## CONTENT OF THE AUD SECTION

To perform successfully on the AUD simulations, you must have an adequate knowledge of the content of the AUD exam. The AICPA Content Specification Outline of the coverage of the AUD section appears below. This outline was issued by the AICPA, and is effective for exams administered after 2005.

## AICPA CONTENT SPECIFICATION OUTLINE: AUDITING & ATTESTATION

I.  Plan the Engagement, Evaluate the Prospective Client and Engagement, Decide Whether to Accept or Continue the Client and the Engagement, and Enter into an Agreement with the Client **(22%-28%)**

   A. Determine Nature and Scope of Engagement

      1. Auditing Standards Generally Accepted in the United States of America (GAAS)
      2. Standards for Accounting and Review Services
      3. Standards for Attestation Engagements
      4. Compliance Auditing Applicable to Governmental Entities and Other Recipients of Governmental Financial Assistance
      5. Other Assurance Services
      6. Appropriateness of Engagement to Meet Client's Needs

   B. Assess Engagement Risk and the CPA Firm's Ability to Perform the Engagement

      1. Engagement Responsibilities
      2. Staffing and Supervision Requirements
      3. Quality Control Considerations
      4. Management Integrity
      5. Researching Information Sources for Planning and Performing the Engagement

   C. Communicate with the Predecessor Accountant or Auditor
   D. Decide Whether to Accept or Continue the Client and Engagement
   E. Enter into an Agreement with the Client about the Terms of the Engagement
   F. Obtain an Understanding of the Client's Operations, Business, and Industry
   G. Perform Analytical Procedures
   H. Consider Preliminary Engagement Materiality
   I. Assess Inherent Risk and Risk of Misstatements from Errors, Fraud, and Illegal Acts by Clients
   J. Consider Other Planning Matters

      1. Using the Work of Other Independent Auditors
      2. Using the Work of a Specialist
      3. Internal Audit Function
      4. Related Parties and Related-Party Transactions

      5. Electronic Evidence
      6. Risks of Auditing Around the Computer

   K. Identify Financial Statement Assertions and Formulate Audit Objectives

      1. Significant Financial Statement Balances, Classes of Transactions, and Disclosures
      2. Accounting Estimates

   L. Determine and Prepare the Work Program Defining the Nature, Timing, and Extent of the Procedures to Be Applied

II. Consider Internal Control in Both Manual and Computerized Environments **(12%-18%)**

   A. Obtain an Understanding of Business Processes and Information Flows
   B. Identify Controls That Might Be Effective in Preventing or Detecting Misstatements
   C. Document an Understanding of Internal Control
   D. Consider Limitations of Internal Control
   E. Consider the Effects of Service Organizations on Internal Control
   F. Perform Tests of Controls
   G. Assess Control Risk

III. Obtain and Document Information to Form a Basis for Conclusions **(32%-38%)**

   A. Perform Planned Procedures

      1. Applications of Audit Sampling
      2. Analytical Procedures
      3. Confirmation of Balances and/or Transactions with Third Parties
      4. Physical Examination of Inventories and Other Assets
      5. Other Tests of Details
      6. Computer-Assisted Audit Techniques, Including Data Interrogation, Extraction, and Analysis
      7. Substantive Tests before the Balance Sheet Date
      8. Tests of Unusual Year-End Transactions

   B. Evaluate Contingencies
   C. Obtain and Evaluate Lawyers' Letters
   D. Review Subsequent Events
   E. Obtain Representations from Management
   F. Identify Reportable Conditions and Other Control Deficiencies

G. Identify Matters for Communication with Audit Committees
H. Perform Procedures for Accounting and Review Services Engagements
I. Perform Procedures for Attestation Engagements

IV. Review the Engagement to Provide Reasonable Assurance That Objectives Are Achieved and Evaluate Information Obtained to Reach and to Document Engagement Conclusions (8%-12%)

A. Perform Analytical Procedures
B. Evaluate the Sufficiency and Competence of Audit Evidence and Document Engagement Conclusions
C. Evaluate Whether Financial Statements Are Free of Material Misstatements
D. Consider Whether Substantial Doubt about an Entity's Ability to Continue as a Going Concern Exists
E. Consider Other Information in Documents Containing Audited Financial Statements
F. Review the Work Performed to Provide Reasonable Assurance That Objectives Are Achieved

V. Prepare Communications to Satisfy Engagement Objectives (12%-18%)

A. Reports

1. Reports on Audited Financial Statements
2. Reports on Reviewed and Compiled Financial Statements
3. Reports Required by *Government Auditing Standards*
4. Reports on Compliance with Laws and Regulations
5. Reports on Internal Control
6. Reports on Prospective Financial Information
7. Reports on Agreed-Upon Procedures
8. Reports on the Processing of Transactions by Service Organizations

9. Reports on Supplementary Financial Information
10. Special Reports
11. Reports on Other Assurance Services
12. Reissuance of Reports

B. Other Required Communications

1. Errors and Fraud
2. Illegal Acts
3. Communication with Audit Committees
4. Other Reporting Considerations Covered by Statements on Auditing Standards and Statements on Standards for Attestation Engagements

C. Other Matters

1. Subsequent Discovery of Facts Existing at the Date of the Auditor's Report
2. Consideration after the Report Date of Omitted Procedures

### References—Auditing and Attestation

- AICPA Statements on Auditing Standards and Interpretations
- AICPA Statements on Standards for Accounting and Review Services and Interpretations
- AICPA Statements on Quality Control Standards
- AICPA Statements on Standards for Attestation Engagements
- US General Accounting Office *Government Auditing Standards*
- AICPA Audit and Accounting Guides *Audit Sampling* *Consideration of Internal Control in a Financial Statement Audit*
- AICPA Audit Risk Alerts and Compilation and Review Alerts
- Single Audit Act, as amended
- Sarbanes-Oxley Act of 2002
- Public Company Accounting Oversight Board (PCAOB) Auditing, Attestation and Quality Control Standards

## COMMUNICATION REQUIREMENTS

As discussed in Chapter 1 every simulation requires you to prepare a written communication. In the AUD section this communication will usually involve preparing a memorandum that describes the implications of audit findings or internal control weakness. The communication may be for someone who would be expected to understand audit and accounting terminology, or someone who would not be expected to have such understanding. To get the maximum score, you should tailor your communication to the recipient. Remember that the communication must address the objectives that are set forth in the requirement. In other words it must be helpful to the recipient. However, it does not have to be technically accurate. Therefore, you should not spend a lot of time thinking about the details of the professional literature. If you are not sure of specific rules, take a guess. If you do not have a clue, you might consider referring to the professional standards database and quickly reviewing the applicable rules. However, you do not have time to spare. Using an excessive amount of time on one written communication will decrease your overall score. Remember you should not quote from the standards, or construct your memorandum in the form of bullets. **You must demonstrate your own writing ability.** Chapter 3 is devoted to suggestions on how to improve your writing ability to maximize your score on the communication requirements of simulations.

# RESEARCH REQUIREMENTS

Research components of simulations in the Auditing and Attestation section will involve a research database that includes

- Statements on Auditing Standards and Interpretations
- Statements on Attestation Standards and Interpretations
- Statements on Standards for Accounting and Review Services and Interpretations
- Statements on Standards for Quality Control

## The AICPA Professional Standards

The AICPA Professional Standards include standards and interpretations issued by senior technical committees of the AICPA (e.g., the Auditing Standards Board). Standards are developed through a due process that includes deliberation in meetings open to the public, public exposure of proposed standards, and a formal vote. Interpretations are not standards, but are issued by the committees to provide recommendations on the application of a particular standard. The codification of the AICPA Professional Standards is shown below.

### Codification of AICPA Professional Standards

| | *Citation* |
|---|---|
| Statements on Auditing Standards | AU Sec. |
|    Introduction | 100 |
|    The General Standards | 200 |
|    The Standards of Fieldwork | 300 |
|    The First, Second, and Third Standards of Reporting | 400 |
|    The Fourth Standard of Reporting | 500 |
|    Other Types of Reports | 600 |
|    Special Topics | 700 |
|    Compliance Auditing | 800 |
|    Special Reports of the Committee on Auditing Procedures | 900 |
| Statements on Standards for Attestation Engagements | AT Sec. |
|    Attestation Standards | 101 |
|    Agreed-Upon Procedures Engagements | 201 |
|    Financial Forecasts and Protections | 301 |
|    Reporting on Pro Forma Financial Information | 401 |
|    Reporting on an Entity's Internal Control Structure over Financial Reporting | 501 |
|    Compliance Attestation | 601 |
|    Management's Discussion and Analysis | 701 |
| Statements on Standards for Accounting and Review Services | AR Sec. |
|    Compilation and Review of Financial Statements | 100 |
|    Reporting on Comparative Financial Statements | 200 |
|    Compilation Reports on Financial Statements Included in Certain Prescribed Forms | 300 |
|    Communications between Predecessor and Successor Accountants | 400 |
|    Reporting on Compiled Financial Statements | 500 |

|                                                                                          | <u>Citation</u> |
|------------------------------------------------------------------------------------------|----------|
| Reporting on Personal Financial Statements Included in Written Personal Financial Plans | 600 |
| Code of Professional Conduct | ET |
| Bylaws of the AICPA | BL |
| Quality Control | QC |

There are two ways to cite a professional standard

1.  Using the original standard number (e.g., Statement on Auditing Standards No. 39, paragraph 12 and 14).
2.  Using the section numbers (e.g., AU section 350.12 - .14).

## Database Searching

Searching a database consists of the following five steps:

1.  Define the issue.  What is the research question to be answered?
2.  Select the database to search (e.g., the Statement on Auditing Standards and Interpretations).
3.  Choose a keyword or table of contents search.
4.  Execute the search.  Enter the keyword(s) or click on the appropriate table of contents item and complete the search.
5.  Evaluate the results.  Evaluate the research to see if an answer has been found.  If not, try a new search.

## Advanced Searches

The advanced search screen allows you to use Boolean concepts to perform more precise searches.  Examples of searches that can be performed in the advanced search mode include

1.  Containing all these words—allows you to retrieve sections that contain two or more specified words.
2.  Not containing any of these words—allows you to retrieve sections that do not contain specific words.
3.  Containing one or more of these words—allows you to retrieve sections that contain any one or more of the specified words.
4.  Containing these words near each other—allows you to retrieve sections that contain words near to each other.

The advanced search also allows you to select options for the search.  One alternative allows you to retrieve alternative word forms.  For example, using this approach with a search on the word "cost" would also retrieve sections containing the word "costing."  A synonyms option allows you to retrieve sections that contain words that mean the same as the specified word.  You also have the option to only search on the selected sections of the literature.

## SOLVING AUD SIMULATIONS

To illustrate how to master the AUD simulations, this chapter will walk you through the process of solving two simulations, some of which have been released by the AICPA.  The chapter will conclude with two AUD simulations that you may use to apply the principles that you have learned.  Recall from Chapter 1 the suggested steps to solving a simulation include the following:

1.  **Review the entire problem.**  Tab through the problem in order to get a feel for the topical area and related concepts that are being tested.  Even though the format of the question may vary, the exam continues to test your understanding of applicable principles or con-

cepts. Relax, take a deep breath, and determine your strategy for conquering the simulation.

2. **Identify the requirements of the problem.** This step will help you focus more quickly on the solution(s) without wasting time reading irrelevant material. Jot down the nature of the requirements on your scratch paper.

3. **Study the items to be answered.** As you do this and become familiar with the topical area being tested, you should think about the concepts of that area. This will help you organize your thoughts so that you can relate logically the requirements of the simulation with the applicable concepts.

4. **With the requirements in mind carefully review the information tabs.** Make notes on your scratch paper (which will be provided) of information from the tabs that will help you answer each requirement.

5. **Answer each tab requirement one at a time.** If the requirements don't build on one another, don't be afraid to answer the tab requirements out of order. Also, if the scenario is long or complex, you may wish to use the split screen function to view the simulation data while answering a particular requirement.

6. **Use the scratch paper and the spreadsheet and calculator tools to assist you in answering the simulation.**

Now let's apply this approach to some actual simulations.

## SIMULATION EXAMPLE 1

Applying step 1 in the solutions approach to the following simulation, you should first review all the tabs, consider the concepts, and jot down the requirements.

In the following simulation, you will be asked various questions regarding an audit engagement. You will use the content in the **Information Tabs** to complete the tasks in the **Work Tabs**. (The following pictures are for illustration only; the actual tabs in your simulation may differ from these.)

**Information Tabs:**

| Directions | Situation | Standards | Resources |
|---|---|---|---|

Beginning with the **Directions** tab at the left side of the screen, go through each of the **Information Tabs** to familiarize yourself with the simulation content. Note that the **Resources** tab will contain useful information, including formulas and definitions, to help you complete the tasks. You may want to refer to this information while you are working.

**Work Tabs:**

| Cost Method | Amt to Report | COGS | Invent Costs | Form 1065 | Communication | Review Letter |
|---|---|---|---|---|---|---|

The **Work Tabs,** on the right side of the screen, contain the tasks for you to complete.

Once you complete any part of a task, the pencil for that tab will be shaded. Note that a shaded pencil does NOT indicate that you have completed the entire task.

You must complete all of the tasks in the **Work Tabs** to receive full credit.

If you have difficulty answering a **Work Tab,** read the tab directions carefully.

*NOTE: If you believe you have encountered a software malfunction, report it to the test center staff immediately.*

| Company Profile | Balance Sheet | Income/Cash Flow | Industry Info | Risks | Audit Findings | Audit Procedures | Analysis and Communication | Auditors Report |
|---|---|---|---|---|---|---|---|---|

Enright Corporation is a **nonpublic** manufacturer of golf balls, golf clubs, and other golf-related equipment. The company has been in business for over fifty years and has its headquarters in San Diego, California.

Enright is divided into two divisions, which represent the major markets for the company's products. One division focuses on new golf clubs and resorts, and providing them with all of the necessary golf equipment to begin operations. The other division focuses on new product development and helps existing golf clubs and resorts to upgrade their existing equipment. Currently, each division accounts for approximately equal amounts of Enright's revenues and net income.

The company experienced its second most profitable year in 2007. However, the financial results did not meet management's expectations. Total reported revenues for the year decreased three percent compared to the prior year. Management recognizes the fact that domestic sales growth has slowed significantly in recent years. As a result, the company is now adopting a global focus for marketing its products and is looking to open up new markets in Australia and Japan.

In order to be competitive in world markets, as well as to improve their domestic market share, management believes that they must strictly control costs and make their overall operations more efficient. At the end of 2007, Enright announced it would make a series of restructuring changes as part of its overall business plan for the future.

Senior management at the company has experienced a significant turnover in recent years. The CEO has been with the company for only two years. He was hired from a major competitor after the prior CEO left to take a position with a large manufacturing company in the Northeast. In addition, the company's long-time CFO retired after twenty-five years of service. The current CFO was hired six months ago. She is a former audit manager from the office that works on Enright's annual audit.

Enright has engaged the same auditing firm for its annual audits for the past decade. There have been no disagreements over accounting issues in any of the past three years.

| Company Profile | Balance Sheet | Income/Cash Flow | Industry Info | Risks | Audit Findings | Audit Procedures | Analysis and Communication | Auditors Report |
|---|---|---|---|---|---|---|---|---|

*Enright Corporation*
**BALANCE SHEET**
*December 31, 2007 and 2006*

|  | 12/31/07 | 12/31/06 |
|---|---|---|
| **Assets** | | |
| Current assets | | |
| Cash and cash equivalents | $300,000 | $235,000 |
| Receivables—net | 750,000 | 816,000 |
| Investments | 600,000 | 545,000 |
| Inventory | 1,000,000 | 1,171,000 |
| Total current assets | 2,650,000 | 2,767,000 |
| Plant and equipment—net | 850,000 | 876,000 |
| Total assets | $3,500,000 | $3,643,000 |

|  | 12/31/07 | 12/31/06 |
|---|---|---|
| **Liabilities and Stockholders' Equity** | | |
| Current liabilities | | |
| Accounts payable | $390,000 | $410,000 |
| Current portion of long-term debt | 620,000 | 620,000 |
| Other current liabilities | 315,000 | 298,000 |
| Total current liabilities | 1,325,000 | 1,328,000 |
| Long-term debt | 475,000 | 1,095,000 |
| Total liabilities | 1,800,000 | 2,423,000 |
| Stockholders' equity | | |
| Common stock | 1,000,000 | 1,000,000 |
| Retained earnings | 700,000 | 220,000 |
| Total stockholders' equity | 1,700,000 | 1,220,000 |
| Total liabilities and stockholders' equity | $3,500,000 | $3,643,000 |

| Company Profile | Balance Sheet | Income/Cash Flow | Industry Info | Risks | Audit Findings | Audit Procedures | Analysis and Communication | Auditors Report |
|---|---|---|---|---|---|---|---|---|

### Enright Corporation
### INCOME STATEMENT
*For the Years Ended December 31, 2007 and 2006*

|  | 12/31/07 | 12/31/06 |
|---|---|---|
| Sales | $5,250,000 | $5,450,000 |
| Cost of goods sold: | 2,100,000 | 2,209,000 |
| Gross profits on sales | 3,150,000 | 3,241,000 |
| Expenses | | |
| Selling expenses | $1,050,000 | $1,124,000 |
| General and administrative | 1,070,000 | 1,215,000 |
| Other operating expenses | | |
| Depreciation | 30,000 | 35,000 |
| Interest expense | 200,000 | 227,000 |
| Total expenses | $2,350,000 | $2,601,000 |
| Income before taxes | $800,000 | $640,000 |
| Provision for income taxes | 320,000 | 256,000 |
| Net income | $480,000 | $384,000 |

**Enright Corporation**
**STATEMENT OF CASH FLOWS**
*For the Year Ended December 31, 2007*

Cash flows from operating activities:

| | |
|---|---|
| Net income (loss) | $480,000 |

Adjustments to reconcile net income (loss) to cash provided by (used for) operating activities

| | |
|---|---|
| Depreciation and amortization | 30,000 |

Changes in certain assets and liabilities:

| | |
|---|---|
| Decrease (increase) in receivables | 66,000 |
| Decrease (increase) in inventory | 171,000 |
| Increase (decrease) in accounts payable | (20,000) |
| Increase (decrease) in other current liabilities | 17,000 |
| Net cash provided by (used for) operating activities | 744,000 |

Cash flows from investing activities:

| | |
|---|---|
| Purchase of property, plant, and equipment | (4,000) |
| Change in short-term investments | (55,000) |
| Net cash provided by (used for) investing activities | (59,000) |

Cash flows from financing activities:

| | |
|---|---|
| Principal payments on long-term debt | (620,000) |
| Net cash provided by (used for) financing activities | (620,000) |
| Net increase (decrease) in cash and cash equivalents | 65,000 |
| Cash and cash equivalents at beginning of year | 235,000 |
| Cash and cash equivalents at end of year | $300,000 |

| Company Profile | Balance Sheet | Income/Cash Flow | Industry Info | Risks | Audit Findings | Audit Procedures | Analysis and Communication | Auditors Report |
|---|---|---|---|---|---|---|---|---|

Market Forecasts
USA Sports Equipment

In 2012, the USA sports equipment market is forecast to reach $47 million, an increase of 19.3% since 2007.

The compounded annual growth rate of the global sports equipment market over the period 2007-2012 is predicted to be 3.5%.

Table 4:  USA Sports Equipment Market Value Forecasts:  $Mn (2006 Prices), 2007-2012

| Market value | $Mn (2006 prices) | % Growth |
|---|---|---|
| 2007 | $40,133.6 | 2.9% |
| 2008 | $41,398.3 | 3.2% |
| 2009 | $42,936.3 | 3.7% |
| 2010 | $44,389.8 | 3.4% |
| 2011 | $46,232.1 | 4.2% |
| 2012 | $46,892.1 | 3.6% |
| CAGR. 2007-2012 | | 3.5% |

Golf:  Play Is Steadying While Sales Struggle

With 1.02 billion participants aged six and over for the year 2006, golf is ranked number 15, compared to other sports.

In what proved to be a disappointing year, sale of golf clubs, balls, bags, gloves, and shoes declined about 6% in wholesale dollars, to about $2.375 billion in 2006.  Sales of irons, which enjoyed strong growth in 2005, accounted for most of the decrease in 2006.

Clearly, the weak economy was the root of the problem and the continuing weakness in 2007 is expected to result in further slight sales declines as players postpone the purchase of the big-ticket items such as clubs and bags.

The total number of golfers grew by 5%, from 28.9 million to 30.4 million, between 1995 and 2005. There are as many as 40 million people who would like to play or play more often. New course development was scaled back in 2006, with 314 construction projects completed through the first nine months, compared to 408 and 379 during the same periods in 2005 and 2004, respectively.

In what might be called a "Tiger Woods" effect, some experienced golfers are trying to open the game to very young players. A small national tournament for players aged four to twelve has been created. Some manufacturers are marketing youth-sized clubs and a few facilities are developing training programs for children once considered too young to play the game.

| Company Profile | Balance Sheet | Income/Cash Flow | Industry Info | Risks | Audit Findings | Audit Procedures | Analysis and Communication | Auditors Report |
|---|---|---|---|---|---|---|---|---|

**(A) (B) (C) (D)**

1. Which of the following correctly identifies an aspect of the company's business model, strategies, and operating environment that is most likely to increase audit risk?      ○  ○  ○  ○

   A. The "Tiger Woods" effect.
   B. The turnover of senior management in recent years.
   C. The company's result in the current year of its second most profitable year in over fifty years of operations.
   D. The company's organization into two divisions, which represent the major markets for the company's products.

| Company Profile | Balance Sheet | Income/Cash Flow | Industry Info | Risks | Audit Findings | Audit Procedures | Analysis and Communication | Auditors Report |
|---|---|---|---|---|---|---|---|---|

The table below presents several ratios that were identified as significant in the current and prior year's audits of Enright. Compare the values for each ratio. Then double-click on each of the shaded spaces in the table and select a possible audit finding that could account for the 2007 value. For each ratio, you should select an audit finding that is consistent with these metrics. Each audit finding may be used once, more than once, or not at all. (Turnover ratios are based on year-end balances.)

*Audit findings*

A. The company uses a periodic inventory system for determining the balance sheet amount of inventory.
B. The company accumulated excess inventories that are physically deteriorating or are becoming obsolete.
C. Merchandise was received, placed in the stockroom, and counted, but not included in the year-end count.
D. A smaller percentage of sales occurred during the last month of the year, as compared to the prior year.
E. A dividend declared prior to the end of the year was not recorded in the general ledger.
F. A dividend declared prior to the end of the year was recorded twice in the general ledger.

| Ratio | 2007 | 2006 | (A) | (B) | (C) | (D) | (E) | (F) |
|---|---|---|---|---|---|---|---|---|
| 1. Inventory turnover | 2.1 | 1.9 | ○ | ○ | ○ | ○ | ○ | ○ |
| 2. Return on equity | 28.2% | 31.5% | ○ | ○ | ○ | ○ | ○ | ○ |

| Company Profile | Balance Sheet | Income/Cash Flow | Industry Info | Risks | Audit Findings | Audit Procedures | Analysis and Communication | Auditors Report |
|---|---|---|---|---|---|---|---|---|

The auditor determines that each of the following objectives will be part of Enright's audit. For each audit objective, select a substantive procedure that would help to achieve the audit objectives by double-clicking on each shaded space and selecting a procedure.  Each of the procedures may be used once, more than once, or not at all.

### Substantive procedures
A.   Review minutes of board of director's meetings and contracts, and make inquiries of management.
B.   Test inventory transactions between a preliminary physical inventory date and the balance sheet date.
C.   Obtain confirmation of inventories pledged under loan agreement.
D.   Review perpetual inventory records, production records, and purchasing records for indication of current activity.
E.   Reconcile physical counts to perpetual records and general ledger balances and investigate significant fluctuation.
F.   Examine sales after year-end and open purchase order commitments.
G.   Examine paid vendors' invoices, consignment agreements, and contracts.
H.   Analytically review and compare the relationship of inventory balance to recent purchasing, production, and sales activity.

| Objective | (A) | (B) | (C) | (D) | (E) | (F) | (G) | (H) |
|---|---|---|---|---|---|---|---|---|
| 1. Confirm that inventories represent items held for sale or use in the normal course of business. | ○ | ○ | ○ | ○ | ○ | ○ | ○ | ○ |
| 2. Confirm that the inventory listing is accurately completed and the totals are properly included in the inventory accounts. | ○ | ○ | ○ | ○ | ○ | ○ | ○ | ○ |

| Company Profile | Balance Sheet | Income/Cash Flow | Industry Info | Risks | Audit Findings | Audit Procedures | Analysis and Communication | Auditors Report |
|---|---|---|---|---|---|---|---|---|

Your firm has been doing the audit of Enright Corporation for several years.  Since last year, Enright changed the board of directors from family members owning stock in the company to independent executives with financial experience.  In a memorandum to your audit team, explain the impact of the new board on audit risk.

*REMINDER: Your response will be graded for both technical content and writing skills.  Technical content will be evaluated for information that is helpful to the intended reader and clearly relevant to the issue. Writing skills will be evaluated for development, organization, and the appropriate expression of ideas in professional correspondence.  Use a standard business memo or letter format with a clear beginning, middle, and end.  Do not convey information in the form of a table, bullet point list, or other abbreviated presentation.*

To:  Audit Team
Re: New board and audit risk

| Company Profile | Balance Sheet | Income/Cash Flow | Industry Info | Risks | Audit Findings | Audit Procedures | Analysis and Communication | Auditors Report |
|---|---|---|---|---|---|---|---|---|

During the fieldwork on Enright, the client asks that you perform a review of the financial statements for the current year only—and not a complete audit. You have now completed your fieldwork and find that you can issue a standard review report.

Research the professional standards to obtain an example of a standard review report.

### Solving the Simulation

Your list from the review of the tabs should be similar to the ones listed below:

1. Identify the items in the company and industry description that increase audit risk.
2. Identify plausible explanations for the changes in ratios.
3. Identify the objectives of the substantive procedures?
4. Write a memorandum to identify the effect of the change in composition of the audit committee.
5. Assemble a review report.

With these requirements in mind, you should carefully read and review the **Profile**, **Balance Sheet**, **Income/Cash Flow**, and **Industry Info** tabs. Then, you should begin the first work tab—the **Risks** tab.

### Requirement 1

The **Risks** tab requires you to identify the factor from the list below that increases audit risk:

A. The "Tiger Woods" effect.
B. The turnover of senior management in recent years.
C. The company's result in the current year of its second most profitable year in over fifty years of operations.
D. The company's organization into two divisions, which represent the major markets for the company's products.

This requirement is fairly simple because the only factor that increases risk is the turnover of senior management. Therefore, the requirement should be answered as follows:

| | (A) (B) (C) (D) |
|---|---|
| 1. Which of the following correctly identifies an aspect of the company's business model, strategies, and operating environment that is most likely to increase audit risk? | ○ ● ○ ○ |

### Requirement 2

The Audit Findings tab requires you to identity the audit findings that are consistent with the change in ratios. This is a common simulation requirement on the Auditing and Attestation section of the CPA examination. Let's start with the first ratio change—inventory turnover increased. Inventory turnover is calculated by dividing cost of sales by average inventory. Therefore, the correct response would involve increased sales with the same inventory levels or a decrease in inventory levels. Response A would have no effect on inventory turnover. Response B would result in a lower inventory turnover. However, response C, not including merchandise in inventory, would reduce ending inventory and increase the level of inventory turnover. Therefore, response C is correct. The last three responses would have no effect on inventory turnover.

The second change in ratio is a reduction in return on equity. Return on equity is calculated by dividing net income by average equity. Therefore, the correct response would have to involve something that decreased net income or increased equity. The responses that would affect equity include E and F. However, response E is the one that would inappropriately reduce equity and result in a decrease in return on equity.

*Audit findings*

A. The company uses a periodic inventory system for determining the balance sheet amount of inventory.
B. The company accumulated excess inventories that are physically deteriorating or are becoming obsolete.
C. Merchandise was received, placed in the stockroom, and counted, but not included in the year-end count.
D. A smaller percentage of sales occurred during the last month of the year, as compared to the prior year.
E. A dividend declared prior to the end of the year was not recorded in the general ledger.
F. A dividend declared prior to the end of the year was recorded twice in the general ledger.

Therefore, the correct responses are presented below:

| | Ratio | 2007 | 2006 | (A) | (B) | (C) | (D) | (E) | (F) |
|---|---|---|---|---|---|---|---|---|---|
| 1. | Inventory turnover | 2.1 | 1.9 | ○ | ○ | ● | ○ | ○ | ○ |
| 2. | Return on equity | 28.2% | 31.5% | ○ | ○ | ○ | ○ | ● | ○ |

## Requirement 3

The **Audit Procedures** tab requires you to identify the objectives of audit procedures. This is also a common type of requirement on the Auditing and Attestation section of the examination. The first requirement is to identify the procedure that is best for confirming that inventories represent items held for sale or use in the normal course of business. Response D is best because a review of perpetual inventory records, production records, and purchasing records for indication of current activity will reveal whether those items are being sold. The second requirement is to identify the best substantive procedure to confirm that the inventory listing is accurately completed and the totals are properly included in the inventory counts. Response E is correct because reconciling physical counts to perpetual records and general ledger balances and investigating significant fluctuations will identify errors in totals.

*Substantive procedures*

A. Review minutes of board of director's meetings and contracts, and make inquiries of management.
B. Test inventory transactions between a preliminary physical inventory date and the balance sheet date.
C. Obtain confirmation of inventories pledged under loan agreement.
D. Review perpetual inventory records, production records, and purchasing records for indication of current activity.
E. Reconcile physical counts to perpetual records and general ledger balances and investigate significant fluctuation.
F. Examine sales after year-end and open purchase order commitments.
G. Examine paid vendors' invoices, consignment agreements, and contracts.
H. Analytically review and compare the relationship of inventory balance to recent purchasing, production, and sales activity.

The correct answer should appear as follows.

| | Objective | (A) (B) (C) (D) (E) (F) (G) (H) |
|---|---|---|
| 1. | Confirm that inventories represent items held for sale or use in the normal course of business. | ○ ○ ○ ● ○ ○ ○ ○ |
| 2. | Confirm that the inventory listing is accurately completed and the totals are properly included in the inventory accounts. | ○ ○ ○ ○ ● ○ ○ ○ |

## Requirement 4

The **Analysis and Communication** tab requires you to draft a memorandum to the audit staff regarding how the change in the composition of the board of directors affects audit risk. Chapter 3 describes how you can improve your writing skills. Before you start writing the memorandum, I suggest that you develop a very short outline. It may be as simple as the one shown below:

1. Introduction and objective of the memorandum
2. A description of change in board composition
3. Effect on audit risk
4. Closing

A suggested memorandum is shown below. Remember after completing the memorandum to use the spell checking function to correct any errors that you have made. With these observations in mind, you can develop your memorandum. In doing so remember the guidance from Chapter 3:

1. Start the memorandum with an introduction indicating its purpose.
2. Use simple sentences.
3. Since you are communicating with management, you should avoid accounting jargon.
4. Use the spell-checker in the exam software.
5. Don't worry that much about getting the requirements of the standard exactly correct. Remember your response will not be graded for technical accuracy.

Review the following memorandum, noting how it applies the principles described above.

---

To:      Audit Team
Re:      New board and audit risk

   This memorandum is designed to describe the effects of the change in the composition of the board of directors of Enright Corporation on audit risk. Enright has altered the composition of its board of directors to include independent executives with financial experience and reduce the number of family members owning the company's stock. This change increases the objectivity and competence of the board of directors. A more independent and competent board of directors should reduce the likelihood that the financial statements are materially misstated. Therefore, it reduces audit risk.
   If any issues arise regarding the board, please refer them to me.

---

## Requirement 5

The **Auditor's Report** tab requires you to research the professional standards to find a standard review report for the engagement. The information indicates that the report should address only the current year.
   You should be aware that review reports for nonpublic companies are addressed in the Statements on Standards for Accounting and Review Services. An efficient search strategy is to review the table of contents of these standards. AR section 100 deals with the compilation and review of financial statements, including reports. By scrolling through AR section 100, you will find the standard review report at paragraph 44 (AR section 100.44).

### Auditor's Review Report

[*Addressee*]

I(we) have reviewed the accompanying balance sheet of XYZ Company as of December 31, 20X1, and the related statements of income, retained earnings, and cash flows for the year then ended, in accordance with Statements on Standards for Accounting and Review Services issued by the American Institute of Certified Public Accountants. All information included in these financial statements is the representation of the management (owners) of XYZ Company.

A review consists principally of inquiries of company personnel and analytical procedures applied to financial data. It is substantially less in scope than an audit in accordance with generally accepted auditing standards, the objective of which is the expression of an opinion regarding the financial statements taken as a whole. Accordingly, I (we) do not express such an opinion.

Based on my (our) review, I am (we are) not aware of any material modifications that should be made to the accompanying financial statements in order for them to be in conformity with generally accepted accounting principles.

## SIMULATION EXAMPLE 2

Now let's try another Auditing and Attestation simulation. Take a few minutes to review and summarize the concepts and requirements of the simulation presented below.

| Directions | Company Profile | Audit Risk | Confirmations | Cutoff Procedures | Communication | Auditor's Report | Resources |
|---|---|---|---|---|---|---|---|

In the following simulation, you will be asked various questions regarding an audit engagement. You will use the content in the **Information Tabs** to complete the tasks in the **Work Tabs**. (The following pictures are for illustration only; the actual tabs in your simulation may differ from these.)

**Information Tabs:**

| Directions | Situation | Standards | Resources |
|---|---|---|---|

Beginning with the **Directions** tab at the left side of the screen, go through each of the **Information Tabs** to familiarize yourself with the simulation content. Note that the **Resources** tab will contain useful information, including formulas and definitions, to help you complete the tasks. You may want to refer to this information while you are working.

**Work Tabs:**

| Cost Method | Amt to Report | COGS | Invent Costs | Form 1065 | Communication | Review Letter |
|---|---|---|---|---|---|---|

The **Work Tabs,** on the right side of the screen, contain the tasks for you to complete.

Once you complete any part of a task, the pencil for that tab will be shaded.    Note that a shaded pencil does NOT indicate that you have completed the entire task.

You must complete all of the tasks in the **Work Tabs** to receive full credit.

If you have difficulty answering a **Work Tab,** read the tab directions carefully.

*NOTE: If you believe you have encountered a software malfunction, report it to the test center staff immediately.*

| Directions | Company Profile | Audit Risk | Confirmations | Cutoff Procedures | Communication | Auditor's Report | Resources |
|---|---|---|---|---|---|---|---|

The year under audit is year 2.

## Company

Aquatic Jet Products, Inc. is a manufacturer of jet boats and personal watercraft, with headquarters in northern Florida. Personal watercrafts are manufactured at the Florida facility. The company's jet boats are manufactured at a facility in Mexico. Finished goods are sold primarily to independent marine stores throughout the United States.

The company, in its ninth year of operations, has experienced two years of declining sales after a period of rapid growth. The overall market demand for watercraft has also declined and many competitors have filed for bankruptcy in recent years. Tough new federal emissions regulations further threaten industry profitability.

## Business Projection

Eager to revive the company's profitability, the board of directors has implemented several new changes, starting with the hiring of a new CEO, lured away from a major competitor. The new CEO is optimistic and ambitious and has set a goal of a 25% increase in sales for year 2. To help achieve this goal, the CEO has changed the sales staff's compensation from salaried to commission-based.

Unhappy with past sales performance, the CEO plans to terminate relationships with several retail customers and identify new outlets for distribution of its product lines. To further protect its bottom line, the board of directors has also restructured the CFO's compensation package, to include a substantial bonus based on the company's net profits. The company's bank, wary of declining trends, has placed strict new covenants on the company's renewed line of credit.

## Auditors

This is the second year that the company has engaged your firm to perform the annual audit of its financial statements. The prior audit firm is upset that they have lost the audit. However, they indicate that no disagreements with management have previously occurred. You learn that a senior accountant from the prior audit firm has taken an accounting position with the company.

The CFO gives your audit team a tour of the Florida facility. During the tour, you note that parts of the facility may require repair. You also note that the finished watercraft inventory is kept in an open lot outside the facility. The CFO explains that due to its rural location, the company has not had any problems with theft of its products. The CFO comments on the collegiality of the workforce. However, in your tour of the office, you overhear two clerical employees complaining about their rate of pay.

## Other Issues

During the year, the company uncovered an embezzlement by the payroll clerk. According to the CFO, the clerk's scheme was to add hours to her time sheet after approval, during processing of the time cards. While the accounting department is not required to take vacations, the company was fortunate to discover the theft while the employee was out sick for two days. The CFO indicates that while this discovery was unexpected, the company is confident that this was an isolated occurrence.

| Directions | Company Profile | Audit Risk | | Confirmations | Cutoff Procedures | Communication | Auditor's Report | Resources |
|---|---|---|---|---|---|---|---|---|

Based on the information in the Company Profile, indicate by clicking the appropriate box next to each item whether or not the item would most likely increase audit risk.

| *Profile Information* | Increase audit risk? | |
|---|---|---|
| | *Yes* | *No* |
| **1.** Finished goods are sold primarily to independent marine stores throughout the United States. | ○ | ○ |
| **2.** Tough new federal emissions regulations further threaten industry profitability. | ○ | ○ |
| **3.** The company's bank, wary of declining trends, has placed strict new covenants on the company's renewed line of credit. | ○ | ○ |
| **4.** The prior audit firm is upset that they have lost the audit. | ○ | ○ |
| **5.** A senior accountant from the prior audit firm has taken an accounting position with the company. | ○ | ○ |
| **6.** Finished watercraft inventory is kept in an open lot outside the Florida facility. | ○ | ○ |
| **7.** In your tour of the office, you overhear two clerical employees complaining about their rate of pay. | ○ | ○ |

| Directions | Company Profile | Audit Risk | Confirmations | | Cutoff Procedures | Communication | Auditor's Report | Resources |
|---|---|---|---|---|---|---|---|---|

As part of the fieldwork on this engagement, the auditor obtained and documented an understanding of the company's internal controls relating to accounts receivable and assessed control risk related to accounts receivable at the maximum level. Susan, the staff person assigned to the engagement, requested and obtained from the company an aged accounts receivable schedule listing the total amount owed by each customer as of December 31, year 2, and sent positive confirmation requests to a sample of the company customers. Review Susan's comments on each of the following confirmations and determine the best conclusion and/or follow-up procedures for each item.

Confirmation letters can be found under the **Resources** tab. Assume that all confirmations received have been appropriately signed, unless otherwise noted. For each customer in the table below, review the relevant confirmation letter and the comments at the bottom of each. Then double-click on the shaded space in the table, and select the procedure that should be followed to clear the exception, if one exists. Choose only one procedure per confirmation. A procedure may be used once, more than once, or not at all.

| Customer | Conclusion/procedure |
|---|---|
| **1.** Performance Marine Sales, Inc. | |
| **2.** West Coast Ski Center, Inc. | |
| **3.** Fish & Ski World, Inc. | |
| **4.** NC Boating Center, Inc. | |

*Selection list*

A. Send a second request for confirmation to the customer.
B. Exception noted; propose adjustment and request that the controller post it to the accounting records.
C. Verify by examining subsequent cash collections and/or shipping documents.
D. Verify that additional invoices noted on confirmation pertain to the subsequent year.
E. Not an exception, no further audit work deemed necessary.
F. Not an exception, no adjustment necessary. Determine the sufficiency of allowance for doubtful accounts.

| Directions | Company Profile | Audit Risk | Confirmations | Cutoff Procedures | Communication | Auditor's Report | Resources |
|---|---|---|---|---|---|---|---|

For each of the potential December 31, year 2, sales cutoff problems listed below, double-click on the shaded space and select the appropriate adjustment for year 2 from the list provided. Each item in the list may be used once, more than once, or not at all.

| | *Potential cutoff problem* | *Adjustment* |
|---|---|---|
| 1. | The company shipped merchandise (FOB destination) to a customer on December 29, year 2, and recorded the sale but not the relief of inventory. The customer received the merchandise on December 31, year 2. | |
| 2. | The company shipped merchandise (FOB shipping point) on December 3, year 2, to a customer, and recorded the sale and relief of inventory. The customer, unhappy with the merchandise, returned the goods on December 29, year 2. The company records the following entry upon receipt of the goods: Inventory (dr.), Cost of Sales (cr.) | |
| 3. | The company shipped merchandise to a consignee on December 16, year 2, and did not record the transaction. The consignee returned the merchandise on December 28, year 2. Upon receipt of the goods, the company made the following entry: Inventory (dr.), Sales (cr.) | |
| 4. | The company shipped merchandise (FOB shipping point) on December 29, year 2, and recorded relief of inventory, but not the sale, on that date. The customer has not received the merchandise and the company has not recorded the sale as of January 3, year 3. | |

*Selection list*

A. No adjustment necessary.
B. Accounts receivable (dr.)
   Sales (cr.)
C. Sales (dr.)
   Accounts receivable (cr.)
D. Inventory (dr.)
   Cost of sales (cr.)
E. Cost of sales (dr.)
   Inventory (cr.)
F. Accounts receivable (dr.)
   Inventory (cr.)
G. Sales (dr.)
   Accounts receivable (cr.)
   Inventory (dr.)
   Cost of sales (cr.)
H. Sales (dr.)
   Inventory (cr.)
I. Accounts receivable (dr.)
   Sales (cr.)
   Cost of sales (dr.)
   Inventory (cr.)
J. Sales (dr.)
   Cost of sales (cr.)

| Directions | Company Profile | Audit Risk | Confirmations | Cutoff Procedures | Communication | Auditor's Report | Resources |
|---|---|---|---|---|---|---|---|

Based on the Company Profile, discuss how the company's discovery of an embezzlement by an accounting department employee might affect your fraud risk assessment, and indicate two fieldwork procedures your firm might utilize to satisfy itself that the extent of the theft has been properly identified in this particular situation.

Type your communication in the response area below the horizontal line using the word processor provided.

*REMINDER: Your response will be graded for both technical content and writing skills. Technical content will be evaluated for information that is helpful to the intended reader and clearly relevant to the issue. Writing skills will be evaluated for development, organization, and the appropriate expression of ideas in professional correspondence. Use a standard business memo or letter format with a clear beginning, middle, and end. Do not convey information in the form of a table, bullet point list, or other abbreviated presentation.*

| Directions | Company Profile | Audit Risk | Confirmations | Cutoff Procedures | Communication | Auditor's Report | Resources |
|---|---|---|---|---|---|---|---|

During the course of your audit of the company for year 2, you identify that the company had purchase transactions with Risotto, LLC. You also determine that Risotto, LLC is owned by the CEO and vice president of the company. The purchases accounted for 28% of materials purchases for the year. Management has declined to disclose the related-party transactions in the footnotes. This is the only item that the auditor wishes to consider for the report on financial statements.

Research the professional standards to find an example of an appropriate report.

| Directions | Company Profile | Audit Risk | Confirmations | Cutoff Procedures | Communication | Auditor's Report | Resources |
|---|---|---|---|---|---|---|---|

## Confirmation Letters

February 1, year 3

Performance Marine Sales, Inc.
1284 River Road
Louisville, Kentucky 40059

Re:  Balance at December 31, year 2 - $267,000

Dear Sirs:

As of December 31, year 2, our records indicate your balance with our company as the amount listed above. Please complete and sign the bottom portion of this letter and return the entire letter to our auditors, JS LLP, PO Box 100, Orlando, Florida 32806.

A stamped, self-addressed envelope is enclosed for your convenience.

Sincerely,

_____

Aquatic Jet Products, Inc.

-------------------------------------------------------------------

| The above balance is | Correct | |
|---|---|---|
| X | Incorrect (show amount) | $325,000 |

If incorrect, please provide information that could help to reconcile your account.

| Response: We placed an order for $58,000 on December 26, year 2. |
|---|
| |

_____

| Signature | Title | Date |

**Susan's note to file:**

| Per discussion with the controller, the order for $58,000 was shipped FOB shipping point on December 30, year 2, and was received by the customer on January 3, year 3. Therefore, no entry has been made to record the sale in year 2. |
|---|

─────────────────────────────────

February 1, year 3

West Coast Ski Center, Inc.
163 Tide Avenue
Monterey, California 93940

Re: Balance at December 31, year 2 - $414,000

Dear Sirs:

As of December 31, year 2, our records indicate your balance with our company as the amount listed above. Please complete and sign the bottom portion of this letter and return the entire letter to our auditors, JS LLP, PO Box 100, Orlando, Florida 32806.

A stamped, self-addressed envelope is enclosed for your convenience.

Sincerely,

_____

Aquatic Jet Products, Inc.

-------------------------------------------------------------------

| The above balance is | Correct | |
|---|---|---|
| X | Incorrect (show amount) | $320,000 |

If incorrect, please provide information that could help to reconcile your account.

| Response: We made a payment of $94,000 on December 12, year 2. |
|---|
| |

_____

| Signature | Title | Date |

**Susan's note to file:**

> Per discussion with the controller, the company received the payment of $94,000 on December 15, year 2, and posted it to "Other Income."

---

February 1, year 3

Fish & Ski World, Inc.
5660 Ocean Blvd.
Port Arkansas, Texas 78373

Re:  Balance at December 31, year 2 - $72,000

Dear Sirs:

As of December 31, year 2, our records indicate your balance with our company as the amount listed above.  Please complete and sign the bottom portion of this letter and return the entire letter to our auditors, JS LLP, PO Box 100, Orlando, Florida 32806.

A stamped, self-addressed envelope is enclosed for your convenience.

Sincerely,

---

Aquatic Jet Products, Inc.

- - - - - - - - - - - - - - - - - - - - - - - - - - - - - - - - - - - - - - - - - - - - - - - - - - -

| The above balance is | Correct | |
|---|---|---|
| X | Incorrect (show amount) | $163,000 |

If incorrect, please provide information that could help to reconcile your account.

> Response:  Per our records, the following invoices are outstanding:
> | | |
> |---|---|
> | Invoice #4212 | $72,000 |
> | Invoice #4593 | $66,000 |
> | Invoice #4738 | $25,000 |

Signature                                    Title                                    Date

**Susan's note to file:**

> Invoices #4593 and 4738 are not on the A/R aging report at December 31, year 2.

---

February 1, year 3

NC Boating Center, Inc.
110 Windward Blvd.
Tierra Verde, Florida 33715

Re:  Balance at December 31, year 2 - $239,000

Dear Sirs:

As of December 31, year 2, our records indicate your balance with our company as the amount listed above.  Please complete and sign the bottom portion of this letter and return the entire letter to our auditors, JS LLP, PO Box 100, Orlando, Florida 32806.

A stamped, self-addressed envelope is enclosed for your convenience.

Sincerely,

_____

Aquatic Jet Products, Inc.

- - - - - - - - - - - - - - - - - - - - - - - - - - - - - - - - - - - - - - - - - -

| The above balance is | Correct | |
|---|---|---|
| | Incorrect (show amount) | $ |

If incorrect, please provide information that could help to reconcile your account.

| Response: We cannot determine the balance due at December 31, year 2. |
|---|

_____
Signature                    Title                    Date

**Susan's note to file:**

| No amount was confirmed on the response letter |
|---|

## Solving the Simulation

You should have summarized on your scratch paper the following requirements for this simulation:

1. Decide whether or not a series of pieces of information from the profile increases audit risk.
2. Review a group of confirmations and decide the conclusion or additional procedures that result.
3. From list of potential cutoff problems identify the appropriate adjusting entry.
4. Draft a memorandum to describe how the discovery of embezzlement might affect your fraud risk assessment and audit procedures.
5. Research and construct the appropriate audit report that includes a modification for a lack of disclosure.

Since there is no advantage to addressing the requirements out of order, let's begin with requirement 1.

### *Requirement 1*

The **Audit** Risk tab requires you to decide whether or not each of the following bits of information increase audit risk. Items that increase audit risk typically are items that indicate a weakness in control or a characteristic of the company or industry which increases business risk. Of the ones listed below, we note that three of them increase audit risk: (2) tough new federal emissions regulations, (3) strict new loan covenants, and (6) finished watercraft inventory is kept in an open lot. Item (1) is just a characteristic of the business which does not significantly affect audit risk. Item (4), the prior audit firm is upset that they lost the audit, obviously does not affect audit risk. If the prior audit firm had resigned, that would present a risk. Item (5), the fact that a senior accountant from the prior audit firm took a position with the company, also does not affect risk. The fact that two clerical clerks were complaining about pay, item (7), would not on its own significantly affect audit risk. The increase in risk in this case arises from the fact that a payroll clerk engaged in embezzlement.

|  | *Profile Information* | Increase audit risk? | |
|---|---|---|---|
|  |  | *Yes* | *No* |
| 1. | Finished goods are sold primarily to independent marine stores throughout the United States. | ○ | ● |
| 2. | Tough new federal emissions regulations further threaten industry profitability | ● | ○ |
| 3. | The company's bank, wary of declining trends, has placed strict new covenants on the company's renewed line of credit. | ● | ○ |
| 4. | The prior audit firm is upset that they have lost the audit. | ○ | ● |
| 5. | A senior accountant from the prior audit firm has taken an accounting position with the company. | ○ | ● |
| 6. | Finished watercraft inventory is kept in an open lot outside the Florida facility. | ● | ○ |
| 7. | In your tour of the office, you overhear two clerical employees complaining about their rate of pay. | ○ | ● |

## Requirement 2

The **Confirmations** tab requires you to review the confirmations returned by three customers and determine the conclusion or procedure that results from information on the confirmation. The conclusion/procedure is selected from the following possibilities:

*Selection list*

A. Send a second request for confirmation to the customer.
B. Exception noted; propose adjustment and request that the controller post it to the accounting records.
C. Verify by examining subsequent cash collections and/or shipping documents.
D. Verify that additional invoices noted on confirmation pertain to the subsequent year.
E. Not an exception, no further audit work deemed necessary.
F. Not an exception, no adjustment necessary. Determine the sufficiency of allowance for doubtful accounts.

Examining confirmation 1, we find that Performance Marine indicates that it placed an additional order on December 26. Investigation by the audit staff indicates that the order was shipped on December 30 with the terms of FOB shipping point. This means that the title to the goods was transferred on the shipping date. Therefore, a sale should be recorded, and the appropriate action is (B), "Exception noted; propose adjustment and request that the controller post it to the accounting records."

The response to confirmation 2 from West Coast Ski Center indicates that the company made a payment prior to year end that was inappropriately recorded. The note from the staff indicates that the controller has not corrected the records. Accordingly, the appropriate course of action is (B), "Exception noted; propose adjustment and request that the controller post it to the accounting records."

The response to confirmation 3 from Fish & Ski World indicates that it owes amounts for additional invoices not confirmed and not included in the year-end receivables balance. Therefore, the appropriate course of action is (D), "Verify that additional invoices noted on confirmation pertain to the subsequent year."

Finally, the response to confirmation 4 from NC Boating Center indicates that the company cannot confirm the amount. This might be a result of the type of accounting system that NC Boating Center has implemented. This is not an exception, nor is it a confirmation. The auditors must verify the amount by using alternative auditing procedures. Thus, response C, "Verify by examining subsequent cash collections and/or shipping documents," is the appropriate course of action.

| *Customer* | *Conclusion/procedure* |
|---|---|
| 1. Performance Marine Sales, Inc. | B |
| 2. West Coast Ski Center, Inc. | B |
| 3. Fish & Ski World, Inc. | D |
| 4. NC Boating Center, Inc. | C |

## Requirement 3

The *Cutoff Procedures* tab requires you to identify the nature of the adjustments necessary for the described situations. You are to select from the following list.

| Selection list | |
|---|---|
| A. No adjustment necessary.<br>B. Accounts receivable (dr.)<br>   Sales (cr.)<br>C. Sales (dr.)<br>   Accounts receivable (cr.)<br>D. Inventory (dr.)<br>   Cost of sales (cr.)<br>E. Cost of sales (dr.)<br>   Inventory (cr.)<br>F. Accounts receivable (dr.)<br>   Inventory (cr.) | G. Sales (dr.)<br>   Accounts receivable (cr.)<br>   Inventory (dr.)<br>   Cost of sales (cr.)<br>H. Sales (dr.)<br>   Inventory (cr.)<br>I. Accounts receivable (dr.)<br>   Sales (cr.)<br>   Cost of sales (dr.)<br>   Inventory (cr.)<br>J. Sales (dr.)<br>   Cost of sales (cr.) |

In the first situation, the company failed to record the entry to reduce inventory for a sale. The entry required involves a debit to cost of sales and a credit to inventory. Accordingly, E. is the correct answer.

1. The company shipped merchandise (FOB destination) to a customer on December 29, year 2, and recorded the sale but not the relief of inventory. The customer received the merchandise on December 31, year 2.

In situation 2, the company recorded the entry to restore the inventory but did not record the sales return. The company needs to reduce sales and accounts receivable for the return. Therefore, C. is the correct answer.

2. The company shipped merchandise (FOB shipping point) on December 3, year 2, to a customer, and recorded the sale and relief of inventory. The customer, unhappy with the merchandise, returned the goods on December 29, year 2. The company records the following entry upon receipt of the goods: Inventory (dr.), Cost of Sales (cr.).

In the third situation, the company did not record an entry when goods were consigned but made an entry to restore the inventory when the items were returned. Also, the entry inappropriately increased sales. Since inventory and sales are both overstated, answer H. is correct.

3. The company shipped merchandise to a consignee on December 16, year 2, and did not record the transaction. The consignee returned the merchandise on December 28, year 2. Upon receipt of the goods, the company made the following entry: Inventory (dr.), Sales (cr.).

In the last situation, the company recorded the relief of inventory but not the sale. Since the items were shipped FOB shipping point, the sale should have been recorded in Year 2. Accordingly, answer B. is correct.

4. The company shipped merchandise (FOB shipping point) on December 29, year 2, and recorded relief of inventory, but not the sale, on that date. The customer has not received the merchandise and the company has not recorded the sale as of January 3, year 3.

The completed answer sheet for this tab is illustrated below.

| Potential cutoff problem | Adjustment |
|---|---|
| **1.** The company shipped merchandise (FOB destination) to a customer on December 29, year 2, and recorded the sale but not the relief of inventory. The customer received the merchandise on December 31, year 2. | E |
| **2.** The company shipped merchandise (FOB shipping point) on December 3, year 2, to a customer, and recorded the sale and relief of inventory. The customer, unhappy with the merchandise, returned the goods on December 29, year 2. The company records the following entry upon receipt of the goods: Inventory (dr.), Cost of Sales (cr.) | C |
| **3.** The company shipped merchandise to a consignee on December 16, year 2, and did not record the transaction. The consignee returned the merchandise on December 28, year 2. Upon receipt of the goods, the company made the following entry: Inventory (dr.), Sales (cr.) | H |
| **4.** The company shipped merchandise (FOB shipping point) on December 29, year 2, and recorded relief of inventory, but not the sale, on that date. The customer has not received the merchandise and the company has not recorded the sale as of January 3, year 3. | B |

## Requirement 4

The **Communication** tab requires you to draft a memorandum to the audit staff regarding how the company's discovery of embezzlement by an accounting department employee might affect your fraud risk assessment, and indicate two fieldwork procedures your firm might utilize to satisfy itself that the extent of the theft has been properly identified in this particular situation. In completing communication requirements, you should remember that the memorandum will not be graded for technical accuracy. As long as it is on point, your score will be determined based the quality of the communication, including its organization. Chapter 3 describes how you can improve your writing skills. Before you start writing the memorandum, I suggest that you develop a very short outline. It may be as simple as the one shown below:

1. Introduction and objective of the memorandum
2. A description of the embezzlement
3. Effect on fraud risk assessment
4. Effect on audit procedures
5. Closing

With these observations in mind, you can develop your memorandum. In doing so remember the guidance from Chapter 3:

1. Start the memorandum with an introduction indicating its purpose.
2. Use simple sentences.
3. Since you are communicating with management, you should avoid accounting jargon.
4. Use the spell-checker in the exam software.
5. Don't worry that much about getting the requirements of the standard exactly correct. Remember your response will not be graded for technical accuracy.

Review the following memorandum, noting how it applies the principles described above.

> To:      Staff on Aquatic Jet Products, Inc. Audit
> From:    Your name
> Date:    Today's date
> Re:      The client's discovery of fraud
>
>     During the year, the company identified embezzlement by the payroll clerk. In the following paragraphs, I provide details on the identified fraud, its effect on our fraud risk assessment, and procedures we should consider performing.
>
>     According to the CFO, the payroll clerk added hours to her time sheet after her supervisor had approved her time card. This was in part possible because the company does not require that employees take vacations, making such embezzlements somewhat easier to commit. The theft was discovered while the employee was out sick for two days. The CFO indicates that while this discovery was unexpected, the company is confident that this was an isolated occurrence.
>
>     The company's discovery of the fraud affects our fraud risk assessment in that we must determine the identified fraud has been properly investigated, and whether other related embezzlements may have occurred. The embezzlement first increases our need to apply audit procedures to the event itself. To begin, we must document the fraud discovered by management and determine whether it has been properly handled from an accounting perspective. Next, we should perform extensive audit procedures in the payroll area to determine whether other periods are affected. We may do this by examining time cards in detail, comparing them to time sheets and, possibly, consulting with the employee's supervisor who approved the time cards prior to their inappropriate modification.
>
>     We might also wish to perform similar procedures relating to other clerical employees in this area. For example, we might select their time cards, time sheets, and payroll records to assure ourselves that this type of embezzlement is not more widespread than has currently been identified. We might also wish to determine that pay rates have not been inappropriately modified. On a staffing basis, we might now, or later, wish to determine whether we wish to staff the engagement with one of our firm's forensic specialists.
>
>     In summary, we have identified a higher than normal expected risk of misstatement due to fraud (misappropriation of assets in the payroll area). Accordingly, we must coordinate more extensive procedures than would normally be the case.

## Requirement 5

The **Auditor's Report** tab requires you to research the professional standards to find an appropriate report. The lack of disclosure is a departure from generally accepted accounting principles resulting in a qualified or an adverse opinion. Because the matter is isolated, the best assumption is that a qualified opinion is appropriate. The information does not tell you whether or not the report should address only the current year, or the current year and comparative financial statements. It is easiest to assume that the report is on only the current year's financial statements.

An efficient search strategy to construct the report is to use the table of contents to locate the standard report on financial statements, which is at AU section 508.08. Next, you need to find the modifying paragraphs for the departure from generally accepted accounting principles. By scrolling down through AU section 508, the modifying paragraphs can be found in AU section 508.42.

## PROBLEMS

The following two simulations are for you to attempt.  As you complete them be sure to apply the principles that you have learned in this text.

### AUD Simulation Problem 1

In the following simulation, you will be asked various questions regarding an audit engagement.  You will use the content in the **Information Tabs** to complete the tasks in the **Work Tabs**.  (The following pictures are for illustration only; the actual tabs in your simulation may differ from these.)

**Information Tabs:**

| Directions | Situation | Standards | Resources |
|---|---|---|---|

Beginning with the **Directions** tab at the left side of the screen, go through each of the **Information Tabs** to familiarize yourself with the simulation content.  Note that the **Resources** tab will contain useful information, including formulas and definitions, to help you complete the tasks.  You may want to refer to this information while you are working.

**Work Tabs:**

| ✏Cost Method | ✏Amt to Report | ✏COGS | ✏Invent Costs | ✏Form 1065 | ✏Communication | ✏Review Letter |
|---|---|---|---|---|---|---|

The **Work Tabs,** on the right side of the screen, contain the tasks for you to complete.

Once you complete any part of a task, the pencil for that tab will be shaded.✏    Note that a shaded pencil does NOT indicate that you have completed the entire task.

You must complete all of the tasks in the **Work Tabs** to receive full credit.

If you have difficulty answering a **Work Tab,** read the tab directions carefully.

*NOTE:  If you believe you have encountered a software malfunction, report it to the test center staff immediately.*

| Situation | Company Profile | Industry Information | Balance Sheet | Income Statement | Statement of Cash Flows | Risks | Financial Statement Analysis | Audit Procedures | Communication | Research |
|---|---|---|---|---|---|---|---|---|---|---|

DietWeb Inc. (hereafter DietWeb) was incorporated and began business in March of 20X1, seven years ago.  You are working on the 20X8 audit—your CPA firm's fifth audit of DietWeb.

| Situation | Company Profile | Industry Information | Balance Sheet | Income Statement | Statement of Cash Flows | Risks | Financial Statement Analysis | Audit Procedures | Communication | Research |
|---|---|---|---|---|---|---|---|---|---|---|

The company's mission is to provide solutions that help individuals to realize their full potential through better eating habits and lifestyles.  Much of 20X1 and 20X2 was spent in developing a unique software platform that facilitates the production of individualized meal plans and shopping lists using a specific mathematical algorithm, which considers the user's physical condition, proclivity to exercise, food preferences, cooking preferences, desire to use prepackaged meals or dine out, among others. DietWeb sold its first online diet program in 20X2 and has continued to market memberships through increasing online advertising arrangements through the years. The company has continued to develop this program throughout the years and finally became profitable in 20X6.

DietWeb is executing a strategy to be a leading online provider of services, information and products related to nutrition, fitness and motivation. In 20X8, the company derived approximately 86% of its total revenues from the sale of approximately 203,000 personalized subscription-based online nutrition plans related to weight management, to dietary regimens such as vegetarianism and to specific medical conditions such as Type 2 diabetes. Given the personal nature of dieting, Diet-Web assures customers of complete privacy of the information they provide. To this point Diet-Web's management is proud of its success in assuring the privacy of information supplied by its customers—this is a constant battle given the variety of intrusion attempts by various Internet hackers.

DietWeb nutrition plans are paid in advance by customers and offered in increments of thirteen weeks with the customers having the ability to cancel and receive a refund of the unused portion of the subscription—this results in a significant level of "deferred revenue" each period. Although some DietWeb members are billed through use of the postal system, most DietWeb members currently purchase programs and products using credit cards, with renewals billed automatically, until cancellation. One week of a basic DietWeb membership costs less than one-half the cost of a weekly visit to the leading classroom-based diet program. The president, Mr. William Readings, suggests that in addition to its superior cost-effectiveness, the DietWeb online diet program is successful relative to classroom-based programs due to its customization, ease of use, expert support, privacy, constant availability, and breadth of choice. The basic DietWeb membership includes

- Customized meal plans, workout schedules, and related tools such as shopping lists, journals, and weight and exercise tracking.
- Interactive online support and education including approximately 100 message boards on various topics of interest to members and a library of dozens of multimedia educational segments presented by experts including psychologists, mental health counselors, dietitians, fitness trainers, a spiritual advisor and a physician.
- 24/7/365 telephone support from a staff of approximately 30 customer service representatives, nutritionists and fitness personnel.

Throughout its nine-year history, Mr. William Readings has served as chief executive officer. The other three founders of the company are also officers. A fifth individual, Willingsley Williamson, also a founder, served as Chief Financial Officer until mid-20X8 when he left the company due to a difference of opinion with Mr. Readings. The four founders purchased Mr. Williamson's stock and invested an additional approximately $1.2 million in common stock during 20X8 so as to limit the use of long-term debt.

The company's board of directors is currently composed of the four individuals who remain active in the company; these four individuals also serve as the company's audit committee; Mr. Readings chairs both the board and the audit committee. Previously, Mr. Readings had also served on the board and the audit committee. With Mr. Williamson's departure, Ms. Jane Jennings, another of the founders, became the company's CFO.

| Situation | Company Profile | Industry Information | Balance Sheet | Income Statement | Statement of Cash Flows | Risks | Financial Statement Analysis | Audit Procedures | Communication | Research |
|---|---|---|---|---|---|---|---|---|---|---|

The nutrition and diet industry in many ways thrives because individuals are becoming more aware of the negative health and financial consequences of being overweight, and consider important both weight loss and healthy weight maintenance. A study by two respected researchers concluded that obesity was linked to higher rates of chronic illness than living in poverty, smoking, or drinking. In addition, the American Cancer Society reported that as many as 14% of cancer deaths in men and 20% of cancer deaths in women could be related to being overweight.

The financial costs of excess weight are also high. A 20X8 study based on data from a major automobile manufacturer's health care plan showed that an overweight adult has annual health care costs that are 7.3% higher than a person in a healthy weight range, while obese individuals have annual health care costs that are 69% higher than a person of a healthy weight. With health care cost inflation running in the double digits in the United States since 20X4, supporters of the industry believe that the implementation of effective weight management tools will attract more attention from insurers, employers, consumers, and the government. As of January 20X9 five nutrition- or fitness-related bills were being considered in Congress, and several states had enacted or were considering enacting legislation relating to the sale of "junk" food in public schools. In addition, the U.S. Food and Drug Administration, Department of Health and Human Services, and Federal Trade Commission are contemplating new labeling requirements for packaged food and restaurant food, new educational and motivational programs related to healthy eating and exercise, and increased regulation of advertising claims for food.

In response to consumers' growing demand for more healthful eating options, quick-service and full-service restaurants have introduced new offerings including salads, sandwiches, burgers, and other food items designed for the weight-conscious person. At the retail level, sales of natural and organic foods have been growing more rapidly than the overall food and over-the-counter drug market for the last several years. Nutritional supplement sales in the US, for instance, are estimated to have grown 34% between 20X4 and 20X8, while natural and organic foods are estimated to be growing at a rate of approximately 15% annually. Also, the industry has a tendency to change quickly as "dieting fads" regularly are introduced; some remain popular for years, some for only months.

Approximately 60% of the U.S. adult population, or 120 million adults, are overweight and, of those, the Calorie Control Council estimates only about 50 million are dieting in a given year. About 15% of these dieters are using a commercial weight loss center, generating revenues of approximately $1.5 billion annually. DietWeb targets dieters who are online, which represents about two-thirds of the world at current Internet penetration rates, or 34 million adults, about 5 million of whom are spending approximately $1 billion at weight loss centers.

At the same time, the online dieting segment of the market is growing rapidly. The online diet industry in the U.S. generated in excess of $100 million in 20X8, compared to revenues of approximately $75 million in 20X2. The industry includes other online nutrition and diet-oriented Web sites.

Another group of competitors to DietWeb are commercial weight loss centers, an industry that has shown marked decline in the last decade. According to Market Analysis Enterprises, the number of commercial weight loss centers in the U.S. declined approximately 50% between 20X2 and 20X8, from over 8,600 to approximately 4,400. DietWeb competes against this segment on the basis of lower price, superior value, convenience, availability, the ability to personalize a meal plan on an ongoing basis, its extensive support capabilities, and the breadth of its meal plan options.

| Situation | Company Profile | Industry Information | Balance Sheet | Income Statement | Statement of Cash Flows | Risks | Financial Statement Analysis | Audit Procedures | Communication | Research |
|---|---|---|---|---|---|---|---|---|---|---|

### DietWeb, Inc.
### BALANCE SHEET
### *December 31, 20X8 and 20X7*
#### *(in thousands)*

|  | 20X8 | 20X7 |
|---|---|---|
| *Assets* | | |
| Current assets | | |
| Cash and cash equivalents | $3,032 | $1,072 |
| Trade receivables | 485 | 450 |
| Prepaid advertising expenses | 59 | 609 |
| Prepaid expenses and other current assets | 175 | 230 |

|                                          | 20X8    | 20X7    |
|------------------------------------------|---------|---------|
| Total current assets                     | 3,751   | 2,361   |
| Fixed assets, net                        | 3,321   | 3,926   |
| Total assets                             | $7,072  | $6,287  |

**Liabilities and shareholders' equity**

Current liabilities

|                                            | 20X8    | 20X7    |
|--------------------------------------------|---------|---------|
| Accounts payable                           | $1,070  | $ 909   |
| Current maturities of notes payable        | 42      | 316     |
| Deferred revenue                           | 1,973   | 1,396   |
| Other current liabilities                  | 171     | 12      |
| Total current liabilities                  | 3,256   | 2,633   |
| Long-term debt, less current maturity      | 34      | 176     |
| Accrued liabilities                        | 792     | 690     |
| Deferred tax liability                     | 15      | 145     |
| Total liabilities                          | 4,097   | 3,644   |

Shareholders' equity

|                                               | 20X8    | 20X7    |
|-----------------------------------------------|---------|---------|
| Common stock                                  | 6,040   | 4,854   |
| Retained earnings                             | (3,065) | (2,211) |
| Total shareholders' equity                    | 2,975   | 2,643   |
| Total liabilities plus shareholders' equity   | $7,072  | $6,287  |

| Situation | Company Profile | Industry Information | Balance Sheet | Income Statement | Statement of Cash Flows | Risks | Financial Statement Analysis | Audit Procedures | Communication | Research |
|-----------|-----------------|----------------------|---------------|------------------|-------------------------|-------|------------------------------|------------------|---------------|----------|

### DietWeb, Inc.
### INCOME STATEMENT
*Two Years Ended December 31, 20X8 and 20X7*
*(in thousands)*

|                                    | 20X8     | 20X7     |
|------------------------------------|----------|----------|
| **Revenue**                        | $19,166  | $14,814  |
| *Costs and expenses*               |          |          |
| Cost of revenue                    | 2,326    | 1,528    |
| Product development                | 725      | 653      |
| Sales and marketing                | 13,903   | 8,710    |
| General and administrative         | 2,531    | 2,575    |
|                                    | 20X8     | 20X7     |
| Depreciation and amortization      | 629      | 661      |
| Impairment of intangible assets    | 35       | -        |
| Total costs and expenses           | 20,149   | 14,127   |
| Net income before taxes            | (983)    | 687      |
| Income tax benefit                 | 129      | 125      |
| Net income (loss)                  | $(854)   | $812     |

| Situation | Company Profile | Industry Information | Balance Sheet | Income Statement | Statement of Cash Flows | Risks | Financial Statement Analysis | Audit Procedures | Communication | Research |
|---|---|---|---|---|---|---|---|---|---|---|

## DietWeb, Inc.
## STATEMENT OF CASH FLOWS
### *Year Ended December 31, 20X8*

|  | 20X8 | 20X7 |
|---|---|---|
| *Cash flows from operations* | | |
| Net income (loss) | $(854) | 812 |
| Adjustments to net income | | |
| Depreciation | 629 | 660 |
| Increase in receivables | (35) | (47) |
| Increase (Decrease) in prepaid advertising | 550 | (650) |
| Increase in other current assets | 55 | 74 |
| Increase (Decrease) in accounts payable | 161 | (540) |
| Increase in accrued liabilities | 102 | 43 |
| Increase (Decrease) in deferred revenue | 432 | (665) |
| Increase in common stock issued | 1,186 | - |
| Increase in other current liabilities | 159 | 43 |
| *Net cash provided (used) by operations* | 2,385 | (270) |
| *Cash flows from investing activities* | | |
| Purchase of property and equipment | (320) | 2,016 |
| *Cash flows from financing activities* | | |
| New debt | 613 | 40 |
| Debt payments | (718) | (918) |
| *Net cash provided (used) by financing activities* | (105) | (878) |
| Net increase in cash and cash equivalents | $1,960 | 868 |
| Cash and equivalents at beginning of year | $1,072 | 204 |
| Cash and equivalents at end of year | $3,032 | 1,072 |

| Situation | Company Profile | Industry Information | Balance Sheet | Income Statement | Statement of Cash Flows | Risks | Financial Statement Analysis | Audit Procedures | Communication | Research |
|---|---|---|---|---|---|---|---|---|---|---|

**(A) (B) (C) (D)**

1. Of the following, which is likely to be one of DietWeb's major risks of doing business on the Internet in the future?          ○ ○ ○ ○

   A. Maintaining privacy of customer information.
   B. Maintaining the ability to pay Federal Communication Commission Internet use fees.
   C. Inability to provide 24/7/365 support.
   D. Inability to reach customers beyond the United States.

**(A) (B) (C) (D)**

2. Which of the following is likely to be the most significant business risk for Diet-Web?          ○ ○ ○ ○

   A. Internal control limitations due to the small size of the company.
   B. Inability of the Internet to provide adequate support for such a business due to its instability.
   C. Entrance of new competitors onto the Internet.
   D. Misstatements of revenues due to difficulties in determining appropriate year-end cutoffs.

| Situation | Company Profile | Industry Information | Balance Sheet | Income Statement | Statement of Cash Flows | Risks | Financial Statement Analysis | Audit Procedures | Communication | Research |
|---|---|---|---|---|---|---|---|---|---|---|

                                                   **(A) (B) (C) (D)**

**1.** The most likely misstatement in the financial statements is       ○ ○ ○ ○

    A. The increase in cash in 20X8.
    B. Treatment of impaired intangible assets as an expense in 20X8.
    C. Treatment of common stock issued as an adjustment to net income.
    D. An income tax benefit on the income statement as contrasted to income tax expense.

                                                     **(A) (B) (C) (D)**

**2.** Which of the following is the most unexpected change on the balance sheet, if   ○ ○ ○ ○
one assumes the revenue increase in 20X8 is correct?

    A. Decrease in prepaid advertising expenses.
    B. Increase in accounts payable.
    C. Decrease in deferred revenues.
    D. Increase in common stock.

| Situation | Company Profile | Industry Information | Balance Sheet | Income Statement | Statement of Cash Flows | Risks | Financial Statement Analysis | Audit Procedures | Communication | Research |
|---|---|---|---|---|---|---|---|---|---|---|

    The auditor determines that each of the following objectives will be part of DietWeb's audit. For each audit objective, select a substantive procedure that would help to achieve that objective. Each of the procedures may be used once, more than once, or not at all.

*Substantive procedure*

    A. Trace opening balances in the summary schedules to the prior year's audit working papers.
    B. Review the provision for deprecation expense and determine that depreciable lives and methods used in the current year are consistent with those used in the prior year.
    C. Determine that responsibility for maintaining the property and equipment records is segregated from the responsibility for custody of property and equipment.
    D. Examine deeds and title insurance certificates.
    E. Perform cutoff test to verify that property and equipment additions are recorded in the proper period.
    F. Determine that property and equipment is adequately insured.
    G. Physically examine all recorded major property and equipment additions.

                                       **(A) (B) (C) (D) (E) (F) (G)**

**1.** DietWeb has legal rights to property and equipment acquired during   ○ ○ ○ ○ ○ ○ ○
the year.

**2.** DietWeb recorded property and equipment acquired during the year   ○ ○ ○ ○ ○ ○ ○
that did not actually exist at the balance sheet date.

| Situation | Company Profile | Industry Information | Balance Sheet | Income Statement | Statement of Cash Flows | Risks | Financial Statement Analysis | Audit Procedures | Communication | Research |
|---|---|---|---|---|---|---|---|---|---|---|

    This is your firm's sixth audit of DietWeb. In a memorandum to the audit team (below) summarize your view of the audit committee's strengths, weaknesses, and any changes that have occurred relating to the audit committee this year.

*REMINDER:  Your response will be graded for both technical content and writing skills.  Technical content will be evaluated for information that is helpful to the intended reader and clearly relevant to the issue. Writing skills will be evaluated for development, organization, and the appropriate expression of ideas in professional correspondence.  Use a standard business memo or letter format with a clear beginning, middle, and end.  Do not convey information in the form of a table, bullet point list, or other abbreviated presentation.*

To:      Audit Team
From:   CPA Candidate
Re:      DietWeb Audit Committee

| | | | | | | | | | | | Research |
|---|---|---|---|---|---|---|---|---|---|---|---|
| Situation | Company Profile | Industry Information | Balance Sheet | Income Statement | Statement of Cash Flows | Risks | Financial Statement Analysis | Audit Procedures | Communication | | |

*NOTE: This section is only possible to work in a meaningful way if you have the professional standards available—preferably in electronic form.*

You are now working on the fieldwork for the DietWeb audit.  Use the Professional Standards to identify risk factors that might indicate misstatements arising from misappropriation of assets.

Find guidance in the AICPA Standards that authoritatively addresses the situation above.  To complete this task, select the appropriate paragraph(s) that answer the requirement.  Use the search capabilities provided by the **Standards** tab to find the numbered paragraph in either the Original Pronouncements or Current Text that addresses the issue above.

**AUD Simulation Problem 2**

In the following simulation, you will be asked various questions regarding an audit engagement.  You will use the content in the **Information Tabs** to complete the tasks in the **Work Tabs**. (The following pictures are for illustration only; the actual tabs in your simulation may differ from these.)

**Information Tabs:**

| Directions | Situation | Standards | Resources |
|---|---|---|---|

Beginning with the **Directions** tab at the left side of the screen, go through each of the **Information Tabs** to familiarize yourself with the simulation content.  Note that the **Resources** tab will contain useful information, including formulas and definitions, to help you complete the tasks. You may want to refer to this information while you are working.

**Work Tabs:**

| ✏Cost Method | ✏Amt to Report | ✏COGS | ✏Invent Costs | ✏Form 1065 | ✏Communication | ✏Review Letter |
|---|---|---|---|---|---|---|

The **Work Tabs,** on the right side of the screen, contain the tasks for you to complete.

Once you complete any part of a task, the pencil for that tab will be shaded. ✏   Note that a shaded pencil does NOT indicate that you have completed the entire task.

You must complete all of the tasks in the **Work Tabs** to receive full credit.

If you have difficulty answering a **Work Tab,** read the tab directions carefully.

*NOTE: If you believe you have encountered a software malfunction, report it to the test center staff immediately.*

You are performing the audit of General Company for the year ended 12/31/07.

| Audit Procedures | | | |
|---|---|---|---|
| | Assessing Audit Risk | Research | Communication |

**Items 1 through 6** represent the items that an auditor ordinarily would find on a client-prepared bank reconciliation. The accompanying **List of Auditing Procedures** represents substantive auditing procedures. For each item, select one or more procedures, as indicated, that the auditor most likely would perform to gather evidence in support of that item. The procedures on the **List** may be selected once, more than once, or not at all.

*Assume*

- The client prepared the bank reconciliation on 10/2/07.
- The bank reconciliation is mathematically accurate.
- The auditor received a cutoff bank statement dated 10/7/07 directly from the bank on 10/11/07.
- The 9/30/07 deposit in transit, outstanding checks #1281, #1285, #1289, and #1292, and the correction of the error regarding check #1282 appeared on the cutoff bank statement.
- The auditor assessed control risk concerning the financial statement assertions related to cash at the maximum.

*List of Auditing Procedures*

A. Trace to cash receipts journal.
B. Trace to cash disbursements journal.
C. Compare to 9/30/01 general ledger.
D. Confirm directly with bank.
E. Inspect bank credit memo.
F. Inspect bank debit memo.
G. Ascertain reason for unusual delay.

H. Inspect supporting documents for reconciling item **not** appearing on cutoff statement.
I. Trace items on the bank reconciliation to cutoff statement.
J. Trace items on the cutoff statement to bank reconciliation.

*General Company*
**BANK RECONCILIATION**
**1ST NATIONAL BANK OF US BANK ACCOUNT**
*September 30, 2007*

| | | | | | |
|---|---|---|---|---|---|
| **1.** | Select 2 Procedures — | Balance per bank | | | $ 28,375 |
| **2.** | Select 5 Procedures — | Deposits in transit | | | |
| | | 9/29/07 | | $4,500 | |
| | | 9/30/07 | | 1,525 | 6,025 |
| | | | | | 34,400 |
| **3.** | Select 5 Procedures — | Outstanding checks | | | |
| | | # 988 | 8/31/07 | 2,200 | |
| | | #1281 | 9/26/07 | 675 | |
| | | #1285 | 9/27/07 | 850 | |
| | | #1289 | 9/29/07 | 2,500 | |
| | | #1292 | 9/30/07 | 7,225 | (13,450) |
| | | | | | 20,950 |
| **4.** | Select 1 Procedure — | Customer note collected by bank | | | (3,000) |
| **5.** | Select 2 Procedures — | Error: Check #1282, written on 9/26/07 for $270 was erroneously charged by bank as $720; bank was notified on 10/2/07 | | | 450 |
| **6.** | Select 1 Procedure — | Balance per books | | | $ 18,400 |

| Audit Procedures | Addressing Audit Risk | Research | Communication |
|---|---|---|---|

**Items 1 through 12** represent possible errors and fraud that you suspect may be present at General Company. The accompanying *List of Auditing Procedures* represents procedures that the auditor would consider performing to gather evidence concerning possible errors and fraud. For each item, select one or two procedures, as indicated, that the auditor most likely would perform to gather evidence in support of that item. The procedures on the list may be selected once, more than once, or not at all.

## *List of Auditing Procedures*

A. Compare the details of the cash receipts journal entries with the details of the corresponding daily deposit slips.

B. Scan the debits to the fixed asset accounts and vouch selected amounts to vendors' invoices and management's authorization.

C. Perform analytical procedures that compare documented authorized pay rates to the entity's budget and forecast.

D. Obtain the cutoff bank statement and compare the cleared checks to the year-end bank reconciliation.

E. Prepare a bank transfer schedule.

F. Inspect the entity's deeds to its real estate.

G. Make inquiries of the entity's attorney concerning the details of real estate transactions.

H. Confirm the terms of borrowing arrangements with the lender.

I. Examine selected equipment repair orders and supporting documentation to determine the propriety of the charges.

J. Send requests to confirm the entity's accounts receivable on a surprise basis at an interim date.

K. Send a second request for confirmation of the receivable to the customer and make inquiries of a reputable credit agency concerning the customer's creditworthiness.

L. Examine the entity's shipping documents to verify that the merchandise that produced the receivable was actually sent to the customer.

M. Inspect the entity's correspondence files for indications of customer disputes for evidence that certain shipments were on consignment.

N. Perform edit checks of data on the payroll transaction tapes.

O. Inspect payroll check endorsements for similar handwriting.

P. Observe payroll check distribution on a surprise basis.

Q. Vouch data in the payroll register to documented authorized pay rates in the human resources department's files.

R. Reconcile the payroll checking account and determine if there were unusual time lags between the issuance and payment of payroll checks.

S. Inspect the file of prenumbered vouchers for consecutive numbering and proper approval by an appropriate employee.

T. Determine that the details of selected prenumbered vouchers match the related vendors' invoices.

U. Examine the supporting purchase orders and receiving reports for selected paid vouchers.

## *Possible misstatements due to errors and fraud*

1. The auditor suspects that a kiting scheme exists because an accounting department employee who can issue and record checks seems to be leading an unusually luxurious lifestyle. (**Select only 1 procedure**)

2. An auditor suspects that the controller wrote several checks and recorded the cash disbursements just before year-end but did not mail the checks until after the first week of the subsequent year. (**Select only 1 procedure**)

3. The entity borrowed funds from a financial institution. Although the transaction was properly recorded, the auditor suspects that the loan created a lien on the entity's real estate that is not disclosed in its financial statements. (**Select only 1 procedure**)

4. The auditor discovered an unusually large receivable from one of the entity's new customers. The auditor suspects that the receivable may be fictitious because the auditor has never heard of the customer and because the auditor's initial attempt to confirm the receivable has been ignored by the customer. (**Select only 2 procedures**)

5. The auditor suspects that fictitious employees have been placed on the payroll by the entity's payroll supervisor, who has access to payroll records and to the paychecks. (**Select only 1 procedure**)

6. The auditor suspects that selected employees of the entity received unauthorized raises from the entity's payroll supervisor, who has access to payroll records. (**Select only 1 procedure**)

7. The entity's cash receipts of the first few days of the subsequent year were properly deposited in its general operating account after the year-end. However, the auditor suspects that the entity recorded the cash receipts in its books during the last week of the year under audit. (**Select only 1 procedure**)

8. The auditor suspects that vouchers were prepared and processed by an accounting department employee for merchandise that was neither ordered nor received by the entity. (**Select only 1 procedure**)

9. The details of invoices for equipment repairs were not clearly identified or explained to the accounting department employees. The auditor suspects that the bookkeeper incorrectly recorded the repairs as fixed assets. (**Select only 1 procedure**)

10. The auditor suspects that a lapping scheme exists because an accounting department employee who has access to cash receipts also maintains the accounts receivable ledger and refuses to take any vacation or sick days. (**Select only 2 procedures**)

11. The auditor suspects that the entity is inappropriately increasing the cash reported on its balance sheet by drawing a check on one account and not recording it as an outstanding check on that account and simultaneously recording it as a deposit in a second account. (**Select only 1 procedure**)

12. The auditor suspects that the entity's controller has overstated sales and accounts receivable by recording fictitious sales to regular customers in the entity's books. (**Select only 2 procedures**)

| Audit Procedures | Addressing Audit Risk | Research | Communication |
|---|---|---|---|

Now assume that the note collected by the bank is from a "related party." Search the Professional Standards to determine procedures that should be performed concerning a related-party transaction that has been identified.

Find guidance in the AICPA Standards that authoritatively addresses the situation above. To complete this task, select the appropriate paragraph(s) that answer the requirement. Use the search capabilities provided by the **Standards** tab to find the numbered paragraph in either the Original Pronouncements or Current Text that addresses the issue above.

| Audit Procedures | Addressing Audit Risk | Research | Communication |
|---|---|---|---|

General Company wishes to put a note in the company's financial statements indicating that the terms of the related-party loan is comparable to those between unrelated parties. Write a brief memorandum to Joe Smith, the CEO of General Company, explaining the implications of this proposed action.

*REMINDER: Your response will be graded for both technical content and writing skills. Technical content will be evaluated for information that is helpful to the intended reader and clearly relevant to the issue. Writing skills will be evaluated for development, organization, and the appropriate expression of ideas in professional correspondence. Use a standard business memo or letter format with a clear beginning, middle, and end. Do not convey information in the form of a table, bullet point list, or other abbreviated presentation.*

To:       Joe Smith, CEO
          General Company
From:   CPA Candidate
Re:       Related-party loan disclosure

# APPENDIX
# SOLUTIONS TO PROBLEMS

## SOLUTIONS TO CHAPTER 2 PROBLEMS

1.  Some efficient search strategies for this problem are

    - Use the topical index and look for accounting for contingencies.
    - If you know that FASB No. 5 contains the guidance, go directly to that pronouncement using the Original Pronouncements Index.
    - Search on the term "litigation."

    The appropriate cite is presented below.

    FASB No. 5, para 8.

    C59.105

    An estimated loss from a loss contingency (as defined in paragraph 1) shall be accrued by a charge to income if *both* of the following conditions are met:

    a.  Information available prior to issuance of the financial statements indicates that it is probable that an asset had been impaired or a liability had been incurred at the date of the financial statements. It is implicit in this condition that it must be probable that one or more future events will occur confirming the fact of the loss.
    b.  The amount of loss can be reasonably estimated.

2.  Some efficient search strategies for this problem are

    - If you know that FASB No. 132R covers this situation go directly to that standard.
    - Use the table of contents and look for guidance regarding pensions and search on "nonpublic."
    - Use the topical index and look under "disclosure" and then under "pension plans."

    The appropriate cite is presented below.

    P16.150A

    FASB No.132R, para. 8

    A nonpublic entity is not required to disclose the information required by paragraphs .150(a)–(c), .150(h), and .150(m)–(p) of this section. A nonpublic entity that sponsors one or more defined benefit pension plans shall provide the following information. [Disclosures required by this section shall not be combined with the disclosures required by Section P40.] Amounts related to the employer's results of operations shall be disclosed for each period for which a statement of income is presented. Amounts related to the employer's statement of financial position shall be disclosed as of the measurement date used for each statement of financial position presented:

    a.  The benefit obligation, fair value of plan assets, and funded status of the plan
    b.  Employer contributions, participant contributions, and benefits paid
    c.  Information about plan assets:

        (1) For each major category of plan assets, which shall include, but is not limited to, equity securities, debt securities, real estate, and all other assets, the percentage of the fair value of total plan assets held as of the measurement date used for each statement of financial position presented.
        (2) A narrative description of investment policies and strategies, including target allocation percentages or range of percentages for each major category of plan assets presented on a weighted-average basis as of the measurement date(s) of the latest statement of financial position presented, if applicable, and other factors that are pertinent to an understanding of the policies or strategies such as investment goals, risk management practices, permitted and prohibited investments including the use of derivatives, diversification, and the relationship between plan assets and benefit obligations.

(3)  A narrative description of the basis used to determine the overall expected long-term rate-of-return-on-assets assumption, such as the general approach used, the extent to which the overall rate-of-return-on-assets assumption was based on historical returns, the extent to which adjustments were made to those historical returns in order to reflect expectations of future returns, and how those adjustments were determined.

(4)  Disclosure of additional asset categories and additional information about specific assets within a category is encouraged if that information is expected to be useful in understanding the risks associated with each asset category and the overall expected long-term rate of return on assets.

d.   For defined benefit pension plans, the accumulated benefit obligation.

e.   The benefits (as of the date of the latest statement of financial position presented) expected to be paid in each of the next five fiscal years, and in the aggregate for the five fiscal years thereafter. The expected benefits should be estimated based on the same assumptions used to measure the company's benefit obligation at the end of the year and should include benefits attributable to estimated future employee service.

f.   The employer's best estimate, as soon as it can reasonably be determined, of contributions expected to be paid to the plan during the next fiscal year beginning after the date of the latest statement of financial position presented. Estimated contributions may be presented in the aggregate combining (1) contributions required by funding regulations or laws, (2) discretionary contributions, and (3) noncash contributions.

g.   The amounts recognized in the statements of financial position, including net pension prepaid assets or accrued liabilities and any intangible asset and the amount of accumulated other comprehensive income recognized pursuant to paragraph .131 of this section.

h.   The amount of net periodic benefit cost recognized and the amount included within other comprehensive income arising from a change in the minimum pension liability recognized pursuant to paragraph .131 of this section.

i.   On a weighted-average basis, the following assumptions used in the accounting for the plans: assumed discount rates, rates of compensation increase (for pay-related plans), and expected long-term rates of return on plan assets specifying, in a tabular format, the assumptions used to determine the benefit obligation and the assumptions used to determine net benefit cost.

j.   The measurement date(s) used to determine pension measurements for the pension plans that make up at least the majority of plan assets and benefit obligations.

k.   If applicable, the amounts and types of securities of the employer and related parties included in plan assets, the approximate amount of future annual benefits of plan participants covered by insurance contracts issued by the employer or related parties, and any significant transactions between the employer or related parties and the plan during the period.

l.   The nature and effect of significant nonroutine events, such as amendments, combinations, divestitures, curtailments, and settlements.

3.  This problem is fairly easy. The most efficient search strategy is an advanced search on the phrase "home equity."
    The appropriate citation is presented below.

    163(h)(3)(C)(i) IN GENERAL—The term "home equity" indebtedness means any indebtedness (other than acquisition indebtedness) secured by a qualified residence to the extent the aggregate amount of such indebtedness does not exceed.

        163(h)(3)(C)(i)(I) the fair market value of such qualified residence, reduced by

        163(h)(3)(C)(i)(II) the amount of acquisition indebtedness with respect to such residence.

    163(h)(3)(C)(ii) LIMITATION—The aggregate amount treated as home equity indebtedness for any period shall not exceed $100,000 ($50,000 in the case of a separate return by a married individual).

4.  This problem is also fairly easy. An efficient search strategy would be an advanced search on all the terms "charitable contribution, corporations, and limitations." Don't perform the search as a term—be sure to use the search on documents containing all of the terms.
    The appropriate citation is presented below.

170(b)(2)(A) IN GENERAL—The total deductions under subsection (a) for any taxable year (other than for <u>contributions</u> to which subparagraph (B) applies) shall not exceed 10 percent of the taxpayer's taxable income.

**5.** An efficient search strategy in this case would be an advanced search in the Statements on Standards for Accounting and Review Services for documents containing all the terms "inquiries and review." The appropriate citation is presented below.

AR 100.33

The following are inquiries the accountant should consider making and other review procedures the accountant should consider performing when conducting a review of financial statements:

a. Inquiries to members of management who have responsibility for financial and accounting matters concerning (see Appendix B [paragraph .85])

   (1) Whether the financial statements have been prepared in conformity with generally accepted accounting principles consistently applied.
   (2) The entity's accounting principles and practices and the methods followed in applying them and procedures for recording, classifying, and summarizing transactions, and accumulating information for disclosure in the financial statements.
   (3) Unusual or complex situations that may have an effect on the financial statements.
   (4) Significant transactions occurring or recognized near the end of the reporting period.
   (5) The status of uncorrected misstatements identified during the previous engagement.
   (6) Questions that have arisen in the course of applying the review procedures.
   (7) Events subsequent to the date of the financial statements that could have a material effect on the financial statements.
   (8) Their knowledge of any fraud or suspected fraud affecting the entity involving management or others where the fraud could have a material effect on the financial statements, for example, communications received from employees, former employees, or others.
   (9) Significant journal entries and other adjustments.
   (10) Communications from regulatory agencies.

b. Inquiries concerning actions taken at meetings of stockholders, board of directors, committees of the board of directors, or comparable meetings that may affect the financial statements.
c. Reading the financial statements to consider, on the basis of information coming to the accountant's attention, whether the financial statements appear to conform with generally accepted accounting principles.
d. Obtaining reports from other accountants, if any, who have been engaged to audit or review the financial statements of significant components of the reporting entity, its subsidiaries, and other investees.

**6.** Since the term public warehouse occurs infrequently, an advanced search on the phrase "public warehouse" would be a very efficient search strategy.
The appropriate citation is presented below.

AU 331.14

If inventories are in the hands of public warehouses or other outside custodians, the auditor ordinarily would obtain direct confirmation in writing from the custodian. If such inventories represent a significant proportion of current or total assets, to obtain reasonable assurance with respect to their existence, the auditor should apply one or more of the following procedures as he considers necessary in the circumstances.

a. Test the owner's procedures for investigating the warehouseman and evaluating the warehouseman's performance.
b. Obtain an independent accountant's report on the warehouseman's control procedures relevant to custody of goods and, if applicable, pledging of receipts, or apply alternative procedures at the warehouse to gain reasonable assurance that information received from the warehouseman is reliable.

c. Observe physical counts of the goods, if practicable and reasonable.
d. If warehouse receipts have been pledged as collateral, confirm with lenders pertinent details of the pledged receipts (on a test basis, if appropriate).

# SOLUTIONS TO CHAPTER 4 PROBLEMS

## FAR Simulation Problem 1

| Directions | Situation | Temporary and Permanent Differences | Deferred Tax Schedule | Calculate Taxable Income | Journal Entries | Disclosures | Communication | Research |
|---|---|---|---|---|---|---|---|---|

|  | *Temporary* | *Permanent* |
|---|---|---|
| Premiums on life insurance of key officer | ○ | ● |
| Depreciation | ● | ○ |
| Interest on municipal bonds | ○ | ● |
| Warranties | ● | ○ |
| Bad debts | ● | ○ |
| Rent received in advance from clients | ● | ○ |

| Directions | Situation | Temporary and Permanent Differences | Deferred Tax Schedule | Calculate Taxable Income | Journal Entries | Disclosures | Communication | Research |
|---|---|---|---|---|---|---|---|---|

| Item | Difference between taxable amount and income statement amount | Classification: Deferred tax asset Deferred tax liability | Current or noncurrent | Deferred tax amount |
|---|---|---|---|---|
| Depreciation | 12,000 | Deferred tax liability | Noncurrent | 4,800 |
| Warranties | 750 | Deferred tax asset | Current | 300 |
| Bad debts | 800 | Deferred tax asset | Current | 320 |
| Rent received | 8,000 | Deferred tax asset | Current | 3,200 |
| Rent received | 16,000 | Deferred tax asset | Noncurrent | 6,400 |

**Explanation of solutions**

The adjustment to warranties is the difference between warranty expense deducted on the income statement and the actual warranty work performed during the period ($4,000 – $3,250 = $750). The adjustment to bad debt is the difference between bad debt expense subtracted on the balance sheet, and the actual bad debts written off during the period ($1,400 – $600 = $800). Note that rent received is taxable in the period received, and for deferred tax purposes, it must be fragmented into two components, current and noncurrent.

| Directions | Situation | Temporary and Permanent Differences | Deferred Tax Schedule | Calculate Taxable Income | Journal Entries | Disclosures | Communication | Research |
|---|---|---|---|---|---|---|---|---|

| | |
|---|---|
| Pretax financial income | $400,000 |
| Premiums on life insurance of key officer | 10,000 |
| Interest on municipal bonds | (5,300) |
| Depreciation for tax in excess of book depreciation | (12,000) |
| Adjustment for warranties | 750 |
| Adjustment for bad debts | 800 |
| Adjustment for rent received in advance | 24,000 |
| | |
| Taxable income | 418,250 |

| Directions | Situation | Temporary and Permanent Differences | Deferred Tax Schedule | Calculate Taxable Income | Journal Entries | Disclosures | Communication | Research |
|---|---|---|---|---|---|---|---|---|

| Account title | Debit | Credit |
|---|---|---|
| Deferred tax asset—Current | 3,820 | |
| Deferred tax asset—Noncurrent | 6,400 | |
| Tax expense | 161,880 | |
| Deferred tax liability—Noncurrent | | 4,800 |
| Income taxes payable | | 167,300 |
| | | |
| | | |

## Explanation of solutions

The total for deferred tax asset—current can be found by adding the current items in the deferred tax schedule in one of the previous simulation tasks.

| Directions | Situation | Temporary and Permanent Differences | Deferred Tax Schedule | Calculate Taxable Income | Journal Entries | Disclosures | Communication | Research |
|---|---|---|---|---|---|---|---|---|

| | |
|---|---|
| Deferred tax asset—Current | 3,820 |
| Deferred tax asset—Noncurrent | 1,600 |
| Deferred tax liability—Current | 0 |
| Deferred tax liability—Noncurrent | 0 |
| | |

## Explanation of solutions

The netting rules for deferred taxes require that current assets be netted against current deferred tax liabilities. Noncurrent deferred tax assets are netted against noncurrent deferred tax liabilities. Using the journal entries from the previous task, we find that total current deferred tax assets are $3,820. There are no current deferred tax liabilities. Netting noncurrent deferred tax assets and liabilities ($6,400 – $4,800) = $1,600 disclosed on the balance sheet as a noncurrent deferred tax asset.

| Directions | Situation | Temporary and Permanent Differences | Deferred Tax Schedule | Calculate Taxable Income | Journal Entries | Disclosures | Communication | | Research |
|---|---|---|---|---|---|---|---|---|---|

> To:     Mr. Dunn
> From:   Mr. Green, CPA
> Re:     Accounting for income taxes
>
>     You have requested that I provide a brief overview of accounting for income taxes in accordance with SFAS 109. The objectives of accounting for income taxes are to recognize (1) the amount of taxes payable or refundable for the current year, and (2) deferred tax liabilities and assets for the estimated future tax consequences of temporary differences and carryforwards. Temporary differences are differences between the tax basis of assets or liabilities and their reported amounts in the financial statements that will result in taxable or deductible amounts in future years.
>
>     Deferred tax assets and liabilities are measured based on the provisions of enacted tax law; the effects of future changes in the tax laws or rates are not anticipated. The measurement of deferred tax assets is reduced, if necessary, by a valuation allowance to reflect the net asset amount that is more likely than not to be realized. Deferred income tax expense or benefit is measured as the change during the year in an enterprise's deferred tax liabilities and assets.
>
>     If you have any other questions, please contact me.

| Directions | Situation | Temporary and Permanent Differences | Deferred Tax Schedule | Calculate Taxable Income | Journal Entries | Disclosures | Communication | Research |
|---|---|---|---|---|---|---|---|---|

### FAS109, Para 16

16. An enterprise shall recognize a deferred tax liability or asset for all temporary differences and operating loss and tax credit carryforwards in accordance with the provisions of paragraph 17. Deferred tax expense or benefit is the change during the year in an enterprise's deferred tax liabilities and assets. For deferred tax liabilities and assets acquired in a purchase business combination during the year, it is the change since the combination date. Total income tax expense or benefit for the year is the sum of deferred tax expense or benefit and income taxes currently payable or refundable.

### FAR Simulation Problem 2

| Situation | Concepts | Uncollectible Accounts | Provision for Uncollectible Accounts Expense | Journal Entries | Transfer of Receivables | Communication | Research |
|---|---|---|---|---|---|---|---|

| | | *Cash* | *Not Cash* |
|---|---|---|---|
| 1. | Checking accounts | ● | ○ |
| 2. | Treasury stock | ○ | ● |
| 3. | Treasury bills | ● | ○ |
| 4. | Money market funds | ● | ○ |
| 5. | Petty cash | ● | ○ |
| 6. | Trading securities | ○ | ● |
| 7. | Savings accounts | ● | ○ |
| 8. | Sinking fund cash | ○ | ● |
| 9. | Compensating balances against long-term borrowings | ○ | ● |
| 10. | Cash restricted for new building | ○ | ● |
| 11. | Postdated check for customers | ○ | ● |
| 12. | Available-for-sale securities | ○ | ● |

| Situation | Concepts | Uncollectible Accounts | Provision for Uncollectible Accounts Expense | Journal Entries | Transfer of Receivables | Communication | Research |
|-----------|----------|------------------------|---------------------------------------------|-----------------|-------------------------|---------------|----------|

Schedule to calculate provision and allowance for bad debts.

### Sigma Company
### SCHEDULE OF CALCULATION OF ALLOWANCE FOR UNCOLLECTIBLE ACCOUNTS
### *December 31, 2007*

|  | Amounts of accounts receivable | Percentage of uncollectible accounts | Estimate of uncollectible accounts |
|--|--------------------------------|--------------------------------------|------------------------------------|
| 0 to 30 days | $300,000 | × 1% | $3,000 |
| 31 to 90 days | 80,000 | × 5% | 4,000 |
| 91 to 180 days | 60,000 | × 20% | 12,000 |
| Over 180 days | 25,000 | × 80% | 20,000 |
| Total accounts receivable | $465,000 | | |
| Total allowance for uncollectible accounts | | | $39,000 |

## Explanation of solutions

**1.**   This problem consists of two related parts:  part a. requires a calculation of the allowance for uncollectible accounts at 12/31/07 using an aging approach, and part b. requires a computation of the 2007 provision for uncollectible accounts (uncollectible accounts expense).  The solutions approach is to quickly review the basics of accounting for uncollectible accounts, visualize the solution format, and begin.  Some candidates may benefit from preparation of T-accounts (see item 4. below).

**2.**   When using the aging approach, the total uncollectible accounts (in other words, the required ending balance in the allowance account) is estimated by applying a different percentage to the various age categories.  The percentage increases as the age of the receivables increases because the older a receivable is, the less likely is its ultimate collection.

**2.1**  In this case, Sigma estimates that 1% of its receivables in the zero-thirty days age category will prove to be uncollectible.  Therefore, of that $300,000 of accounts receivable, it is estimated that $3,000 (1% × $300,000) will be uncollectible.  Similar computations are performed for the other age categories, resulting in an estimate that $39,000 of the $465,000 accounts receivable will prove to be uncollectible.  This is the required 12/31/07 balance in the allowance account.

**3.**   When using the aging approach, the first step is to compute the required ending balance in the allowance account (as discussed in items 2. and 2.1 above).  The second step is to compute the uncollectible accounts expense necessary to bring the **unadjusted** allowance balance up to the **required** allowance balance.

**3.1**  The only item affecting the allowance account in 2006 was the recording of uncollectible accounts expense of $28,000 (1% × $2,800,000 credit sales).  Therefore, the 1/1/07 balance in this account is $28,000.  No adjustment is necessary for the change in the method of estimating this expense (from percent of sales to aging schedule) because any such change is handled prospectively.

*NOTE:  Using the aging percents given also results in a $28,000 balance at 1/1/07.  Even if the result was different, though, no adjustment is necessary.*

**3.2**  During 2007, this $28,000 credit balance was decreased by write-offs of $27,000 (debit allowance, credit AR) and increased by $7,000 of recoveries (debit AR, credit allowance; and debit cash, credit AR).  Therefore, the 12/31/07 balance in the allowance account, before adjustment, is $8,000 ($28,000 − $27,000 + $7,000).

**3.3**  To increase the allowance account from $8,000 (see 3.2 above) to $39,000 (see 2.1 above), a provision for uncollectible accounts (uncollectible accounts expense) of $31,000 must be recorded for 2007.

**4.** Some candidates may benefit from the preparation of T-accounts for the allowance account and accounts receivable. These T-accounts are provided below.

### T-accounts for 2007

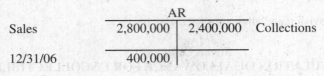

|  | AR |  |  |
|---|---|---|---|
| Sales | 2,800,000 | 2,400,000 | Collections |
| 12/31/06 | 400,000 |  |  |

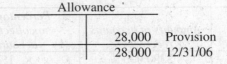

|  | Allowance |  |  |
|---|---|---|---|
|  |  | 28,000 | Provision |
|  |  | 28,000 | 12/31/06 |

| Situation | Concepts | Uncollectible Accounts | Provision for Uncollectible Accounts Expense | Journal Entries | Transfer of Receivables | Communication | Research |
|---|---|---|---|---|---|---|---|

### Computation of 2007 provision

| Balance December 31, 2006 | $28,000 |
|---|---|
| Write-offs during 2007 | (27,000) |
| Recoveries during 2007 | 7,000 |
| Balance before 2007 provision | 8,000 |
| Required allowance at December 31, 2007 | 39,000 |
| 2007 Provision | $31,000 |

| Situation | Concepts | Uncollectible Accounts | Provision for Uncollectible Accounts Expense | Journal Entries | Transfer of Receivables | Communication | Research |
|---|---|---|---|---|---|---|---|

#### Write-offs

| Allowance for uncollectible accounts | 27,000 |  |
|---|---|---|
| Accounts receivable |  | 27,000 |

#### Recoveries

| Accounts receivable | 7,000 |  |
|---|---|---|
| Allowance for uncollectible accounts |  | 7,000 |
| *To reinstate the account receivable* |  |  |
| Cash | 7,000 |  |
| Accounts receivable |  | 7,000 |
| *To show payment on the account* |  |  |

#### Provision for uncollectible accounts expense at December 31, 2007

| Uncollectible accounts expense | 31,000 |  |
|---|---|---|
| Allowance for uncollectible accounts |  | 31,000 |

| Situation | Concepts | Uncollectible Accounts | Provision for Uncollectible Accounts Expense | Journal Entries | Transfer of Receivables | Communication | Research |
|---|---|---|---|---|---|---|---|

| | | | |
|---|---|---|---|
| Cash | | 144,226 | |
| Interest expense (150,000 × .15 × 45/365) | | 2,774 | |
| Factoring fee (2% × 150,000) | | 3,000 | |
| Accounts receivable | | | 150,000 |

| Situation | Concepts | Uncollectible Accounts | Provision for Uncollectible Accounts Expense | Journal Entries | Transfer of Receivables | Communication | Research |
|---|---|---|---|---|---|---|---|

To:      CEO, Sigma Company
From:    CPA Candidate
Re:      Estimating uncollectible accounts

This memorandum is designed to answer your questions about the accounting for uncollectible accounts. Under generally accepted accounting principles there are two acceptable methods for estimating uncollectible accounts. One method uses an income statement approach, and the other method uses a balance sheet approach. Either method is acceptable; however, a company should select a method and continue to use it over time.

The income statement (percent-of-credit-sales) approach estimates uncollectible accounts based on credit sales. This approach focuses on income determination by attempting to match uncollectible accounts expense with the revenues generated during the period. A company may use a historical analysis to estimate the percent of credit sales that will not be collected. This percent is multiplied by the credit sales for the period to arrive at uncollectible accounts expense.

The second approach, the aging of accounts receivable method, uses a balance sheet approach to estimate uncollectible accounts. The aging approach groups the accounts receivable by the number of days the receivables have been outstanding. Management then uses historical data or loss experience in the industry to estimate a percent of each grouping that may not be collected. The estimated percent is multiplied by the outstanding balance of receivables for that period of time, and the sum of these estimated uncollectible accounts is totaled. The total of estimated uncollectible accounts should be the ending balance in the allowance for uncollectible accounts. The uncollectible accounts expense for the period will be the difference between the year-end balance in the allowance for uncollectible accounts (before adjustment) and the target number for the allowance account based on the most recent aging schedule.

If you would like assistance in preparing the aging schedule, please contact my office.

| Situation | Concepts | Uncollectible Accounts | Provision for Uncollectible Accounts Expense | Journal Entries | Transfer of Receivables | Communication | Research |
|---|---|---|---|---|---|---|---|

**1.** With regard to transfers of financial assets, what is the financial components approach?

**FAS140, Para 7**

7. Before FASB Statement No. 125, *Accounting for Transfers and Servicing of Financial Assets and Extinguishments of Liabilities*, accounting standards generally required that a transferor account for financial assets transferred as an inseparable unit that had been either entirely sold or entirely retained. Those standards were difficult to apply and pro-

duced inconsistent and arbitrary results. For example, whether a transfer "purported to be a sale" was sufficient to determine whether the transfer was accounted for and reported as a sale of receivables under one accounting standard or as a secured borrowing under another. After studying many of the complex developments that have occurred in financial markets during recent years, the Board concluded that previous approaches that viewed each financial asset as an indivisible unit do not provide an appropriate basis for developing consistent and operational standards for dealing with transfers and servicing of financial assets and extinguishments of liabilities. To address those issues adequately and consistently, the Board decided to adopt as the basis for the statement a financial-components approach that focuses on control and recognizes that financial assets and liabilities can be divided into a variety of components.

**2.** Describe the criteria for determining when control has been surrendered in a transfer of receivables.

**FAS140, Para 9**

9. A transfer of financial assets (or all or a portion of a financial asset) in which the transferor surrenders control over those financial assets shall be accounted for as a sale to the extent that consideration other than beneficial interests in the transferred assets is received in exchange. The transferor has surrendered control over transferred assets if and only if all of the following conditions are met:

a. The transferred assets have been isolated from the transferor—put presumptively beyond the reach of the transferor and its creditors, even in bankruptcy or other receivership (paragraphs 27 and 28).

b. Each transferee (or, if the transferee is a qualifying SPE (paragraph 35), each holder of its beneficial interests) has the right to pledge or exchange the assets (or beneficial interests) it received, and no condition both constrains the transferee (or holder) from taking advantage of its right to pledge or exchange and provides more than a trivial benefit to the transferor (paragraphs 29-34).

c. The transferor does not maintain effective control over the transferred assets through either (1) an agreement that both entitles and obligates the transferor to repurchase or redeem them before their maturity (paragraphs 47-49) or (2) the ability to unilaterally cause the holder to return specific assets, other than through a cleanup call (paragraphs 50-54).

**3.** How are transfers of receivables accounted for if one or more of the criteria for determining whether control has been surrendered are not met?

**FAS140, Para 12**

12. If a transfer of financial assets in exchange for cash or other consideration (other than beneficial interests in the transferred assets) does not meet the criteria for a sale in paragraph 9, the transferor and transferee shall account for the transfer as a secured borrowing with pledge of collateral (paragraph 15).

# SOLUTIONS TO CHAPTER 5 PROBLEMS

## REG Simulation Problem 1

| Introduction | Schedule M-1 Adjustments | Deductibility | Taxability | Alternative Minimum Tax | Communication | Research |
|---|---|---|---|---|---|---|

*NOTE:  Schedule M-1 is the schedule of the corporate income tax return that provides a reconciliation of net income (loss) per books with the corporation's taxable income before the net operating loss and dividends received deductions.  If an item's treatment per books differs from its treatment for tax purposes, an M-1 adjustment will result.*

| | Schedule M-1 Adjustment | (I) | (D) | (N) |
|---|---|---|---|---|
| 1.  Reliant's disbursements included reimbursed employees' expenses in 2007 for travel of $100,000, and business meals of $30,000.  The reimbursed expenses met the conditions of deductibility and were properly substantiated under an accountable plan.  The reimbursement was not treated as employee compensation. | $15,000 | ● | ○ | ○ |
| 2.  Reliant's books expensed $7,000 in 2007 for the term life insurance premiums on the corporate officers.  Reliant was the policy owner and beneficiary. | $ 7,000 | ● | ○ | ○ |
| 3.  Reliant's books indicated an $18,000 state franchise tax expense for 2007.  Estimated state tax payments for 2007 were $15,000. | $0 | ○ | ○ | ● |
| 4.  Book depreciation on computers for 2007 was $10,000.  These computers, which cost $50,000, were placed in service on January 2, 2006.  Tax depreciation used MACRS with the half-year convention.  No election was made to expense part of the computer cost or to use a straight-line method. | $ 6,000 | ○ | ● | ○ |
| 5.  For 2007, Reliant's books showed a $4,000 short-term capital gain distribution from a mutual fund corporation and a $5,000 loss on the sale of Retro stock that was purchased in 2005.  The stock was an investment in an unrelated corporation.  There were no other 2007 gains or losses and no loss carryovers from prior years. | $ 5,000 | ● | ○ | ○ |
| 6.  Reliant's 2007 taxable income before the charitable contribution and the dividends received deductions was $500,000.  Reliant's books expensed $15,000 in board of director authorized charitable contributions that were paid on January 5, 2008.  Charitable contributions paid and expensed during 2007 were $35,000.  All charitable contributions were properly substantiated.  There were no net operating losses or charitable contributions that were carried forward. | $0 | ○ | ○ | ● |

### Explanation of solutions

1.  **($15,000; I)**  The $100,000 reimbursement for employee travel is deductible for both book and tax purposes and no adjustment is necessary.  However, since only 50% of the $30,000 of reimbursed business meals that was deducted per books is deductible for tax purposes, an M-1 increase adjustment results in the amount of $15,000 ($30,000 × 50%).

**2.** **($7,000; I)** The $7,000 of term life insurance premiums on corporate officers that was deducted per books is not deductible for tax purposes because Reliant was the policy owner and beneficiary. As a result there is an M-1 increase adjustment of $7,000.

**3.** **($0; N)** The $18,000 of state franchise taxes and $15,000 of estimated state tax payments are fully deductible for both book and tax purposes and no M-1 adjustment is necessary.

**4.** **($6,000; D)** Since the computers are five-year recovery property and Reliant used MACRS and the half-year convention, depreciation would be computed using the 200% declining balance method (i.e., twice the straight-line rate) and the tax depreciation for 2006 would be ($50,000 × 40% × 1/2) = $10,000. The tax depreciation for 2007 would then be ($50,000 – $10,000) × 40% = $16,000. Since book depreciation was only $10,000, the book to tax difference in depreciation would result in an M-1 decrease adjustment of $6,000.

**5.** **($5,000; I)** Since only long-term capital gain distributions from a mutual fund pass through as capital gain, the $4,000 of short-term capital gain distribution from a mutual fund corporation must be reported by Reliant as ordinary dividend income, and cannot be netted against the $5,000 capital loss from the sale of the Retro stock held as an investment. As a result, Reliant's sale of the Retro stock results in a net capital loss of $5,000 for 2007. Since a corporation cannot deduct a net capital loss for tax purposes, the $5,000 of net capital loss deducted per books results in a book to tax difference and an M-1 increase adjustment of $5,000.

**6.** **($0; N)** Since Reliant had taxable income before the charitable contribution deduction of $500,000 for 2007, Reliant can deduct a maximum of ($500,000 × 10%) = $50,000 of charitable contributions for tax purposes. Reliant can deduct the $35,000 of contributions made during 2007, as well as the $15,000 paid on January 5, 2008, because Reliant is an accrual-basis taxpayer, the $15,000 contribution was authorized by Reliant's board of directors, and the $15,000 was paid within 2 1/2 months after the end of 2007. Since Reliant is deducting $50,000 of contributions for both book and tax purposes, there is no M-1 adjustment.

| Introduction | Schedule M-1 Adjustments | Deductibility | Taxability | Alternative Minimum Tax | Communication | Research |
|---|---|---|---|---|---|---|

|  | (F) | (P) | (N) |
|---|---|---|---|
| **1.** Reliant purchased theater tickets for its out-of-town clients. The performances took place after Reliant's substantial and bona fide business negotiations with its clients. | O | ● | O |
| **2.** Reliant accrued advertising expenses to promote a new product line. Ten percent of the new product line remained in ending inventory. | ● | O | O |
| **3.** Reliant incurred interest expense on a loan to purchase municipal bonds. | O | O | ● |
| **4.** Reliant paid a penalty for the underpayment of 2006 estimated taxes. | O | O | ● |
| **5.** On December 9, 2007, Reliant's board of directors voted to pay a $500 bonus to each nonstockholder employee for 2007. The bonuses were paid on February 3, 2008. | ● | O | O |

**Explanation of solutions**

**1.** **(P)** The cost of the theater tickets qualifies as a business entertainment expense which is only 50% deductible for 2007.

**2.** **(F)** Indirect costs that do not directly benefit a particular activity or are not incurred because of a particular activity may be currently deducted and are not required to be capitalized as part of the cost of inventory. Indirect costs that can be currently deducted include such costs as marketing, selling, advertising, distribution, and general and administrative expenses.

**3.** **(N)** Since the proceeds of the loan were used to purchase municipal bonds which generate tax-exempt income, the interest expense on the loan is not deductible.

**4.** **(N)** No deduction is allowed for the penalty that results from the underpayment of estimated income tax.

**5.   (F)** An accrual method taxpayer can deduct compensation for nonstockholder employees when there is an obligation to make payment, economic performance has occurred, the amount is reasonable, and payment is made not later than 2 1/2 months after the end of the tax year.  Here, the amount of bonus was determined on December 9, 2007, and was paid February 3, 2008.

| Introduction | Schedule M-1 Adjustments | Deductibility | Taxability | Alternative Minimum Tax | Communication | Research |
|---|---|---|---|---|---|---|

|  |  | **(F)** | **(P)** | **(N)** |
|---|---|---|---|---|
| **1.** | The portion of Reliant's refund that represented the overpayment of the 2005 federal taxes. | ○ | ○ | ● |
| **2.** | The portion of Reliant's refund that is attributable to the interest on the overpayment of federal taxes. | ● | ○ | ○ |
| **3.** | Reliant received dividend income from a mutual fund that solely invests in municipal bonds. | ○ | ○ | ● |
| **4.** | Reliant, the lessor, benefited from the capital improvements made to its property by the lessee in 2007.  The lease agreement is for one year ending December 31, 2007, and provides for a reduction in rental payments by the lessee in exchange for the improvements. | ● | ○ | ○ |
| **5.** | Reliant collected the proceeds on the term life insurance policy on the life of a debtor who was not a shareholder.  The policy was assigned to Reliant as collateral security for the debt.  The proceeds exceeded the amount of the debt. | ○ | ● | ○ |

**Explanation of solutions**

**1.   (N)** Since the payment of federal income tax does not result in a deduction, a subsequent refund of federal income tax will be nontaxable.

**2.   (F)** Interest is generally fully included in gross income, including the interest on an overpayment of federal taxes.

**3.   (N)** A mutual fund that invests in tax-exempt municipal bonds is permitted to pass the tax exemption on the bond interest on to its shareholders when the tax-exempt interest is distributed in the form of dividends.  To qualify, the mutual fund has to have at least 50% of the value of its total assets invested in tax-exempt municipal bonds at the close of each quarter of its taxable year.

**4.   (F)** Generally, a lessor will not recognize any income as a result of the capital improvements made by a lessee that revert to the lessor at the expiration of the lease.  However, if the parties intend the improvements to be, in whole or in part, a substitute for rental payments, then the lessor must recognize the improvements as rental income equal in amount to the reduction in rental payments.

**5.   (P)** Since Reliant was a collateral assignee as a result of the insured's indebtedness, Reliant received the insurance proceeds as payment on the debt, rather than as life insurance proceeds paid "by reason of death of the insured."  Consequently, the insurance proceeds are tax-free only to the extent of the amount of unpaid debt, and any proceeds in excess of the debt repayment must be included in Reliant's gross income.

| Introduction | Schedule M-1 Adjustments | Deductibility | Taxability | Alternative Minimum Tax | Communication | Research |
|---|---|---|---|---|---|---|

|  |  | **(I)** | **(D)** | **(N)** |
|---|---|---|---|---|
| **1.** | Reliant used the 70% dividends received deduction for regular tax purposes. | ○ | ○ | ● |
| **2.** | Reliant received interest from a state's general obligation bonds. | ○ | ○ | ● |

|  | (I) | (D) | (N) |
|---|---|---|---|

3.  Reliant used MACRS depreciation on seven-year personal property placed into service January 3, 2007, for regular tax purposes. No expense or depreciation election was made. ● ○ ○

4.  Depreciation on nonresidential real property placed into service on January 3, 2007, was under the general MACRS depreciation system for regular tax purposes. ○ ○ ●

5.  Reliant had only cash charitable contributions for 2007. ○ ○ ●

**Explanation of solutions**

1.  **(N)** The dividends received deduction is not an adjustment in computing AMTI before the ACE adjustment. However, note that the 70% dividends received deduction is an increase adjustment in computing a corporation's ACE.

2.  **(N)** The tax-exempt interest on a state's general obligation bonds is not an adjustment in computing AMTI before the ACE adjustment. However, note that the interest from state and local private activity bonds would be an increase adjustment in computing AMTI prior to the ACE adjustment.

3.  **(I)** Generally for seven-year property, the 200% declining balance method would be used under MACRS for regular tax purposes, while the 150% declining balance method must be used for AMT purposes, resulting in an increase adjustment in computing AMTI prior to the ACE adjustment for the year placed in service.

4.  **(N)** For real property placed in service after December 31, 1998, the AMT adjustment has been eliminated because for AMT purposes, the recovery period is the same as that used for regular tax MACRS depreciation (e.g., 39 years or 27 1/2 years). On the other hand, for real property that was placed in service before January 1, 1999, an AMT adjustment is necessary because for AMT purposes, real property must be depreciated using the straight-line method over a 40-year recovery period, rather than the 39-year or 27 1/2-year period used for regular tax purposes.

5.  **(N)** Allowable charitable contributions do not result in an adjustment in computing AMTI or ACE.

| Introduction | Schedule M-1 Adjustments | Deductibility | Taxability | Alternative Minimum Tax | Communication | Research |
|---|---|---|---|---|---|---|

Dear Ms. Evans:

You have requested information regarding the accounting for the costs of forming a wholly owned subsidiary of Reliant Corporation. A corporation may elect to deduct up to $5,000 of organizational expenditures for the tax year in which the corporation begins business for organizational expenditures incurred or paid after October 22, 2004. The $5,000 amount must be reduced by the amount by which organizational expenditures exceed $50,000. Remaining expenditures are allowed as a deduction ratably over the 180-month period beginning with the month in which the corporation begins business.

Organizational expenditures include fees for accounting and legal services incident to incorporation (e.g., fees for drafting the corporate chapter, bylaws, terms of stock certificates) expenses of organizational meetings and of temporary directors meetings, and fees paid to the state of incorporation. However, the costs incurred in issuing and selling stock and securities (e.g., professional fees to issue stock, printing costs, underwriting commissions) do not qualify as organizational expenditures and are not tax deductible. The election to deduct organizational expenditures is made by attaching a statement to the corporation's tax return for the tax year in which it begins business.

If you require any additional information, please contact me.

| Introduction | Schedule M-1 Adjustments | Deductibility | Taxability | Alternative Minimum Tax | Communication | Research |
|---|---|---|---|---|---|---|

Internal Revenue Code Section 170(b)(2) limits a corporation's deduction for charitable contributions to 10% of its taxable income before certain specified deductions.

## REG Simulation Problem 2

| Situation | Schedule D | Communication | Research |
|---|---|---|---|

### SCHEDULE D (Form 1040)
**Capital Gains and Losses**
OMB No. 1545-0074
2006
Attachment Sequence No. 12

Department of the Treasury Internal Revenue Service (99)

► Attach to Form 1040 or Form 1040NR. ► See Instructions for Schedule D (Form 1040).
► Use Schedule D-1 to list additional transactions for lines 1 and 8.

Name(s) shown on return: **Lou Tomsik**
Your social security number: **324 65 7037**

**Part I — Short-Term Capital Gains and Losses—Assets Held One Year or Less**

| (a) Description of property | (b) Date acquired | (c) Date sold | (d) Sales price | (e) Cost or other basis | (f) Gain or (loss) |
|---|---|---|---|---|---|
| 1  200 shs. King Corp. | 2-24-06 | 11-15-06 | 5,000 | 4,000 | 1,000 |

| | |
|---|---|
| 2 Enter your short-term totals, if any, from Schedule D-1, line 2 | 2 |
| 3 Total short-term sales price amounts. Add lines 1 and 2 in column (d) | 3  5,000 |
| 4 Short-term gain from Form 6252 and short-term gain or (loss) from Forms 4684, 6781, and 8824 | 4 |
| 5 Net short-term gain or (loss) from partnerships, S corporations, estates, and trusts from Schedule(s) K-1 | 5 |
| 6 Short-term capital loss carryover. Enter the amount, if any, from line 10 of your Capital Loss Carryover Worksheet on page D-7 of the instructions | 6  (7,300) |
| 7 Net short-term capital gain or (loss). Combine lines 1 through 6 in column (f) | 7  (6,300) |

**Part II — Long-Term Capital Gains and Losses—Assets Held More Than One Year**

| (a) Description of property | (b) Date acquired | (c) Date sold | (d) Sales price | (e) Cost or other basis | (f) Gain or (loss) |
|---|---|---|---|---|---|
| 8  100 shs Copperleaf Ind. | 3-1-05 | 10-20-06 | 4,200 | 2,500 | 1,700 |

| | |
|---|---|
| 9 Enter your long-term totals, if any, from Schedule D-1, line 9 | 9 |
| 10 Total long-term sales price amounts. Add lines 8 and 9 in column (d) | 10  4,200 |
| 11 Gain from Form 4797, Part I; long-term gain from Forms 2439 and 6252; and long-term gain or (loss) from Forms 4684, 6781, and 8824 | 11 |
| 12 Net long-term gain or (loss) from partnerships, S corporations, estates, and trusts from Schedule(s) K-1 | 12 |
| 13 Capital gain distributions. See page D-2 of the instructions | 13  1,500 |
| 14 Long-term capital loss carryover. Enter the amount, if any, from line 15 of your Capital Loss Carryover Worksheet on page D-7 of the instructions | 14 ( ) |
| 15 Net long-term capital gain or (loss). Combine lines 8 through 14 in column (f). Then go to Part III on the back | 15  3,200 |

For Paperwork Reduction Act Notice, see Form 1040 or Form 1040NR instructions. Cat. No. 11338H Schedule D (Form 1040) 2006

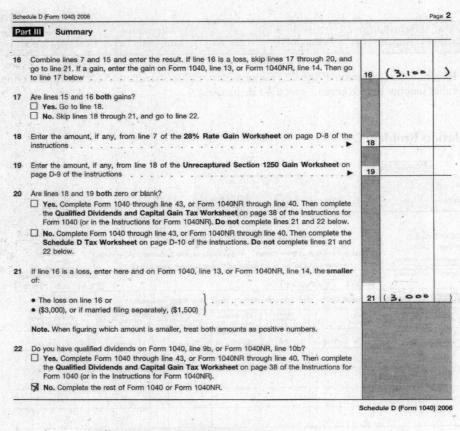

Schedule D (Form 1040) 2006                                                                    Page **2**

**Part III**    Summary

16   Combine lines 7 and 15 and enter the result. If line 16 is a loss, skip lines 17 through 20, and
     go to line 21. If a gain, enter the gain on Form 1040, line 13, or Form 1040NR, line 14. Then go
     to line 17 below . . . . . . . . . . . . . . . . . . . . . . .   **16**   ( 3,100 )

17   Are lines 15 and 16 **both** gains?
     ☐ **Yes.** Go to line 18.
     ☐ **No.** Skip lines 18 through 21, and go to line 22.

18   Enter the amount, if any, from line 7 of the **28% Rate Gain Worksheet** on page D-8 of the
     instructions . . . . . . . . . . . . . . . . . . . . . . . ▶   **18**

19   Enter the amount, if any, from line 18 of the **Unrecaptured Section 1250 Gain Worksheet** on
     page D-9 of the instructions . . . . . . . . . . . . . . . . ▶   **19**

20   Are lines 18 and 19 **both** zero or blank?
     ☐ **Yes.** Complete Form 1040 through line 43, or Form 1040NR through line 40. Then complete
        the **Qualified Dividends and Capital Gain Tax Worksheet** on page 38 of the Instructions for
        Form 1040 (or in the Instructions for Form 1040NR). **Do not** complete lines 21 and 22 below.
     ☐ **No.** Complete Form 1040 through line 43, or Form 1040NR through line 40. Then complete the
        **Schedule D Tax Worksheet** on page D-10 of the instructions. **Do not** complete lines 21 and
        22 below.

21   If line 16 is a loss, enter here and on Form 1040, line 13, or Form 1040NR, line 14, the **smaller**
     of:

     • The loss on line 16 or             } . . . . . . . . . . .   **21**   ( 3,000 )
     • ($3,000), or if married filing separately, ($1,500)

     **Note.** When figuring which amount is smaller, treat both amounts as positive numbers.

22   Do you have qualified dividends on Form 1040, line 9b, or Form 1040NR, line 10b?
     ☐ **Yes.** Complete Form 1040 through line 43, or Form 1040NR through line 40. Then complete
        the **Qualified Dividends and Capital Gain Tax Worksheet** on page 38 of the Instructions for
        Form 1040 (or in the Instructions for Form 1040NR).
     ☒ **No.** Complete the rest of Form 1040 or 1040NR.

                           Schedule D (Form 1040) 2006

|  | **Communication** |  |
|---|---|---|
| **Situation** | **Schedule D** | **Research** |

Tomsik contacts you and indicates that he expects to incur a substantial net capital loss for calendar year 2007 and wonders what the treatment of the carryforwards will be in future years. Write a letter to Tomsik explaining the treatment of an individual's capital loss carryforwards.

---

Dear Mr. Tomsik:

     You have requested that I provide you with information about the treatment of a net capital loss for federal tax purposes. Individuals may carry over a net capital loss to future tax years until the loss is used. A capital loss that is carried over to a later tax year retains its short-term or long-term character for the year to which it is carried. A short-term capital loss carryover first offsets short-term gain in the carryover year. If a net short-term capital loss results, this loss first offsets net long-term capital gain and then up to $3,000 of ordinary income. A long-term capital loss carryover first reduces long-term capital gain in the carryover year, then net short-term capital gain, and finally up to $3,000 of ordinary income.

     If you have any additional questions about the treatment of capital losses, please contact me.

| Situation | Schedule D | Communication | Research |
|---|---|---|---|

Internal Revenue Code Section 1221 provides a definition of capital assets.

## SOLUTIONS TO CHAPTER 6 PROBLEMS

### AUD Simulation Problem 1

| Situation | Company Profile | Industry Information | Balance Sheet | Income Statement | Statement of Cash Flows | Risks | Financial Statement Analysis | Audit Procedures | Communication | Research |
|---|---|---|---|---|---|---|---|---|---|---|

| | (A) | (B) | (C) | (D) |
|---|---|---|---|---|
| 1. Of the following, which is likely to be one of DietWeb's major risks of doing business on the Internet in the future? | ● | ○ | ○ | ○ |
| 2. Which of the following is likely to be the most significant business risk for DietWeb? | ○ | ○ | ● | ○ |

**Explanation of solutions**

1.   (A) The requirement is to identify DietWeb's major listed risk of doing business on the Internet.  Answer (A) is correct because DietWeb must carefully maintain the privacy of their customers' information—both due to law and due to DietWeb's assurance provided to its customers.  Answer (B) is incorrect because there are no major Federal Communications Commission Internet use fees.  Answer (C) is incorrect because the case indicates no particular problem in providing 24/7/365 support.  Answer (D) is incorrect because the Internet is able to reach customers beyond the United States.

2.   (C) The requirement is to identify the most significant business risk listed for DietWeb.  Answer (C) is correct because barriers to entrance on the Internet are ordinarily not high.  Another organization might develop similar (or more accepted) software, and/or charge lower prices than those charged by DietWeb.  Answer (A) is incorrect because internal control limitations need not necessarily be a major problem, and because internal control relates to control risk more directly than to the company's business risk.  Answer (B) is incorrect because while Internet instability may cause difficulties, few would consider it as significant a problem as new competitors.  Answer (D) is incorrect because determining appropriate year-end cutoffs is not likely to create major difficulties.

| Situation | Company Profile | Industry Information | Balance Sheet | Income Statement | Statement of Cash Flows | Risks | Financial Statement Analysis | Audit Procedures | Communication | Research |
|---|---|---|---|---|---|---|---|---|---|---|

| | (A) | (B) | (C) | (D) |
|---|---|---|---|---|
| 1. The most likely misstatement in the financial statements is | ○ | ○ | ● | ○ |
| 2. Which of the following is the most unexpected change on the balance sheet, if one assumes the revenue increase in 20X8 is correct? | ● | ○ | ○ | ○ |

**Explanation of solutions**

1.   (C) The requirement is to identify a likely misstatement in the financial statements.  Answer (C) is correct because common stock issued should be treated under financing rather than operations.  Answer (A) is incorrect because an increase in cash may well occur—even during a year in which the company encounters a loss.  Answer (B) is incorrect because there is no indication that the impairment expense is inappropriate.

Answer (D) is incorrect because previous years' pattern of income and losses may create a situation in which a net income tax benefit occurs.

**2.    (A)** The requirement is to identify, of the balance sheet changes listed, the most unexpected one.  Answer (A) is unexpected in that prepaid advertising expenses decreased by more than 90%—at a time when the company increased its sales and marketing expenses so significantly.  Answer (B) is incorrect because the relatively small increase in accounts payable may be expected given the increase in revenues.  Answer (C) is incorrect because one would expect such an increase in deferred revenues as revenues increase.  Answer (D) is incorrect since the company simply issued more stock—as indicated in the company profile.

| Situation | Company Profile | Industry Information | Balance Sheet | Income Statement | Statement of Cash Flows | Risks | Financial Statement Analysis | Audit Procedures | Communication | Research |
|---|---|---|---|---|---|---|---|---|---|---|

|   | | (A) | (B) | (C) | (D) | (E) | (F) | (G) |
|---|---|---|---|---|---|---|---|---|
| 1. | DietWeb has legal rights to property and equipment acquired during the year. | ○ | ○ | ○ | ● | ○ | ○ | ○ |
| 2. | DietWeb recorded property and equipment acquired during the year that did not actually exist at the balance sheet date. | ○ | ○ | ○ | ○ | ○ | ○ | ● |

**Explanation of solutions**

**1.    (D)** The requirement is to identify the best substantive procedure to determine that DietWeb has legal rights to the property and equipment acquired during the year.  Answer (D) is correct because the deeds and title insurance certificates will provide evidence that the company owns the property and equipment.

**2.    (G)** The requirement is to identify the best substantive procedure to determine that DietWeb recorded property and equipment actually exists.  Answer (G) is correct because physically examining the items will provide this evidence.

| Situation | Company Profile | Industry Information | Balance Sheet | Income Statement | Statement of Cash Flows | Risks | Financial Statement Analysis | Audit Procedures | Communication | Research |
|---|---|---|---|---|---|---|---|---|---|---|

---

To:        Audit Team
From:    CPA Candidate
Re:        DietWeb Audit Committee

   We have identified a number of concerns regarding the makeup of DietWeb's audit committee.  The audit committee membership is identical to that of the board of directors.  Accordingly, there are no independent members.  Mr. Readings, the company's CEO, serves as chairman of both the board of directors and the audit committee.  On the other hand, the committee members are competent and interested.
   We will make a recommendation to the board of directors to correct this matter by bringing on independent board and audit committee members.  In addition, we should consider the implications of this weakness in control environment on our audit.

| Situation | Company Profile | Industry Information | Balance Sheet | Income Statement | Statement of Cash Flows | Risks | Financial Statement Analysis | Audit Procedures | Communication | Research |
|---|---|---|---|---|---|---|---|---|---|---|

AU 316.85 presents the following examples of risk factors related to misstatements arising from misappropriation of assets:

## Incentives/Pressures

   a.  Personal financial obligations may create pressure on management or employees with access to cash or other assets susceptible to theft to misappropriate those assets.

   b.  Adverse relationships between the entity and employees with access to cash or other assets susceptible to theft may motivate those employees to misappropriate those assets. For example, adverse relationships may be created by the following:

- Known or anticipated future employee layoffs
- Recent or anticipated changes to employee compensation or benefit plans
- Promotions, compensation, or other rewards inconsistent with expectations

## Opportunities

   a.  Certain characteristics or circumstances may increase the susceptibility of assets to misappropriation. For example, opportunities to misappropriate assets increase when there are the following:

- Large amounts of cash on hand or processed
- Inventory items that are small in size, of high value, or in high demand
- Easily convertible assets, such as bearer bonds, diamonds, or computer chips
- Fixed assets that are small in size, marketable, or lacking observable identification of ownership

   b.  Inadequate internal control over assets may increase the susceptibility of misappropriation of those assets. For example, misappropriation of assets may occur because there is the following:

- Inadequate segregation of duties or independent checks
- Inadequate management oversight of employees responsible for assets, for example, inadequate supervision or monitoring of remote locations
- Inadequate job applicant screening of employees with access to assets
- Inadequate recordkeeping with respect to assets
- Inadequate system of authorization and approval of transactions (for example, in purchasing)
- Lack of complete and timely reconciliations of assets
- Lack of timely and appropriate documentation of transactions, for example, credits for merchandise returns
- Lack of mandatory vacations for employees performing key control functions
- Inadequate management understanding of information technology, which enables information technology employees to perpetrate a misappropriation
- Inadequate access controls over automated records, including controls over and review of computer systems event logs.

## Attitudes/Rationalizations

Risk factors reflective of employee attitudes/rationalizations that allow them to justify misappropriations of assets, are generally not susceptible to observation by the auditor. Nevertheless, the auditor who becomes aware of the existence of such information should consider it in identifying the risks of material misstatement arising from misappropriation of assets. For example, auditors may become aware of the following attitudes or behavior of employees who have access to assets susceptible to misappropriation:

- Disregard for the need for monitoring or reducing risks related to misappropriations of assets
- Disregard for internal control over misappropriation of assets by overriding existing controls or by failing to correct known internal control deficiencies
- Behavior indicating displeasure or dissatisfaction with the company or its treatment of the employee
- Changes in behavior or lifestyle that may indicate assets have been misappropriated

## AUD Simulation Problem 2

| Audit Procedures | Assessing Audit Risk | Research | Communication |
|---|---|---|---|

1. **(D, I)** The balance per bank may be traced to a standard form used to confirm account balance information with financial institutions and to the cutoff statement (on which will appear the beginning balance).

2. **(A, G, H, I, J)** One of the deposits in transit does not appear on the cutoff bank statement (the 9/29/07 deposit for $4,500). Accordingly, that deposit should be traced to the cash receipts journal (procedure A), the reason for the delay should be investigated (procedure G), and supporting documents should be inspected (procedure H). Both deposits should be traced to and from the bank reconciliation and the cutoff statement (procedures I and J).

3. **(B, G, H, I, J)** One of the checks does not appear on the cutoff statement (check #988 dated 8/31/07 for $2,200). Accordingly, that check should be traced to the cash disbursements journal (procedure B), the reason for the delay should be investigated (procedure G), and supporting documents should be inspected (procedure H). All checks should be traced to and from the bank reconciliation and cutoff statement (procedures I and J).

4. **(E)** The credit memo from the bank for the note collected should be investigated.

5. **(E, I)** The credit for the check that was charged by the bank for an incorrect amount should be investigated on both the bank credit memo and on the cutoff statement.

6. **(C)** The only source of the balance per books is the cash general ledger account as of 9/30/07.

| Audit Procedures | Addressing Audit Risk | Research | Communication |
|---|---|---|---|

1. **(E)** Kiting involves manipulations causing an amount of cash to be included simultaneously in the balance of two or more bank accounts. Kiting schemes are based on the float period—the time necessary for a check deposited in one bank to clear the bank on which it was drawn. To detect kiting, a bank transfer schedule is prepared to determine whether cash is improperly included in two accounts.

2. **(D)** A comparison of the cleared checks to the year-end bank reconciliation will identify checks that were not mailed until after the first week of the subsequent year because most of those checks will not be returned with the cutoff statement and will appear to remain outstanding an abnormally long period of time.

3. **(H)** Among the terms confirmed for such a borrowing arrangement will be information on liens.

4. **(K,L)** A reply to the second request, or information from the credit agency, may confirm the existence of the new customer. Also, examination of shipping documents will reveal where the goods were shipped, and ordinarily to which party.

5. **(P)** Observing the payroll check distribution on a surprise basis will assist in detection since the auditor will examine details related to any paychecks not picked up by employees.

6. **(Q)** Vouching data in the payroll register to document authorized pay rates will reveal situations in which an employee is earning income at a rate that differs from the authorized rate.

7. **(A)** A comparison of the details of the cash receipts journal to the details on the daily deposit slips will reveal a circumstance since the details will have been posted to accounts during the last week of the year under audit.

8. **(U)** When vouchers are processed for merchandise not ordered or received, there will be no supporting purchase orders and receiving reports and this will alert the auditor to the problem.

9. **(B)** Scanning the debits to the fixed asset accounts and vouching selected amounts will reveal repairs that have improperly been capitalized.

**10.  (A,J)** Lapping involves concealing a cash shortage by delaying the recording of journal entries for cash receipts.  Since lapping includes differences between the details of postings to the cash receipts journal and corresponding deposit slips, comparing these records will reveal it.  Also, confirmation requests may identify lapping when payments of receivables (as indicated by confirmation replies) appear to have taken too much time to be processed.

**11.  (E)** Increasing cash by drawing a check in this manner is a form of kiting (see answer 1).  Preparation of a bank transfer schedule will assist the auditor in identifying such transactions.

**12.  (J,L)** Confirmations will identify overstated accounts receivable when customers disagree with the recorded balance due.  Also, the related overstated sales will not have shipping documents indicating that a shipment has occurred.

| Audit Procedures | Addressing Audit Risk | Research | | Communication |
|---|---|---|---|---|

The first step is to determine the manner in which the candidate wishes to identify the pertinent research in the area.  If a keyword or index search is to be used, words such as "identified related-party transactions" or "identified related-party" may be helpful.  Even using "related party" will get the candidate to AU 334 which provides the needed information.  AU 334 indicates the following with respect to identified related-party transactions:

.09  After identifying related-party transactions, the auditor should apply the procedures he considers necessary to obtain satisfaction concerning the purpose, nature, and extent of these transactions and their effect on the financial statements.  The procedures should be directed toward obtaining and evaluating sufficient appropriate audit evidence and should extend beyond inquiry of management.  Procedures that should be considered include the following:

   a.  Obtain an understanding of the business purpose of the transaction.
   b.  Examine invoices, executed copies of agreements, contracts, and other pertinent documents, such as receiving reports and shipping documents.
   c.  Determine whether the transaction has been approved by the board of directors or other appropriate officials.
   d.  Test for reasonableness the compilation of amounts to be disclosed, or considered for disclosure, in the financial statements.
   e.  Arrange for the audits of intercompany account balances to be performed as of concurrent dates, even if the fiscal years differ, and for the examination of specified, important, and representative related-party transactions by the auditors for each of the parties, with appropriate exchange of relevant information.
   f.  Inspect or confirm and obtain satisfaction concerning the transferability and value of collateral.

.10  When necessary to fully understand a particular transaction, the following procedures, which might not otherwise be deemed necessary to comply with generally accepted auditing standards, should be considered.

   a.  Confirm transaction amount and terms, including guarantees and other significant data, with the other party or parties to the transaction.
   b.  Inspect evidence in possession of the other party or parties to the transaction.
   c.  Confirm or discuss significant information with intermediaries, such as banks, guarantors, agents, or attorneys, to obtain a better understanding of the transaction.
   d.  Refer to financial publications, trade journals, credit agencies, and other information sources when there is reason to believe that unfamiliar customers, suppliers, or other business enterprises with which material amounts of business have been transacted may lack substance.
   e.  With respect to material uncollected balances, guarantees, and other obligations, obtain information about the financial capability of the other party or parties to the transaction.  Such information may be obtained from audited financial statements, unaudited financial statements, income tax returns, and reports issued by regulatory agencies, taxing authorities, financial publications, or credit agencies.  The auditor should decide on the degree of assurance required and the extent to which available information provides such assurance.

| Audit Procedures | Addressing Audit Risk | Research | Communication |
|---|---|---|---|

---

To:       Joe Smith, CEO
          General Company
From:   CPA Candidate
Re:       Related-party loan disclosure

   You have asked me to provide you with information regarding disclosures about related-party transactions.  By their nature, related-party transactions are not at arm's length—they do not involve independent bargaining.  Except for routine transactions, it is generally not possible to determine whether a particular transaction would have occurred if the parties were not related, or assuming it would have occurred, what the terms would have been.  Therefore, it is difficult to support representations that the transaction's terms are similar to those that would have occurred between unrelated parties.  Accordingly, we do not recommend that this representation be included in the notes to the financial statements.  Also, if this information is included in the footnotes, our firm would be required to disclaim an opinion on the assertion.

   If you have any additional questions about this matter, please contact me.